THE CHICAGO SCHOOL OF ARCHITECTURE

THE CHICAGO SCHOOL

OF ARCHITECTURE

*A History of Commercial
and Public Building
in the Chicago Area, 1875–1925*

CARL W. CONDIT

Chicago and London

THE UNIVERSITY OF CHICAGO PRESS

Publication of this book has been aided by a generous grant from the
GRAHAM FOUNDATION FOR ADVANCED STUDY IN THE FINE ARTS

Library of Congress Catalog Card Number: 64-13287

THE UNIVERSITY OF CHICAGO PRESS, CHICAGO & LONDON
The University of Toronto Press, Toronto 5, Canada

PREFACE

This book is an outgrowth of *The Rise of the Skyscraper*, published in 1952. In addition to substantial changes within various chapters, I have nearly doubled the length of the text and the number of illustrations. Several factors which have appeared since the earlier work was published made a new volume desirable. Most important of them has been the continued and growing interest in the architecture of the Chicago school. This is particularly the case in the city of Chicago itself, where the press, the municipal government, and leading citizens have now become aware of the city's unique architectural heritage and have made heroic efforts to preserve the buildings that are constantly threatened by the tide of new construction. The existence of this interest required and in part made possible a more thorough examination of the Chicago school, with the aim of a fuller understanding of its relation to the vernacular building of the nineteenth century and its ultimate meaning for the architecture of our own day. To this end I have added material on the technical and formal background of the Chicago work and on the structural details of the buildings themselves, on the genesis of the major buildings, the social, economic, and intellectual history of the city, and contemporary attitudes toward the work of the school.

The balance of the new additions has been devoted to the commercial and public buildings of the architects who constitute the second generation of the Chicago movement. The decision as to what proportion of this work ought to be included was based on principles that determined the limits of the earlier book. Most of the second-generation work is residential architecture and consequently does not belong in the book as I have planned it. Among the commercial and public buildings, many are outside the city and its metropolitan area. I decided to include a few illustrations of the residential designs to show how the creative power of the Chicago movement invigorated every kind of building and how its rich formal vocabulary offered solutions to every kind of architectural problem. Since the work of Sullivan and Wright has been widely studied, I have confined the treatment of domestic architecture to a few houses by Griffin, Maher, Tallmadge, and Van Bergen. Of the commercial and public buildings of the late Chicago group (sometimes

v

called the Prairie school), I followed the principle established for the original text of limiting consideration to buildings located within the metropolitan area of the city.

The past ten years have seen a steady outpouring of scholarly papers and monographs on the history of vernacular building in England and the United States and on various figures of the Chicago school. The most fruitful of these for an adequate understanding of Chicago's place in modern building art are A. W. Skempton's articles on the development of iron framing in England, Turpin C. Bannister's detailed monograph on James Bogardus and his influence, Winston Weisman's and J. Carson Webster's articles on the New York and Chicago skyscrapers during their pioneer phase, Willard Connely's biography of Sullivan and Albert Bush-Brown's interpretive essay on his work, H. Allen Brooks's initial article on the residential designs of what he chooses to call the Prairie school, and David Gebhard's article and exhibition catalogue on Purcell, Feick and Elmslie. The most valuable of all the studies continues to be the exhaustive documentation of Chicago building in Frank A. Randall's *Development of Building Construction in Chicago.* I have made liberal use of all this material, as my notes and bibliography indicate. Richard Nickel's comprehensive survey of Sullivan's architectural and ornamental designs has not yet been published, but he has given generously of his knowledge and his photographic talents, which have recently been devoted to making a graphic record of all the great works of Chicago architecture that are threatened by the construction of new buildings and expressways. Few of the classics are likely to remain if the present rate of destruction continues.

In addition to Mr. Nickel, other individuals and organizations responded willingly to my requests for information and photographs. I am especially indebted to Graham Aldis, of Aldis and Company; Russell Ballard, director of Hull-House; Joseph Benson, municipal reference librarian of Chicago; William Deknatel, architect; Leonard K. Eaton, of the University of Michigan Department of Architecture; Florence Stewart, of the Northwestern University Archives Department; and J. Carson Webster and William Rudd, of the Northwestern University Art Department; and to the Chicago Board of Education, Chicago Park District, Illinois Central Railroad, Illinois Institute of Technology, Inland Steel Company, Skidmore, Owings and Merrill, and the University of Chicago. Credits to individual photographers and to publications from which I have copied prints are given in the list of illustrations, and sources of quotations in the notes. I extend my thanks to all photographers and publishers for their kind permission to reprint this material. The costs of assembling illustrations and preparing the text were borne by grants from the Committee on Reseach Funds of Northwestern University. I am grateful to the members of this committee, who made it possible for me to meet the heavy expenses involved in a work of this kind.

An extensive part of my concluding evaluation of Sullivan's work in chapter xi was originally published as an article, "Sullivan's Skyscrapers as the Expression of Nineteenth Century Technology," in *Technology and Culture*, Volume I (Winter, 1959). I have reprinted it here with the permission of the Wayne State University Press and the Society for the History of Technology.

CARL W. CONDIT

MORTON GROVE, ILLINOIS

CONTENTS

ILLUSTRATIONS

xi

following page 142

CHAPTER I

ARCHITECTURE IN THE NINETEENTH CENTURY

The architectural and technical achievement of the Chicago school marked the establishment of a new style of architecture, but at the same time it was the culmination of a structural evolution that extended over the century preceding it. This dual character was reflected in the two major developments of the school, which existed side by side throughout the central portion of its history. One was highly utilitarian, marked by a strict adherence to function and structure, and was in great part derived from certain forms of urban vernacular building in Europe and the eastern United States. The other was formal and plastic, the product of a new theoretical spirit and the conscious determination to create rich symbolic forms—to create, in short, a new style expressive of contemporary American culture. Thus the architecture of the Chicago school must be interpreted from several standpoints: first, in terms of the structural techniques and building forms from which it grew; second, in relation to the architectural dress, so to speak, of the revivalistic building of the nineteenth century; and finally, in comparison with the later development of the stylistic revolution which it set in motion.

Style in architecture represents or stands for those essential characteristics of construction, form, ornament, and detail that are common to all the important structures of any definable period in history. But it also stands for those technical and aesthetic qualities of the artistic product that grow directly and organically out of the conditions of human existence and out of the aspirations and powers of human beings. We rightly feel that the buildings of a certain style—if it is a genuine style—symbolize in their form the realities of man's experience and the attempt to master and give adequate emotional expression to those realities. These buildings are constituent facts of man's history, and their revelation is a part of truth itself.

The refined architectural classicism that became dominant in the latter half of the eighteenth century eventually faced the social and economic revolution brought about by the large-scale application of steam power to industrial techniques and by the new mechanical inventions that accompanied this application. The first clumsy steam engine might have seemed remote from the proud dignity of the Royal Crescent or Cumberland Terrace; yet it represented a force that soon engulfed all the arts and all the modes of action of Western civilization. In the face of this unprecedented phenomenon, the ancient and vital art of architecture was threatened by powerful disintegrative forces. With respect to utilitarian needs, the traditional techniques of construction eventually fell hopelessly short of meeting the requirements and taking advantage of the opportunities presented by the new age of mechanized industrialization. Architectural revivalism struggled bravely with the social and technical forces of the age and frequently produced functionally successful and aesthetically valid works of building art, but as the century moved on revivalism grew increasingly out of touch with the realities of the time. The ultimate artistic failure of architecture in the nineteenth century can be stated very simply as the failure to form a consistent style. It was the failure to provide, in its own vocabulary, an aesthetic discipline that would combine the expression of science, technology, mechanized industry, and modern urban life with the deeper-lying emotional needs of the human spirit.

Architecture had once been what it ought to be—the *structural art*. It is the combined art and technique of designing, shaping, organizing, and decorating the stone, iron, wood, and glass of which a building is composed. It is not one of these activities alone, but all of them together, making an organic unit with a form and expression and use of its own. But as the nineteenth century progressed, the architect, instead of being a master builder or a designer of a whole structure, increasingly became the person who applies an arbitrary dress to a structure which was largely designed and wholly built by others who cared little about the niceties of scale, proportion, and rhythm. The architect did the best that he could in the face of unprecedented demands, but it became more and more difficult for him to develop an exterior form that grew out of and gave expression to the dominant social factors of the time, chiefly the new conditions of urban life in the great centers of trade and manufacture.

The failure of the nineteenth-century architects, however, cannot be ascribed simply to perversity or to ignorance; nor can it be understood as an escape into fantasies that seemed more pleasing than the harsh realities of the time. It is true that before the challenge of the machine they sought refuge in styles with literary, historical, and even ethical associations. But that challenge was so extreme, so complex, and so unprecedented that much of the best talent went to finding ways in which well-known architectural forms could be adapted to the new exigencies. In a positive sense, the architects of the time reflected the extent to which the age was imbued with the historical spirit and its associated points of view. In this respect the nine-

2

teenth century was unique: no other period was so deeply conscious of the historical process as an essential dimension of man's self-awareness. The borrowing of exterior architectural details was often indiscriminate and sometimes merely capricious, so that when we view the century as a whole from our own vantage point, we feel that styles came and went like fashions in dress. But if we consider the names of only a few of the best American architects of the past century, we realize that, however much the succession of revivals prevented them from forming an architectural style, they were in no way inhibited from creating impressive individual buildings. Some of them, indeed, are superior to anything we have produced today, at least in the richness of the visual experience that they can offer.

American architecture in the nineteenth century began with the variations on Palladian and allied classical forms which are generally comprehended in the term "Federal style." Thomas Jefferson was the best-known exponent of its Roman enthusiasm, but many others contributed to a body of architectural work distinguished by a harmony, dignity, and repose that seem remote from our frantic time. The Greek Revival might be regarded as a simplification of the earlier movement, sometimes combining a dedicated antiquarianism with a perfectly sound understanding of its adaptability to the needs of the young republic. The possibilities of this romantic classicism, as it has sometimes been called, are most fully revealed in the work of William Strickland, Robert Mills, and Thomas Ustick Walter.

The revivals which followed the Greek came at shorter intervals. By mid-century, Gothic was in the ascendant. It is best represented in the ecclesiastical designs of James Renwick and Richard Upjohn in New York. Shortly after the Civil War the restless age demanded another change, and the Gothic was superseded by the Romanesque, most powerfully and creatively exploited by Henry Hobson Richardson in ways that ultimately pointed toward genuinely contemporary forms.[1] The last phase before the end of the century was the Renaissance Revival, dominated by the great town houses and public buildings of McKim, Mead and White. In the heyday of their lavish practice, however, Sullivan was enjoying his largest commissions and thus providing the perfect antithesis to the revivalistic spirit of the age. Yet eclecticism was to continue as the dominant mode of building until the third decade of the twentieth century.

For all the excellence of individual buildings, the whole pattern of architectural development revealed to a growing degree a serious malaise at the roots of nineteenth-century culture. The artist in part creates the character of his time, but he must at the same time be nourished by what his age gives him. Architecture, in the period of its decline, reflected certain cultural fail-

[1] For Richardson's Chicago work and its influence, see pp. 60–63.

ures of the new industrial age. Most pervasive, as we can now see, was the collapse of the traditional well-ordered cosmos that embraced a moral, or at least a rational, as well as a physical order. Associated with this loss was the progressive decline of a public or civic world in which human beings might find scope for meaningful action and the potential self-realization that accompanies it. The growth of the industrial megalopolis of the nineteenth century quickly destroyed the remaining vestiges of the humane urban order that once provided some measure of self-identity and dignity to the citizen. The past century seemed stable on the surface, but in truth the unstable and ephemeral quality of many of its cultural achievements provided increasing evidence of an inner disharmony and confusion that persist to this day, although in different forms.

What the nineteenth century suffered from was in part a split personality, a "cultural schizophrenia," as Sigfried Giedion explained it. This state has been characteristic of other highly creative periods of confused or rapidly changing spiritual orientation. The emotional satisfactions and the aesthetic experiences of people were split off from their intellectual and practical activities. Science and technology parted company from art, and both were ultimately divided into an ever growing number of separate, isolated compartments. Eventually specialization reached such a point that one could not even see the world beyond one's own special activity, much less comprehend it.

Thus at a time when the technical and intellectual elements of culture were most in need of a humanizing discipline, the one best calculated to achieve it in the public world failed to realize its highest function. Architecture in one of its aspects is a utilitarian art. Function, structure, and form are indissolubly wedded. Applied science and technology provide it with materials and with their known mechanical, thermal, and chemical properties; the artist's sense of form and order and harmony, his capacity to create symbolic images transform the physical elements into emotionally satisfying objects that live in the imaginations of men while giving voice to their ideals, aspirations, and capacities. A genuine architecture is a technical-aesthetic synthesis that makes it possible for the world of technology to enter into the domain of feeling and morality.

In order to achieve this end architects in the nineteenth century eventually had to turn their backs on imitations of the past, for they were faced with conditions and opportunities that had no precedent. They had to master new materials and offer solutions to new problems. The forms of the past, however vital they once were, came to have little meaning in the face of the conditions which came to exist in New York or Chicago. But just as the great majority of nineteenth-century architects seemed to have lost contact with the

4

social and technical realities of their time, individuals began to appear who, consciously or unconsciously, accepted the challenge of their age and built directly and boldly on its basis.

It was the engineers who first pointed the way that a new structural art might profitably take. They built primarily for use, and whatever form their structures took at least had the merit of expressing directly, simply, and honestly the system of construction they employed. However, some of the bridge engineers had a strong sense of form. They looked upon techniques somewhat as the artist looks on the material of his painting or poetry, and they wanted to celebrate the powers they possessed by means of a new kind of monumentalism. Industry had provided them with new structural materials, cast and wrought iron, and they exploited their possibilities with an exuberance unparalleled in the history of building. Early in the nineteenth century some of the bridge engineers, imbued with a sense of harmony and proportion characteristic of trained architects, developed structural forms that pointed toward an organic architecture appropriate to a mechanized industrial culture.

The first cast-iron structure was a small arch bridge over the River Severn at Coalbrookdale, England. It was built by the iron founders Abraham Darby and John Wilkinson between the years 1775 and 1779. Following the precedent of two thousand years of masonry bridge construction, the builders employed the fixed semicircular arch as the only acceptable form. Thomas Telford's great project of 1801 for a bridge over the Thames at London involved a flattened arch of 600-foot span. In its size, its effortless grace, and the delicacy of its iron ornament, it would have been a major aesthetic achievement. Telford's finest completed span was the suspension bridge over Menai Strait, built between 1819 and 1826, the first big bridge to embody the new system of suspended construction.

The success of Telford's Menai Bridge led to the extensive employment of the suspension principle in Europe, England, and America. The triumph of the cable form came with the Brooklyn Bridge, built by John and Washington Roebling over the years from 1869 to 1883. Contemporary with this structure was James B. Eads's bridge over the Mississippi at St. Louis, built between 1868 and 1874. For this bridge Eads returned to the older form, using a series of fixed steel arches of 520-foot span. Most significant for Chicago architecture was the profound effect that the bridge exercised on Louis Sullivan.[2] Equal in its architectonic excellence was Gustave Eiffel's Garabit Viaduct, completed in 1884. The great engineer of the Eiffel Tower used the two-hinged arch in the Garabit span and thus provided the structural art

[2] For the importance of bridges in the development of Sullivan's architectural principles, see pp. 168–71.

with a large-scale demonstration of another impressive form, the crescent-shaped arched truss. These immense bridges stand today, monumental pioneer exhibitions of a new building technology rich in promise for the whole architectural art.

Of more immediate significance for the architects, especially those of the Chicago school, was the application of iron to conventional types of building. Cast-iron structural elements began to appear in the eighteenth century. An early and extensive use of the material was in St. Anne's Church, Liverpool (1770–72), in which all the interior columns—that is, the compressive members—were of cast iron. An even larger installation formed part of the internal frame of William Strutt's Calico Mill at Derby, England (1792–93), which was composed of iron columns and timber beams. Within the following decade Matthew Boulton and James Watt began to build multistory factories with complete internal frames of cast iron. In the United States the new system of framing was first adopted by the architect-engineer William Strickland, who introduced cast-iron columns as balcony supports in the Chestnut Street Theater in Philadelphia (1820–22). Within a generation Daniel Badger and James Bogardus, the two most influential builders in the pioneer phase of iron construction, established their respective factories in New York (Badger in 1847 and Bogardus the following year). Their buildings often revealed great refinement of form, with street elevations reduced to a rhythmic pattern of rectangular openings enframed by the columns and spandrel girders of the iron frame.[3] An early example of large-scale iron framing that prefigured the dominant mode of the Chicago work was the John Shillito Store in Cincinnati, Ohio (1876–77), designed by James McLaughlin. By combining interior iron columns and beams with narrow masonry piers in the exterior enclosure, McLaughlin turned all four elevations of the block-long six-story building into the open cellular walls that the Chicago school later developed into forms of great architectonic power.

Meanwhile, the builders of England and the Continent were rapidly exploiting the potentialities of the structural techniques introduced by Strutt and by Boulton and Watt. One of the most promising and original works of the nineteenth century was Joseph Paxton's Crystal Palace, erected for the London International Exhibition of 1851. Paxton reduced the huge building to a transparent, neutral skin of glass stretched over a delicate frame of iron members. The construction of the Crystal Palace was carried out by assembling prefabricated elements of curtain wall and skeleton. It was an invention the useful consequences of which are just beginning to be realized by the

[3] Certain structures erected by Badger and Bogardus clearly anticipated the systems of iron and steel framing developed by the Chicago builders. For these works and their possible influence on Chicago architects, see p. 81, under the Home Insurance Building.

building industry. A similar system of construction was embodied in Carsten-sen and Gildemeister's Crystal Palace for the New York Exhibition of 1853. The great significance of both these buildings was largely lost on the archi-tects of the nineteenth century. The fact that they were erected for the ephem-eral purposes of an exposition contributed to the feeling that they were novelties without serious architectural meaning. More influential because of its relative permanence is Hippolyte Fontaine's warehouse for the St. Ouen docks near Paris (completed in 1866). There is good evidence that this extraordinary building is the first multistory structure carried entirely on an iron frame without any assistance from masonry bearing elements.[4] Within five years Jules Saulnier produced one of the curiosities of early iron fram-ing in his Menier Chocolate Works at Noisiel, France (1871–72). The braced framing in the curtain walls of this building, undoubtedly derived from the iron bridge truss, is an important step in the development of wind-bracing for the tall building.[5]

A peculiar problem posed by the industrial demands of the nineteenth cen-tury was the need to span wide enclosures without intermediate supports. The early market halls and theaters were examples in traditional forms. The train shed of the metropolitan railway terminal, however, offered novel difficulties because of its great size and unique function. The engineers attacked the problem with characteristic directness and courage, and by mid-century they had produced the great balloon shed that was once the most striking feature of the transportation structures. I. K. Brunel and M. D. Wyatt, in Paddington Station, London (1852–54), created a huge vault of wrought-iron ribs carry-ing a shell of glass and iron. The two materials were perfectly integrated in a form of great size. St. Pancras Station (1863–76), the creation of W. H. Barlow, R. M. Ordish, and Sir George Gilbert Scott, revealed further refine-ments of the glass and iron vault in a structure of even greater dimensions. The first Grand Central Terminal in New York (1869–71), designed by John B. Snook and Isaac Buckhout, was the first American structure com-parable to these extraordinary British achievements. The train sheds of the nineteenth century embodied a prevision of the twentieth-century builder's treatment of space, not as an inclosed volume, but as a free-flowing element integrated with an open and buoyant structure.

The great bulk of iron-framed buildings in the past century belong to the domain of vernacular architecture. Although it is impossible to define this type of building exactly and to separate it from architecture consciously de-signed for expressive and symbolic ends, one can readily distinguish its

[4] The St. Ouen warehouse is another antecedent of "skyscraper construction" in Chicago. For structural details and its relation to William Le Baron Jenney's work, see p. 82.

[5] For pioneer essays in windbracing in Chicago, see pp. 67, 91–92, 123–24.

dominant visual and utilitarian characteristics. Vernacular building comprehends all those structures erected by carpenters, masons, ironworkers, and others with the requisite technical skills but without formal training in architectural design, and planned usually for strictly utilitarian ends such as shelter, containment, and protection. Vernacular form is thus purely functional, but this does not preclude the possibility of its possessing a genuine aesthetic distinction. The earliest colonial residences and churches belonged to the vernacular tradition of the carpenter-builder, but as the American economy expanded, such building was progressively restricted to barns, mills, warehouses, factories, and the like. These structures are usually marked by extreme severity of form, an elemental geometry of flat rectangular wall planes and gabled roofs. The timber mill building, for example, might consist simply of a New England braced frame covered by a sheathing of clapboard siding. The common structural alternative was a building of masonry bearing walls with an interior frame of wooden columns and beams, wooden trusses, or combinations of timber and iron. Materials were generally directly presented, and openings were as simple in shape, as regularly spaced, and as large as structural exigencies permitted. The use of cast and wrought iron for wall framing, as in the buildings of James Bogardus, allowed the builder to open the exterior walls almost entirely to glass. Many of the surviving vernacular classics of the pre-iron age are the early mills of New England and the barns of eastern Pennsylvania.

Chicago's first major contribution to the building art grew out of the vernacular tradition. The balloon frame, invented in 1833 by Augustine D. Taylor, was an enormously useful and influential variation on the heavy New England frame (Fig. 1). For the stout girts and posts of the older system, Taylor substituted a closely ranked series of light studs, joists, roof rafters, and purlins joined by simple nailing. The resulting structure was usually covered with clapboard siding nailed to the studs. St. Mary's Church in Chicago, built by Taylor, was the first building carried on a balloon frame. From it grew a countless progeny in the towns and on the farms of the West. One can trace a fairly direct line from the little church through the cast-iron fronts of Badger and Bogardus to the mature architecture of steel framing that Chicago produced at the end of the century.

A good example of vernacular building in masonry, wood, and iron is one of the few survivors of the Chicago fire of 1871: the Inbound Freight House of the Illinois Central Railroad, on South Water Street a block east of Michigan Avenue (Fig. 2). Originally built in 1855, the interior timber work of the station was destroyed by the fire and replaced in 1872. The building measures 45 by 572 feet 6 inches on the exterior in plan, with a clear interior space of 40-foot span. The bearing walls, 2 feet 6 inches thick, are composed of irregular blocks of Niagara limestone, which was available in great quantities following the completion of the Illinois and Michigan Canal in 1847. The gable roof is supported by purlins in turn resting on curious trusses built up of heavy timbers and wrought-iron rods. In its homely simplicity, relieved only by the texture of the limestone walls, it represents a perfectly functional approach to building. Yet it was this strict utilitarian functionalism that formed the very foundation of even the most sophisticated designs of the Chicago school. Only a short step removed from this vernacular essay was the first passenger terminal of the Illinois Central in Chicago. Known as Great Central Station, it was designed by Otto H. Matz and built in 1856. With its vaulted shed of wood and its arched openings in the masonry end wall for the passage of trains, it actually belonged to the vernacular phase of the metropolitan terminal. It was demolished in 1892, when the present Central Station was completed.

The transmutation of vernacular building, with its exclusive emphasis on immediate utility, into a genuine architectural style was in part the product of a relatively long theoretical preparation. The growth of a functionalist and organic theory of architecture was one of the numerous by-products of the pragmatic and evolutionary currents in nineteenth-century thought. Among European theorists the most influential was Eugène Emmanuel Viollet-le-Duc. The English translation of his *Discourses on Architecture* was published in the United States in 1881, but his proposals for a new architecture consistent with the physical properties and the structural potentialities of iron had gained wide currency before that date. Gottfried Semper, a German historian and theorist who derived his organic doctrine of architectural style partly from the Darwinian hypothesis, was read and discussed in Chicago around 1890.[6] A native organic theory, however, had begun to develop before the middle of the century. Its founder was Andrew Jackson Downing, who proposed in his *Landscape Architecture* (1844) that a building ought to be adapted to its site and ought to express its end or purpose. A more thoroughly developed organic theory, with transcendentalist elements, was worked out by Emerson in a series of disconnected fragments scattered through his journals and lectures. The essential idea in his doctrine is that architecture is the only art that is both utilitarian and aesthetic and hence ought to express its practical function as well as the inspiration that leads to the creation of beauty. Emerson held that the architect derives his forms from nature—that is, from natural structures such as trees and shells—and that his work is the imaginative embodiment of the physical laws of natural processes.

The first strictly functionalist theory of design was developed around the

[6] For further details of Semper's thought and his influence in Chicago, see pp. 97–98.

middle of the century by the sculptor Horatio Greenough, who was a con-temporary of Emerson and possibly an influence on his thought. Greenough's friend and admirer Henry T. Tuckerman provided a comprehensive statement of the artist's ideas in *A Memorial of Horatio Greenough* (1853). Like Emerson, Greenough believed that nature is the primary source of form in architecture and that just as the form of an organism reveals its functional capacity, so should the form of a building reveal its function. The chief characteristic of the natural organism, he said, "is the consistency and har-mony of the parts juxtaposed, the subordination of details to masses, and of masses to the whole. The law of adaptation is the fundamental law of nature in all structure."[7] As examples of human creations in which this law is embodied, he cites various machines and the clipper ships. His extreme admiration for ships led him to assert that if civil architecture were as well designed as the sailing vessels, public buildings would soon become superior to the Parthenon. Beauty in architecture, then, is simply the promise of function. Greenough's concept of the aesthetic quality is thus highly empiri-cal and positivistic and is strictly bound up with a scientific understanding of nature.

I call therefore upon science in all its branches to arrest the tide of sensuous-ness and arbitrary embellishment . . . not negatively by criticism thereof alone, but positively by making the instrument a many-sided response to the multiform demands of life. The craving for completeness will then obtain its normal food in results, not the opiate and deadening stimulus of decoration. Then will structure and its dependent sister arts emerge from the standstill of *ipse dixit* and, like the ship, the team, the steam engine, proceed through phases of development toward a response to need.[8]

Greenough's organic and functionalist theory remained the most extensive and thorough until Sullivan elaborated his own aesthetic philosophy at the end of the century. However, the twin themes of natural adaptation and empirical fitness continued to be presented with variations in a steady stream of essays and books. Attacks on eclecticism began to appear in the engineer-ing press in the 1860's. Calvert Vaux argued in his *Villas and Cottages* (1857) for an architecture built to suit the needs of the American people and the local climate. James J. Jarves, in *The Art-Idea* (1864), repeated

---

[7] Tuckerman, *A Memorial of Horatio Greenough*, reprinted in Lewis Mumford (ed.), *Roots of Contemporary American Architecture* (New York: Reinhold Publishing Corp., 1952), p. 35. It is noteworthy that Greenough used the concept of adaptation before the appearance of *Origin of Species* (1859), although the idea is clearly presented in Darwin's *Voyage of the Beagle* (1839).

[8] Mumford, *op. cit.*, p. 48.

Greenough's doctrine that if the functional and pragmatic basis of American technical creations was applied to the design of buildings America could quickly create an original and beautiful native architecture. John Burroughs, whose *Signs and Seasons* (1886) was extremely popular, presented a romantic naturalistic variation on the fundamental theme. In addition to adaptation to site and need, he argued for the honest presentation of natural materials in their rudeness and simplicity. By the last decade of the century, these doctrines were beginning to impress the architects themselves, some of whom, most notably Joseph W. Yost, began to demand a modern style emancipated from tradition and consistent with the new structural materials and utilitarian demands.[9] Thus many of the ideas from which a new philosophy and a new style of architecture might be derived had been given a wide currency in numerous writings by the time the Chicago movement began the material revolution in the building arts.

The architects who came together in Chicago following the fire of 1871 included men of rare creative talent who had no formal education in architecture but who had a remarkable capacity for learning their craft through direct attack on the problems of large-scale commercial building. Few of the leading figures were born or grew to manhood in Chicago. The city had no schools of architecture and only a handful of architects who could train apprentices. Yet in little more than a decade after the fire they invented and mastered the modern technique of riveted steel framing and were thus able to develop the office building, hotel, and apartment block as we know them today. But these categories hardly exhaust the areas in which the architects of the Chicago school worked. These included every type of building: residences, railway terminals and way stations, warehouses, factories, churches, schools, hospitals, museums, theaters, and even tombs. Nor was their work confined to a single city. They designed buildings erected in New York, Buffalo, Cincinnati, St. Louis, New Orleans, Kansas City, Omaha, Milwaukee, Minneapolis, Pueblo, Salt Lake City, San Francisco, and Seattle. They were the acknowledged leaders of their profession in the Middle West and among those few critics in the East who were willing to risk their reputations by making an objective assessment of what the Chicago group was doing. That they were either forgotten or condemned in the period between the two world wars is one of the major ironies of American history.

Their achievement was not an accident, and we now know that they belonged in the mainstream of a world movement. They knew exactly what

[9] Yost presented a theoretical formulation of what was then going on in Chicago in a paper read before the national convention of the American Institute of Architects in 1896. The title was "The Influence of Steel Construction and Plate Glass upon the Development of Modern Style" (Mumford, *op. cit.*, pp. 152–58).

they were doing and why they ought to do it. They recognized their problem with relentless clarity of insight, and the solutions they developed represented a mode of attack very much in the spirit of creative scientific inquiry and theorizing. They believed that they had created a new style of architecture by means of a new kind of thinking about it. Several of them, most notably John Wellborn Root and Louis Sullivan, wrote extensively about the technical and aesthetic aspects of their art. Architectural journals and societies were founded in Chicago to preserve their words. Sullivan, the most sensitive and subtle personality among them, in developing his own aesthetic philosophy recognized the true value of their achievement: that they had taken a long step toward the development of an aesthetic discipline of the powerful forces of nineteenth-century industrialism. The whole forward movement of contemporary architecture lies in the direction of that synthesis.

The recorders of building progress in Chicago were also aware of the unique success of the local architects. The best evidence of this understanding lies in the pages of *Industrial Chicago,* whose anonymous authors were tireless in their praise of the originality and greatness of what they called "Chicago construction." They coined the phrase "commercial style" to designate a form of building that had no counterpart in the past. What is most remarkable, however, is their recognition of the union of science, technology, and art that reveals itself in the structural-utilitarian-aesthetic unity of the best Chicago buildings.

Among the critics and scholars of the East, a few saw the importance of the architecture that was growing up in the city of the prairies. Chief among them were Montgomery Schuyler and Russell Sturgis, the leading exponents of a rational and realistic architecture. The latter consistently maintained that work like that of the Chicago school represented the only genuine structural art of the time. He pointed out in numerous articles that no school of architecture could train men like Sullivan, Jenney, and Root, that it could not, as a matter of fact, turn out an architect at all, and that any real imagination and technical skill would be corrupted by it.

By the time of Sullivan's death in 1924, the ideal that he stood for seemed to be a lost cause. As a consequence, the Chicago school had to be rediscovered by a later generation. Perhaps the first to do so was Lewis Mumford, whose discerning chapter on Richardson, Root, and Sullivan in *The Brown Decades* (1931) awakened interest in the background of the modern movement in the building arts. In 1932 the Museum of Modern Art in New York showed a small exhibit entitled "Early Modern Architecture in Chicago" and issued a slim catalogue on some of the architects and their works. Hugh Morrison, in connection with another exhibit of the Museum of Modern Art, wrote a comprehensive critical and biographical study of Sullivan that was published in 1935. The most thorough treatment of the school in its full historical setting appeared in Giedion's *Space, Time and Architecture*, first published in 1941. Today recognition of the school is world-wide, and its once forgotten principles now constitute the basis of architecture as it is practiced on every continent.

CHAPTER II

CHICAGO: 1871

By 1871 Chicago had become the focal point of commerce in the United States. Forty years earlier it was a collection of cabins, a few houses with some claim to comfort, and at least one tavern, located on a swamp near the point where a sluggish stream flowed into Lake Michigan. By the end of the Civil War the expansive forces within it had reached an explosive pitch. The population had increased tenfold in twenty years, from 29,963 in 1850 to 298,977 in 1870. The prairies of the Mississippi Valley had been opened to intensive agricultural exploitation. With agriculture came the institutions of finance and the facilities for the storage and milling of grain. The meat-packing industry soon followed the establishment of the grain exchange. The Union Stock Yards was founded in 1865 to centralize the processes of slaughter. The growth of operations at the mills and the stockyards was astronomical. It is no exaggeration to say that before another decade had passed the price of the world's bread was decided on the Chicago grain market.

Parallel with the development of agriculture was the growth of the railway network. The first company to operate trains in and out of Chicago was the Galena and Chicago Union, which began service in 1848 and within a few years connected the city with the lead mines in the northwestern corner of the state. In 1869 it joined the recently completed Union Pacific Railroad at Omaha to provide the first rail route to the Pacific coast. The Chicago and Rock Island was chartered in 1847 and began to run trains in 1854, when it became the first line to cross the Mississippi River. The Aurora Branch Railroad, established in 1849, joined Chicago and Aurora in 1852 and reached Quincy, Illinois, as the Chicago, Burlington and Quincy Railroad in 1855. Service south of Chicago was promised in 1851 with the incorporation of the Illinois Central. The original line, completed in 1856, extended to Cairo on the Ohio River. The Michigan Central, Michigan Southern, and Northern Illinois railroads were opened to service by 1853 and became the first companies to operate trains east of the city. In 1869 the last two were merged with seven other lines to form the Lake Shore and Michigan Southern Railroad, thus providing links in a through route

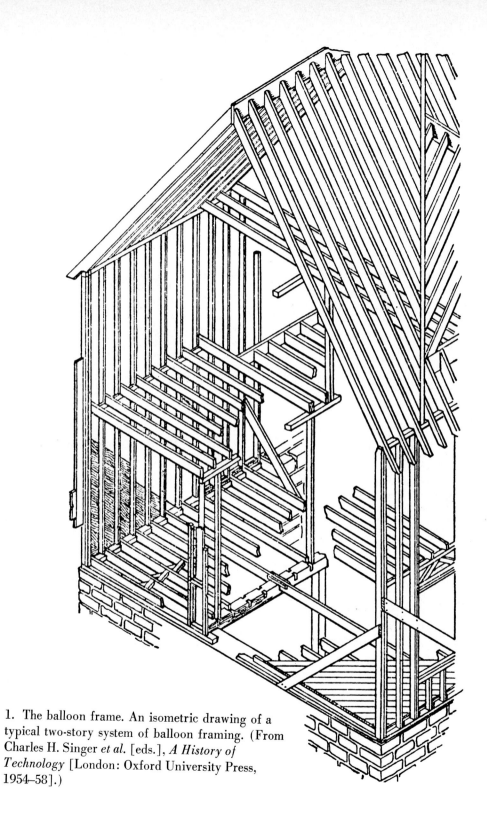

1. The balloon frame. An isometric drawing of a
typical two-story system of balloon framing. (From
Charles H. Singer *et al.* [eds.], *A History of
Technology* [London: Oxford University Press,
1954–58].)

2. INBOUND FREIGHT HOUSE, ILLINOIS CENTRAL RAILROAD, 1855, 1872

East South Water Street near Michigan Avenue.
(*Illinois Central Railroad.*)

3. NIXON BUILDING, 1871 OTTO H. MATZ

Formerly at the northeast corner of La Salle and
Monroe streets; demolished in 1889. (From
Frank A. Randall, *History of the Development
of Building Construction in Chicago* [Urbana:
University of Illinois Press, 1949].)

4. CENTRAL MUSIC HALL, 1879 Dankmar Adler

Formerly at the southeast corner of State and
Randolph streets; demolished in 1901. (*Commercial
Photographic Co.*)

5. SCHILLER BUILDING, 1891–92   ADLER AND SULLIVAN
   BORDEN BLOCK, 1879–80   ADLER AND SULLIVAN

The Schiller (*center*), later the Garrick Theater Building, stood
at 64 West Randolph Street before its demolition in 1961. The
Borden (*right*), formerly at the northwest corner of Randolph
and Dearborn streets, was demolished in 1916. (*Chicago
Architectural Photographing Co.*)

6. ROTHSCHILD STORE, 1881   Adler and Sullivan

Now known by its address, 210 West Monroe Street.
(*Kaufmann & Fabry Co.*)

7. JEWELERS BUILDING, 1881–82   ADLER AND SULLIVAN

15 South Wabash Avenue (*center, with sign
"Harmony Cafeteria"*); now known by its address.
(*Kaufmann & Fabry Co.*)

8. REVELL BUILDING, 1881–83 ADLER AND SULLIVAN

Northeast corner of Wabash Avenue and Adams Street.
The first two stories were remodeled in 1929. (*Commercial
Photographic Co.*)

9. REVELL BUILDING, 1881–83   Adler and Sullivan

Part of the south elevation as it was originally constructed.
(*Kaufmann & Fabry Co.*)

10. THIRD McVICKERS THEATER, 1883, 1885   ADLER AND SULLIVAN

Formerly at 25 West Madison Street; demolished in 1922. (*Commercial Photographic Co.*)

11. THIRTY-NINTH STREET PASSENGER STATION, ILLINOIS
CENTRAL RAILROAD, 1886   ADLER AND SULLIVAN

Demolished in 1934. (*Illinois Central Railroad.*)

12. WIRT DEXTER BUILDING, 1887 ADLER AND SULLIVAN

Now known by its address, 630 South Wabash Avenue.
(*Kaufmann & Fabry Co.*)

13. STANDARD CLUB, 1887–88   ADLER AND SULLIVAN

Formerly at the southwest corner of Michigan Avenue and
Twenty-fourth Street; demolished in 1910. (*Chicago
Architectural Photographing Co.*)

14. WALKER WAREHOUSE, 1888–89   Adler and Sullivan

Formerly at 210 South Market Street (now Wacker Drive);
demolished in 1953. (*Commercial Photographic Co.*)

15. MONTAUK BUILDING, 1881–82   BURNHAM AND ROOT

Formerly at 64 West Monroe Street; demolished in 1902.
(From A. T. Andreas, *History of Chicago* [Chicago:
A. T. Andreas, 1884–86].)

16. HIRAM SIBLEY WAREHOUSE, 1882–83   George H. Edbrooke

315 North Clark Street. (From Frank A. Randall,
History of the Development of Building Construction in Chicago
[Urbana: University of Illinois Press, 1949].)

17. DEXTER BUILDING, 1883   Clinton J. Warren,
    Burnham and Root

Formerly at 39 West Adams Street; demolished in 1961.
(*Kaufmann & Fabry Co.*)

18. CHICAGO OPERA HOUSE, 1884–85   Cobb and Frost

Formerly at the southwest corner of Clark and Washington Streets; demolished in 1912. (*Commercial Photographic Co.*)

19. GLESSNER HOUSE, 1886–87   Henry Hobson Richardson

Now owned by the Lithographers Research Association,
at the southwest corner of Prairie Avenue and Eighteenth Street.
(*Municipal Reference Library of Chicago.*)

20. MARSHALL FIELD WHOLESALE STORE, 1885–87
HENRY HOBSON RICHARDSON

Formerly on the block bounded by Adams, Wells, Quincy, and Franklin streets; demolished in 1930. (*Chicago Architectural Photographing Co.*)

21. THE ROOKERY, 1885–86   BURNHAM AND ROOT

209 South La Salle Street. (*Commercial Photographic Co.*)

22. THE ROOKERY, 1885–86   Burnham and Root

Detail of the court walls. (*Thomas Knudtson.*)

23. THE ROOKERY, 1885–86   Burnham and Root

Glass and iron dome above the light court. (*Peter Weil.*)

24. THE ROOKERY, 1885–86 Burnham and Root

Suspended stairway at the west side of the light court. (*Peter Weil.*)

25. THE ROOKERY, 1885–86 BURNHAM AND ROOT

Main stairway above the second floor. (*Thomas Knudtson.*)

26. THE ROOKERY, 1885–86   BURNHAM AND ROOT

Detail of the glass and iron housing of the stairway. (*Thomas Knudtson.*)

27. THE ROOKERY, 1885–86   BURNHAM AND ROOT

La Salle Street entrance. (*Thomas Knudtson.*)

28. MONADNOCK BUILDING, 1889–91   Burnham and Root
53 West Jackson Boulevard. (*Commercial Photographic Co.*)

29. MONADNOCK BUILDING, 1889–91   Burnham and Root
East elevation. (*Richard Nickel.*)

30. MONADNOCK BUILDING, 1889–91 BURNHAM AND ROOT
Detail of the east elevation. (*Richard Nickel.*)

31. AUDITORIUM BUILDING, 1887–89 ADLER AND SULLIVAN

Now Roosevelt University, at the northwest corner of Michigan Avenue and Congress Parkway. (*Chicago Architectural Photographing Co.*)

32. AUDITORIUM BUILDING, 1887–89   ADLER AND SULLIVAN

The tower above the theater entrance on the south elevation.
(*Ralph M. Line.*)

from Chicago to Buffalo, where Cornelius Vanderbilt's newly created New York Central and Hudson River Railroad offered connecting service to Albany and New York. A number of small companies established during the mid-century decade were merged in 1862 to form the Pittsburgh, Fort Wayne and Chicago Railway, which joined the city to Pittsburgh and a connection with the Pennsylvania Railroad to Philadelphia.[1] Thus, by the time of the Civil War rail lines extended from the city in all directions to the eastern seaboard and the midwestern waterways and by 1869 to the Pacific coast. In 1871 Chicago was the hub of railroad systems embracing 10,750 miles of line, with aggregate annual revenues of $82,777,000. The carriers operated 75 passenger trains per day to and from the city's terminals.

With respect to waterway transportation, Chicago was ideally located. Traffic on the Great Lakes followed immediately upon the establishment of communities along their shores and grew at a constantly accelerating rate. The city was quick to take advantage of its focal position. The digging of the Illinois and Michigan Canal was undertaken in 1836 and completed eleven years later, when it joined the South Branch of the Chicago River with the Illinois River at La Salle, Illinois. The narrow but valuable waterway was superseded by the present Chicago Sanitary and Ship Canal in 1900. The chief function of the early waterway was the transportation of agricultural products from the farms to the slaughterhouses and grain elevators of the city. The discovery of deposits of natural cement in La Salle County and the inauguration of coal mining in southern Illinois quickly expanded the traffic on the original canal. The subsequent construction of the Illinois-Mississippi Canal provided another artery to the Mississippi River. The constant extension and improvement of the streams and canals of the Midwest ultimately made Chicago the focus of the largest system of inland waterways in the world.

With the railroads and the canals came the steel, coal, and lumber industries. From 1860 to 1871 the total shipments and receipts of lumber increased three and one-third times, from 488,000,000 board-feet to 1,581,000,000 board-feet. In the same period total traffic in coal increased six and two-

[1] The Galena and Chicago Union, extended by merger with the Chicago, Iowa and Nebraska Railroad, is now the Galena Division of the Chicago and North Western Railway, although it no longer serves the town from which it took its original name. The Chicago and Rock Island was steadily pushed westward to Colorado and New Mexico and eventually became the present Chicago, Rock Island and Pacific. The Lake Shore and Michigan Southern was leased to the New York Central and Hudson River in 1873 and merged with the latter company in 1914, when the name was shortened to the present New York Central. (One of the twin medallions flanking the entranceway of La Salle Street Station still bears the letters "L. S. and M. S.") The Pittsburgh, Fort Wayne and Chicago was leased to the Pennsylvania in 1890 and is still the proprietary company of Chicago Union Station by virtue of 50 per cent ownership of the property.

thirds times, from 151,000 tons to 998,000 tons. There were no blast furnaces in the city in 1860; in 1871 there were four, with a total capacity of 160 tons of pig iron per day. The total value of manufactured iron and steel products increased five times, from $2,140,000 in 1860 to $10,467,000 in 1871.

But the bare statistics serve only as a mathematical measure of quantity. The dynamic quality of the city's life had no parallel. The fervor and devotion and energy that went into the production of agricultural and industrial wealth would have done credit to the most enthusiastic crusader. The discipline would have broken a martyr. Chicagoans "were born into the world to take no rest themselves and to give none to others," as Thucydides said of the Athenians.[2] The achievement was staggering, but so was the cost. Lewis Mumford characterized the Chicago of the early 1870's as "a brutal network of industrial necessities." Most of the dwellings were flimsy houses and cabins. Railway tracks, yards, warehouses, factories, slaughterhouses, elevators, and dumps literally choked the interior city. The internal pressures knew no bounds once the riches of an undeveloped continent were opened to exploitation.

The economic demands clearly established the need for a highly developed building art, but it was the creative spirit and the stimulating intellectual climate of the city that made such an art possible. The traditional view—still persisting among historians—that Chicago was a crude and illiterate frontier town with no intellectual and artistic culture is wholly false. To accept such a view makes it impossible to explain the phoenix that arose from the ashes of 1871. Even at the time of its incorporation in 1837 the city included a bookstore, a theater, a newspaper, and three debating societies and offered regular musical concerts by amateur and professional musicians. Consciousness of and interest in its regional past led to the establishment of the Chicago Historical Society in 1856. By the time of the fire, there were sixty-eight bookstores in the city, or one for every 4,396 inhabitants, a higher ratio than can be found in most cities today. In fact, the eastern publishers regarded the city as one of the best book markets in the nation.

The interest in literature was paralleled by an equal enthusiasm for the visual arts, which led to the inauguration of regular exhibits in 1859. The systematic teaching of painting and sculpture soon followed with the establishment in 1866 of the Chicago Academy of Design. The school expanded rapidly during the following decade. It was renamed the Chicago Academy of Fine Arts and merged with the newly founded Art Institute in 1879, when the Institute was incorporated by a special act of the Illinois State Legisla-

[2] *The Peloponnesian War* (Modern Library ed.; trans. Richard Crawley), I, 70.

ture.[3] This celebrated school and museum, one of the first four in the United States, was thus the culmination of an interest in collecting, exhibiting, and teaching in the arts which began to be implemented on an informal basis during the early years of the city's history. As Charles L. Hutchinson wrote in 1888: "Chicago was not without earlier art movements, which were sustained by old citizens with a public spirit which ought not to be forgotten, and which were perhaps only prevented from permanent success by the catastrophe of the great fire. To these movements the Art Institute is in some sense a successor."[4]

Many of the wealthy families of Chicago lived a cultivated and sophisticated life, often in the European style, which they had discovered at first hand through frequent travels abroad. The most impressive evidence of a rich intellectual life appears in the number of large private libraries among the leading families of the city. The systematic collection of books seems to have been well under way when the city was incorporated. In 1841 several prominent citizens, among them Walter L. Newberry, the founder of the Newberry Library, established the Young Men's Association primarily to provide the city with a subscription library, which proved to be the forerunner and the nucleus of the present public library. Again we can see that what began as private activity eventually flowered into civic institutions. This vigorous intellectual life made the citizens receptive to new ideas and enthusiastic about their implementation. At the time of the fire, Chicago had thirty-five years of a well-developed cultural life behind it. The real intellectual character of the early city has been exactly summed up by one of the few students of the city's history who have understood its true nature.

Historians of the early city have dwelt largely on three things: the inadequacy of, and even the danger represented by, jerry-built houses and stores; the extraordinary promise of the early settlement; and the surprising swiftness with which that promise was fulfilled as the marshy little town at the mouth of the Checagou took its place as the greatest city of the northwest and the second largest in the country. This is so pat a summary of the American frontier experience that it has been generally accepted as the whole truth, but only a little probing beneath the surface reveals that early Chicago was very far from typical of frontier society. On the contrary, the city was cosmopolitan almost from its beginning; in weighted counterpart to the bass notes of the materialistic theme there sound always the higher tones of a cultural motif, a culture Chicago shared with the rest of mid-nineteenth century urban America and, to some degree, with the cities of Europe. From its swaddling days, Chicago was actively interested in things of the mind and the spirit, possessing a degree of refinement in its society which was deemed

[3] On the construction of the present Art Institute building, see p. 96.

[4] Quoted in Allan McNab, "The School of the Art Institute—a Brief History," *Art Institute of Chicago Quarterly*, LV (June, 1961), 25.

remarkable by visitors from abroad. Harriet Martineau, for example, in her *Society in America*, says of Chicago in 1836: "There is some allowable pride in the place about its society. It is a remarkable thing to meet such an assemblage of educated, refined and wealthy persons as may be found there, living in small, inconvenient houses on the edge of a wild prairie." . . . The people of whom Miss Martineau speaks came largely from New York, New England, and the aristocracy of the South, and they brought with them the tastes and pretensions of the world they'd left behind.[5]

One reason for the failure to appreciate the importance attached to things of the intellect in early Chicago is that most of the evidence of the city's cultural life was in the form of letters, diaries, and books, the bulk of which were destroyed in the fire. This represented, perhaps, the most serious material loss.

Most of the buildings of the city reflected the tempo of its commercial life. About two-thirds of them were built wholly of wood, particularly the houses, stockyard structures, warehouses, railway facilities, and the many barns that were uniformly scattered over the urban area. The larger commercial buildings of the central portion were of brick with wood floors and roofs supported by timber or cast-iron columns and, here and there, cast-iron beams. For the most part, however, where masonry was used, the interior bearing members consisted entirely of wood. Persistent wind, the carelessness of a business community operating on a narrow, pragmatic basis, and the absence of any safety precautions—these, together with the physical substance of the city, extended the most generous invitation to fire.

When it came, it struck with devastating fury. At nine o'clock on the night of October 8, 1871, a small blaze started in a barn on De Koven Street not far west of Clinton. The fire department, such as it was, had exhausted itself the day before fighting several fires that were traced to a planing mill near the intersection of Canal and Van Buren streets. The general area was a tinderbox. The great fire swept across the river and burned its way to the lake in a few hours. Northward it moved along Canal Street to the intersection of the North and South branches of the river, thence up the west bank of the North Branch. The old eastward-flowing portion of the river proved no barrier at all. The flames leaped over it and started to consume the northside area. The fire finally burned itself out along open ground at the lower end of Lincoln Park. In about forty-eight hours the flames destroyed $192,-000,000 worth of property out of a total property evaluation of $575,-000,000. Approximately one hundred thousand people were rendered homeless.

[5] Archibald Byrne, "Walter L. Newberry's Chicago," *Newberry Library Bulletin*, III (August, 1955), 262–63.

The scene that one would have observed from a high point near Canal and De Koven streets was one of almost total destruction. Broken fragments of masonry walls stood up at infrequent intervals. Between them the ground was covered with blackened rubble. The so-called fireproof construction of the larger commercial and governmental buildings proved to be a tragic joke. In a heat of three thousand degrees exposed cast-iron members melted into a completely fluid state. Molten iron set fire to whatever the flames could not reach. It was a dreadful lesson, but it had its effect.

Reconstruction began immediately and progressed with amazing rapidity for about eighteen months, but the panic and depression of 1873 to 1874 seriously retarded it. Genuine fireproof construction marked nearly every building that was erected in the burned area. In the first year following the fire, 598 permanent buildings were erected. During the seven years from 1872 to 1879 a total of about 10,200 permits for construction were issued. The average was 1,275 per year, the low being 712 in 1874 and the high 2,698 in 1877. In the two decades following the fire the total cost of new buildings erected was $316,220,000, or about $2,900,000,000 at the current price level (1963). It was this vast program of reconstruction and expansion that gave the architects their immense opportunity and forced upon them the necessity of developing a new form and technique of building.

If we exclude the human loss, the fire proved in one respect to be a blessing. Looking back over the new city that had grown out of the ashes of the old, the authors of *Industrial Chicago* could say: "Those fires were fortunate events for the Garden City as a whole, and none profited directly by them, so much as art and architects, for the flames swept away forever the greater number of monstrous libels on artistic house-building, while only destroying the few noble buildings, of which Old Chicago could boast."[6]

The fireproof commercial building that appeared immediately and in enormous volume during the years following the fire was an evolutionary outgrowth of the more advanced commercial structures that had been developing in the East since the middle of the century. As we have seen, there was nothing novel about iron construction, and its early history in Chicago was in no way distinguished. The manufacture of architectural ironwork began about 1843, when Frederick Letz established a foundry for the casting of ornamental details. The Union Iron Works, established by Bouton and Hurlburt in 1852, seems to have been the first to cast iron structural members, but they do not appear to have been widely used. Before that date, however, iron columns had been imported in small quantity from New York. The use of cast-iron members in the first story of a building façade had been inaugurated by New York builders around 1835 to provide for a maximum

[6] *Industrial Chicago* (Chicago: Goodspeed Publishing Co., 1891), I, 115.

window area at the base. A similar technique appeared in Chicago as early as 1848. The small office building generally referred to as the Lind Block, at the northwest corner of Wacker Drive and Randolph Street, was built no later than 1852 with masonry bearing walls and interior cast-iron columns. It stood until 1963, when it was demolished, and thus enjoyed the distinction of being one of the four structures built before the fire to survive to the present time.[7]

The first complete cast-iron front in the form that Badger and Bogardus were multiplying in New York was that of the Lloyd Block, built in 1855 at Randolph and Wells streets. The columns and beams of the façade were cast by Daniel Badger's foundry and shipped to Chicago for assembly on the site. In the same year Chicago's pioneer architect, John M. Van Osdel, introduced cast-iron columns and possibly wrought-iron floor beams into the Post Office and Customs House. During the next four years he designed a number of store buildings on Lake Street immediately east and west of State, so that by 1860 a four-block length of the street was solidly lined on both sides with nicely harmonized cast-iron façades that were very impressive to visitors of the time. All the buildings were five stories in height and followed the Venetian Renaissance forms so popular in the East.[8] Although the cast-iron

[7] The other three are the Illinois Central Freight House (masonry walls only [see pp. 8–9]), the celebrated Water Tower (1868–69) at Michigan and Chicago avenues, the city's most popular monument to its extravagant past, and St. Mary's Church (1868) at Wabash Avenue and Ninth Street.

[8] John Mills Van Osdel was born in 1811 and began the practice of architecture in Chicago in 1837, the year of incorporation. By the time of his death in 1891, he had designed at least seventy-three commercial and public buildings in the Loop area alone (according to Frank A. Randall's compilation, in his *History of the Development of Building Construction in Chicago*).

The claim of wrought-iron beams in the Post Office was made by the authors of *Industrial Chicago,* but it is open to question. The first lot of such beams was rolled in 1854 for the Cooper Union and the printing plant of Harper and Brothers in New York. All of them were rolled by the Trenton Iron Works, founded by Peter Cooper and Abram Hewitt, the only manufacturer at the time, and it seems unlikely that novel and costly structural members of this kind would have been shipped from Trenton to Chicago at that early date.

Exactly which of the Lake Street stores were Van Osdel's work is now impossible to determine. An illustration of the street elevation of one of the buildings immediately east of State Street survives; if it was not Van Osdel's design, it was certainly typical of his hand. The five-story building provided store and warehouse space for three firms of dry-goods merchants: Buell, Hill and Granger; Wadsworth and Wells; Williams, Case and Rhodes. The first story, devoted entirely to stores, was divided into narrow bays (probably no more than six feet in span) by thirty-three fluted Corinthian columns and two heavy corner piers of square section. At the second story the columns were continued as pilasters, while the corner piers retained their ground-floor shape. Between each pair of pilasters there was a double-arched window. At the third story a row of columns supported an arcade. The fourth story repeated the second, and the fifth story the third. Interior columns, beams, and joists were undoubtedly timber, a common characteristic of the iron-fronted

20

front was fairly common in Chicago by the time of the Civil War, it began to lose popularity in the late 1860's, when the architects returned to masonry for the street elevations of store and office buildings. No iron fronts survive in Chicago, in spite of the fact that a good many were built in the first few years after the fire.

The number of five-story buildings the upper floors of which provided warehouse space for the stores at the ground level soon convinced the owners of the advantages of the power-driven elevator. The first steam-driven elevator in Chicago was installed in the Charles B. Farwell Store, at 171 North Wabash Avenue, in 1864. This was superseded in 1870 by the hydraulic elevator, the first of which was built and installed by C. W. Baldwin in the store and warehouse of Burley and Company on West Lake Street. At the time of the fire, enthusiasm for the elevator and the increasing number of installations led to the designation "elevator building" for the new multistory commercial structure. The successful application of the elevator to relatively low buildings, and its rapid mechanical improvement, made possible in the decade of the 1870's a sudden and marked increase in the number of stories; at the same time the insatiable demands of commerce made the increase a necessity. Together with the rise in height went a simplicity of formal treatment and a decreasing dependence on historical styles for the ornamental detail and the over-all form of the building. In few cases, however, did the architects abandon the precedents of the past. The materials of construction were for the most part brick, dressed stone, plain concrete, cast iron, small quantities of wrought iron, and wood. The best buildings revealed a simple dignity growing out of flat, unadorned wall surfaces and fairly large, nicely proportioned, uniformly spaced windows.

The structural system of the post-fire elevator building was uniform and simple. Interior cast-iron columns connected by cast- or wrought-iron floor girders supported iron or timber joists, which in turn carried the loads of floors and roof. Column spacing was the same in both directions and relatively small, seldom more than ten feet. Windbracing was either unknown or thought to be irrelevant. The exterior walls of the elevator building were generally of solid masonry divided into piers of brick or dressed stone and strong enough to support themselves, wind loads, and the floor and roof loads of the half-bays immediately adjacent to the walls. The foundations were usually pyramid footings of coursed stone spread widely at the base and contracted upward by steps to receive the lower surface of column or wall.

---

building. The open, well-articulated façade and the subordination of ornamental detail to the primary forms of structural members were typical of the commercial block of New York and constituted a major source of the mature commercial architecture of the Chicago school.

The building height was roughly proportional to the speed and safety of the elevator.

The fact that the thickness of a masonry bearing wall must increase in direct proportion to its height eventually placed a sharp restriction on the over-all height of the building. The Chicago architects generally thought that at least a 12-inch wall was necessary for one story and that the base thickness had to be increased 4 inches for each additional story. Consequently, they felt that ten stories was the limit for a building with masonry walls or piers. The astonishing exception to this rule helps to prove the point. Burnham and Root's sixteen-story Monadnock Building, the highest building with masonry bearing walls ever constructed, rests on walls 72 inches thick at the base.[9] The problems of adequate lighting and the desire for the utmost economy of construction eventually forced the architects to turn against the masonry structure once and for all in the case of commercial buildings.

The description of the typical elevator building that we have just given fits the great majority of large office blocks, stores, and multistory warehouses constructed during the 1870's and early 1880's. Among these were a number of structures which belong to the architecture of the Chicago school, and we shall discuss them at length in their appropriate places. With a few important exceptions, virtually all the buildings designed by the leaders of the school were constructed in this way until Jenney developed the skeleton framework in 1883. A good example of the more pretentious and elegant commercial structure by an architect of national reputation was H. H. Richardson's first building in Chicago, the six-story office block of the American Express Company, erected between 1872 and 1873 at 21 West Monroe Street. Associated with Richardson in the design of this building were Charles D. Gambrill and Peter B. Wight. The total load of floors and roof was divided between the masonry bearing walls and the interior columns of cast iron. In a functional sense the building marked a step in the right direction: the wide windows, nearly filling each bay defined by the masonry piers, admitted a generous quantity of light; the interior frame provided for a relatively free disposition of office partitions; the general rectangularity of the elevations expressed the structure of piers, spandrels, and inner columns and hence the utilitarian aim. But the main elevation was overloaded with pointless changes in pier and spandrel width and with a quasi-Gothic ornament cluttering up the high mansard roof behind which the sixth story was lighted by dormer windows. It was clear that the architects did not fully understand the problem posed by the urban office building, but they were beginning to grasp its fundamental terms. The nature of that problem was most succinctly summarized by Albert Bush-Brown.

[9] For details of the Monadnock, see pp. 65–69.

22

Essentially the problem had two parts; there was the group of technical problems: how to utilize iron so that the tall building would be least heavy, how to anchor it in Chicago's mud, and how to give it the light, air, heat, and mechanical circulation its occupants required; second, there were the aesthetic problems: how to express the iron structure in the exterior fireproof cladding, and how to unify the composition by using proportions, scale, rhythms, and ornament that were appropriate to its size and function.[10]

The structure that revealed more fully and with much greater clarity how the problems would have to be solved was the Nixon Building, a remarkable example of indestructibility and the most advanced work of building technique in the city at the time of the fire (Fig. 3). Designed by Otto H. Matz and erected at the northeast corner of La Salle and Monroe streets, the Nixon was very nearly complete when the fire struck in October, 1871. All the primary structural elements—exterior walls and inner framing members—survived intact; these were cleaned, the flooring, roof, and interior fixtures were quickly installed, and the building was opened to occupancy before the year ended. This astonishing capacity to survive a fire that destroyed everything else in the area was not an accident or an inexplicable freak. The five-story building was painstakingly designed for maximum fireproofing, in so far as that could be achieved at the time. The walls were of heavy masonry construction, divided into deep, narrow piers spaced about 6 feet on centers. The interior frame was composed of cast-iron columns and girders carrying wrought-iron floor joists and roof rafters. The maximum span of the interior bays was 16 feet. The upper surfaces of all members in the floor-framing system were covered with a 1-inch layer of concrete, and the ceilings were protected by another 1-inch layer of plaster of Paris.[11] The elevations of the

[10] Albert Bush-Brown, *Louis Sullivan* (New York: George Braziller, Inc., 1960), p. 14. The soil above bedrock in the Chicago area is not mud but sand, clay, and some gravel interspersed with water pockets. The depth of bedrock (Niagara limestone) along the lake shore is about 125 feet below grade level.

[11] Concrete was scarcely known in Chicago at the time that it was specified for the Nixon Building. It was first used in the form that was then called "artificial stone," or as we should now say, precast concrete block. This kind of block, cast in imitation of dressed natural stone, was patented by George A. Frear in 1868 and initially used in a house built for H. B. Horton in the same year. The Frear Stone Manufacturing Company flourished: in 1873 it employed fifty men and made $100,000 worth of block. The most notable building in which Frear's concrete was used was the Phoenix (1885–86), designed by Burnham and Root. The discovery of deposits of natural cement in La Salle County and its early use in the lock walls of the Illinois and Michigan Canal stimulated the development of the new structural technique. Frear had two competitors the year after he secured his patent, and by 1873 there were at least seven companies manufacturing artificial stone. The most important of these for the subsequent history of concrete construction was the Ransome Artificial Stone Company, founded in 1872 by Ernest L. Ransome, the foremost pioneer in the development of reinforced concrete structures in the United States. There were several

Nixon, with their subdued classical detail and generous window area, were perfectly appropriate to the functional and structural character of the building. The two-story base (one of the early examples of the so-called double first floor) was particularly fine: in its great open area and narrow piers it clearly foreshadowed some of the advanced designs that were to come in the eighties. The Nixon was a model of the new fire-resistant building, but it could not withstand the forces of economic expansion. It was demolished in 1889 to make way for the larger La Salle–Monroe Building of Jenney and Mundie.

The most important innovation in the direction of complete fireproofing was George H. Johnson's invention of hollow-tile construction for subflooring and partitions. A designer on the staff of Daniel Badger's Architectural Iron Works in New York, Johnson came to Chicago in 1871 to promote his new invention.[12] He won the contract for fireproofing the Kendall Building, designed by John M. Van Osdel and constructed at 40 North Dearborn Street during 1872 and 1873. The building was originally six stories in height but was later increased to eight. The floors rested on hollow terra-cotta arches spanning between the wrought-iron joists, and the fixed partitions were built of hollow terra-cotta blocks. The Kendall enjoyed a comparatively long life: it eventually became the Equitable Building and finally the Real Estate Exchange before its demolition in 1940.

The application of tile to the covering of exposed iron members soon followed and was the next major step in rounding out the program of fireproofing. The result of these decisively important inventions was that two of the greatest sources of danger in the event of fire were largely eliminated. The tile, being fire-resistant up to very high temperatures, remained intact in the heat of direct flames. The reduction in the amount of inflammable material in the floor brought about a consequent reduction in the total amount of material that could be consumed by fire. The tile covering of iron members was even more beneficial. The hollow space inclosed by the individual tiles acted as an insulator, and the iron could thus be prevented from melting and often from excessive buckling.

---

spectacular demonstrations of the value of concrete block as a primary building material. The façade of a store on East Monroe Street (1871) was built entirely of block. The wall collapsed in the fire, but the blocks were recovered, cleaned, and laid up once more to form what was claimed to be a perfectly sound wall. The huge warehouse of J. V. Farwell and Company (1882) had a first story of concrete block, finished with chamfered edges and laid up in courses like those of traditional masonry. It was estimated that the cost of the concrete was one-quarter that of limestone or sandstone. For concrete framing, see pp. 175, 191–93.

[12] Johnson was a practical builder of unusual inventive ability. For his most important structures and their possible influence on William Le Baron Jenney, see pp. 81–82.

With the rapid progress in the technique of iron framing came many possibilities for even more radical changes in the design of the large, many-storied building. The elevator made such a building practical from the standpoint of easy movement to upper floors. Fireproof construction made it safe. Within a few years the exploitation of these technical factors brought about the revolution in form and construction that became the basis of a fully modern architecture, emancipated from the last vestige of dependence on the past. But even before this revolution was launched, and for a short time during the course of it, the architects of the Chicago school were concerned with the technical and aesthetic problem of creating in the older combination of masonry and iron a form appropriate to the needs and the spirit of the new industrial culture.

CHAPTER III

NEW FORMS IN TRADITIONAL MATERIALS

Many changes in the size, design, and construction of large urban buildings would have occurred whether the architects were capable of directing them or not. As we have seen, enormous pressures lay behind the whole building process. The architects and engineers had first of all to develop a new type of structure, the big office block of the crowded commercial area. The growing complexity of modern industry demanded concentrated administrative centers where large numbers of people could work at detailed and correlated tasks. The increasing centralization of the business process, along with other social and economic determinants arising from urban growth, led to an ever increasing intensity of land use. By 1880 in Chicago the price of land in the Loop district was $130,000 per quarter-acre. By 1890 it had risen to $900,-000 per quarter-acre. Population growth continued to follow its rising curve: in 1870 it was 298,977; in 1880, 505,185; in 1890, 1,099,850. The total urban area expanded nearly six times, from 35.15 square miles in 1870 to 178.05 square miles in 1890.

These conditions meant that the architect was no longer a free agent, molding the material of a building into a form expressive of his own spirit and feeling. He had a commission from society that he had to accept if he was to survive in his profession. The Chicago architects faced the challenge with rare boldness and imagination. They met all the utilitarian requirements of the big office building by introducing a bewildering number of innovations in structure and mechanical facilities. They designed buildings to be erected in unbroken ranks along the city blocks. They developed structural devices and methods of construction that constantly increased the speed and efficiency of the building process.

The 1880's saw not only the creation of the wind-braced iron frame and the curtain wall but also the architectonic mastery of these technical factors. The period brought the first use of winter construction, which was adopted about 1881. By means of salt introduced into the mortar, bricklaying could be carried on in subfreezing temperatures. Through the insulation of concrete with straw and tarpaulin, pouring could be accomplished in freezing weather. A few years later the practice of using electric lights under temporary roofing over excavated areas made it possible for workers to complete foundations and basements in rain and snow. The next step was the employment of electric floodlights for night work. Only by methods such as these could the industry maintain the vast tide of building that came in the 1880's.

Working often from the standpoint of strict empirical functionalism, the architects nevertheless avoided a deadening monotony of profile and detail (such as we now have in our blocks of glass curtain walls). They designed structures in quantity, story on story, block after block. As Giedion wrote: "Each [building] had its own individual appearance and its own name, and yet the aggregate appearance was not chaotic. . . . In the eighties the Loop . . . became the perfect illustration of American audacity in the direct assault that was made upon its problems. Whole streets were developed in a way that had never been seen before."[1]

With characteristic directness the authors of *Industrial Chicago* summed up the factors that determined what they called the "commercial style": "The requirements of commerce and the business principles of real estate owners called this style into life. Light, space, air, and strength were demanded by such requirements and principles as the first objects and exterior ornamentation as the second."[2] One sees here the genesis of the extreme functionalism and structuralism of modern architecture, of Mies van der Rohe's theory of "more through less."

Enthusiasm for these architectural marvels is the leading theme of *Industrial Chicago*, whose authors felt that they were witnessing the creation at last of an indigenous architectural style.

Commercial architecture is the just title to be applied to the great airy buildings of the present. They are truly American architecture in conception and utility. The style is a monument to the advance of Chicago in commerce and commercial greatness and to the prevailing penchant for casting out art where it interferes with the useful. It is a commanding style without being venerable. . . . The commercial style, if structurally ornamental, becomes architectural.[3]

The last sentence is particularly significant: it presents the basis for any aesthetic analysis of the major stream of the Chicago school and, indeed, of the central tendency in modern commercial architecture.

The general architectural achievement of the city and the social and economic situation out of which it came was summarized by Paul Bourget, a

---

[1] Sigfried Giedion, *Space, Time and Architecture* (Cambridge, Mass.: Harvard University Press, 1941), pp. 291–92.

[2] *Industrial Chicago* (Chicago: Goodspeed Publishing Co., 1891), I, 168.

[3] *Ibid.*, p. 70.

French visitor of the nineties who was not motivated by any great enthusiasm for things American.

At one moment you have around you only "buildings." They scale the sky with their eighteen, their twenty stories. The architect who has built them, or rather who has plotted them, has renounced colonnades, mouldings, classical embellishments. He has frankly accepted the conditions imposed by the speculator; multiplying as many times as possible the value of the bit of ground at the base in multiplying the supposed offices. It is a problem capable of interesting only an engineer, one would suppose. Nothing of the kind. The simple force of need is such a principle of beauty, and these buildings so conspicuously manifest that need that in contemplating them you experience a singular emotion. The sketch appears here of a new kind of art, an art of democracy, made by the crowd and for the crowd, an art of science in which the certainties of natural laws give to audacities in appearance the most unbridled the tranquility of geometrical figures.[4]

We may best understand the building forms that evolved organically out of this rigorous context by the analysis of specific works of the commercial style. The first generation of architects after the fire brought about a vigorous and progressive evolution of the new style before the invention and mastery of iron and steel framing. As a matter of fact, the high point of masonry architecture in Chicago came six years after the first completely framed structure was built. The leading figures in this early phase were Jenney, Adler, Sullivan, Root, and Burnham. The first of these pioneers was William Le Baron Jenney, who launched into the current established by the Nixon Building with his Portland Block, built in 1872 at Dearborn and Washington streets, where it survived until 1933.

Jenney was perhaps the most original structural talent of the Chicago school, but at the same time he was least conscious of the aesthetic problem fixed by his new constructions. He belonged to that type of American genius of which John A. Roebling and James B. Eads were leading representatives. A creative builder of the front rank, willing to break with precedent when he recognized the need, he was so imbued with the ruling pragmatic spirit of the market place that he was largely unaware of the aesthetic implications of what he had achieved. As an engineer he had that kind of easy confidence in his ability that seldom led to self-questioning or to theoretical considerations. But Jenney knew what he was doing, and it had to be done before others could move on to greater heights.

He was born at Fairhaven, Massachusetts, in 1832, the son of a successful owner of a whaling fleet. He studied at Lawrence Scientific School for about

[4] Paul Bourget, *Outre Mer*, as translated and quoted by Montgomery Schuyler in "Architecture in Chicago: Adler and Sullivan" ("Great American Architects Series," No. 2, Part I), *Architectural Record*, December, 1895, p. 8.

two years and in 1853 enrolled as an engineering student at the École Centrale des Arts et Manufactures in Paris, from which he graduated in 1856. He got his early practical experience in war. He entered the Union Army in 1861 as an assistant in the Engineering Department at Cairo. His rise was rapid. He became staff engineer to Grant at Corinth, and shortly thereafter served with Sherman at Memphis. The next step took him to the rank of chief engineer of the Fifteenth Army Corps, Army of Tennessee. When the Civil War ended, he was engineer-in-charge of the Engineer Headquarters at Nashville. He was discharged in 1866 with the rank of major, a title which he retained throughout his life.

Jenney came to Chicago in 1867 and established an architectural office in the following year. Except for a brief appointment as professor of architecture at the University of Michigan in 1876, he remained at his Chicago office. The high level of his career, in both the number and excellence of his buildings, came in 1891, the year he formed the partnership of Jenney and Mundie. His appointment to the Commission of Architects for the World's Columbian Exposition of 1893 seems to have aroused his enthusiasm for the new classical fashion. After he designed the Horticultural Building for the fair his work shows a progressive departure from the tough-minded empiricism of the years from 1889 to 1891.

Jenney was not a narrow specialist. His learning in the history and science of his art brought him to the attention of editors and university administrators. His most important contribution outside the work of design and supervision was a series of lectures on the history of architecture delivered at the old Chicago University in 1883 and published in the *Inland Architect and Builder* during 1883 and 1884. The lectures included much new material on the results of recent archeological investigations into Babylonian and early Hellenic architecture. He contributed several important technical papers to the *Inland Architect*. One of them, an expansion of an address given at the Chicago Academy of Sciences, dealt with the subject of the preservation of building stone. It showed an unusual amount of chemical and mineralogical learning.

As a personality Jenney impressed all who met him, although the impression varied extremely depending on whether they met him in the office or in his life after hours. The question whether he was an architect or an engineer has been debated off and on since he first entered the profession. There is little doubt that he was both, but he was certainly not an architect in the class of Richardson or Sullivan. We will consider this question at length in our discussion of the Home Insurance Building and its successors.[5]

Sullivan considered the matter in the amusing portrait of the Major that he

[5] For Jenney's Home Insurance and later buildings, see pp. 81–87.

29

drew in his *Autobiography*. Sullivan regarded him as one of the few architects who "were intelligently conscientious in the interest of their clients," but beyond that the younger man was little disposed to hero worship.

The Major was a free-and-easy cultured gentleman, but not an architect except by courtesy of terms. His true profession was that of engineer. . . . He spoke French with an accent so atrocious that it jarred Louis's teeth, while his English speech jerked about as though it had St. Vitus's dance. He was monstrously pop-eyed, with hanging mobile features, sensuous lips, and he disposed of matters easily in the manner of a war veteran who believed he knew what was what. Louis soon found out that the Major was not, really, in his heart, an engineer at all, but by nature, and in toto, a *bon vivant*, a gourmet. . . . The Major was effusive; a hale fellow well met, an officer of the Loyal Legion, a welcome guest anywhere, but by preference a host.[6]

Sullivan remained in the Major's office for six months. He was one of many Chicago architects who were trained by Jenney, the most notable being, besides Sullivan, William Holabird, Martin Roche, D. H. Burnham, and R. H. Turnock. "William Le Baron Jenney," Giedion wrote, "played much the same role in the younger generation of Chicago architects that Peter Behrens did in Germany around 1910, or Auguste Perret in France. He gave young architects the preparation they needed to tackle the new problems for which the schools could offer no solutions."[7]

The commercial style was prefigured in Jenney's seven-story Portland Block (1872), at the southeast corner of Dearborn and Washington streets. Except for interior columns and beams of cast iron, the bearing construction was masonry. The piers were of pressed brick separating relatively large windows. The flat walls were unadorned except for narrow quoins at the corners and shallow rustication. The windows at the end bays of the façade were grouped into units of three; otherwise, the openings were single and uniformly spaced over the whole wall area. A continuous projecting stone course at the top of the first story and a small cornice provided a horizontal division that recalled the traditional base-shaft-capital treatment of the elevation that Jenney continued to use in many of his larger and more advanced buildings. Lintels of full-centered or semicircular arches formed the only interruption of the dominant rectangularity of the structure. The Portland Block was a simple and straightforward design that took its form almost entirely from the requirements of a small office building. Every office had an outside exposure. There was little precedent for buildings like this and the Nixon except for the American vernacular predilection for plane walls with few

[6] Louis Sullivan, *The Autobiography of an Idea* (New York: Press of the American Institute of Architects, 1922), pp. 203–4.

[7] Giedion, *op. cit.*, p. 293.

projecting courses, sills, and lintels, or ornamental details. The Portland was popular as an office block and survived for almost sixty years, until its demolition in 1933.

Jenney's next major commission was the Lakeside Building, erected in 1873 at the southwest corner of Clark and Adams streets. A six-story combination of masonry walls and interior cast-iron columns, it was a work of pure Gothic revivalism and gave no indication of what Jenney was to accomplish before the end of the decade in the first Leiter Building.[8]

Dankmar Adler began in a hesitant way to enter into the mainstream of the Chicago movement with his Central Music Hall, completed in 1879. Another combination of traditional masonry bearing walls and internal iron members, this forerunner of the Auditorium provided an early demonstration of the technical ingenuity that Adler revealed so magnificently in the later structure.

Eighteen rather undistinguished years of engineering and architectural experience lay behind the design of the Central Music Hall. Adler had come to Chicago in 1861, at the age of seventeen, and had begun his career in the office of Augustus Bauer. He was born in 1844 in Lengsfeld, Germany, which he left with his parents at the age of ten to emigrate to Detroit. His father became the rabbi of Congregation Beth-el in Detroit and later of the well-known KAM Temple in Chicago. Adler had some elementary schooling in Detroit and later in Ann Arbor, but he cut his education short to become an apprentice draftsman in the office of the Detroit architect E. Willard Smith, who later moved to Chicago.

As in the case of Jenney, the Civil War interrupted Adler's career. He joined the Union Army as an engineer in 1862 and served in the Chattanooga and Atlanta campaigns. During the last six months of the conflict, he was an officer of the Topographical Engineer Corps in Tennessee. His experience with the Union Army during the war was his education, as he himself was fond of saying. Actually, everything that Adler learned was self-taught or acquired from his professional associates.

He returned to Chicago in 1866 and entered the office of O. S. Kinney, with whose son he formed the partnership of Kinney and Adler in 1869. Their work consisted mostly of churches, synagogues, schools, and courthouses. Commissions for office buildings came shortly after the fire, following the establishment of the firm of Burling and Adler in 1871. This partnership was dissolved in 1878 and replaced by D. Adler and Company. The Central Music Hall was thus Adler's first independent commission and his most important until 1881, when he joined Louis Sullivan in one of the nation's most famous and most productive architectural offices. Adler by

[8] For the first Leiter Building and Jenney's subsequent work, see pp. 79–94.

himself or in association with men of only ordinary competence produced little to command the attention of historians. It was the partnership with the imaginative Sullivan that gave him exactly the opportunity he needed to exploit his amazing technical virtuosity. While Sullivan concerned himself with the problems of planning and architectonic design, Adler handled the matters of business and engineering. It was a perfect symbiosis.

The chief importance of the Central Music Hall (Fig. 4) is historical and possibly technical. In it lay the genesis of the great Auditorium Building, which was to follow it by a decade. The Music Hall stood on the southeast corner of Randolph and State streets, where it was opened for use late in 1879 and served its purpose for little more than twenty years, being demolished in 1901 to make way for the first block of the present Marshall Field Store of D. H. Burnham. Adler showed no particular originality in the elevations and depended for the most part on a simplified mixture of Renaissance and earlier Italian styles for the treatment of walls, openings, and masonry details. The structure had a certain force and dignity, especially in the simplicity and regularity of the long State Street elevation. The nearly continuous window groups at the base and the second story and the large number of uniformly spaced openings above pointed toward the open-wall construction that became the distinguishing mark of the Chicago school.

The Central Music Hall was probably of masonry construction throughout except for iron trusses, girders, and columns in the theater and iron mullions in the second-story window groups. The ceiling over the orchestra floor was suspended from trusses, a technique later employed on a grand scale in the Auditorium, but it is no longer possible to determine the construction exactly. The exterior facing consisted of dressed Lemont stone, and the columns flanking the entrance were of granite.

The most important feature of the Central Music Hall was the functional arrangement of interior elements in what was then a unique kind of building. The Music Hall included in its six stories not only a theater but also a dozen stores and seventy-five offices. The stores were located at the base and the offices on the periphery of the theater, which was in the interior of the building. The acoustical properties of the theater were nationally famous and served to give Adler the reputation of the leading acoustical "engineer" of his time. This reputation justly became world-wide with the completion of the Auditorium. The acoustical excellence of the Music Hall theater resulted from three characteristics: (1) the upward curve of the orchestra floor away from the stage; (2) the transverse projections below the ceiling (the furring around the trusses over the theater); and (3) the lateral curve of the ceiling vault. Adler's mastery of acoustical design appears to have been the product of a direct empirical approach to the problem. In 1885 he made a careful study of the Mormon Tabernacle in Salt Lake City as preparation for the design of the Auditorium. Adler was particularly proud of the Central Music Hall throughout the remainder of his life and often said that he wanted it, more than any other building, to stand as his memorial. In tribute to him Marshall Field saved one of the entrance columns and had it erected as a monument over Adler's grave in Mount Mayriv Cemetery.

The partnership that united the talents of Adler and Sullivan was as essential to the full growth of the younger man as it was to the older. The facts of Louis Sullivan's life are now well known through his own *Autobiography of an Idea* and the critical and biographical studies by Hugh Morrison and Willard Connely. It is valuable, however, to recall certain aspects of his youth—his childhood character and experiences and the decisive episodes of his irregular education—for these prefigure fundamental characteristics of the mature man and are essential to the understanding of his art. His life as a boy and an adolescent was strongly marked by the powerful enthusiasms and the equally violent hostilities that later appeared in the grown man.

Sullivan was born in Boston of Irish and German-French parentage. As a child he was especially fond of drawing flowers and leaves, a love that he indulged with passionate absorption throughout his architectural career. According to his own account, he acquired the love of books and of buildings around the age of twelve and found both more interesting than people. Neither flowers, books, nor buildings, however, aroused in him the peculiarly intense emotions stimulated by bridges. From childhood they were closely associated with powerful unconscious impulses that eventually sought expression in his art.[9] One of his exciting childhood experiences was the discovery of the chain suspension bridge over the Merrimack River near Newburyport, Massachusetts, an experience that provoked one of the liveliest passages in his *Autobiography*. A little later, at the age of fourteen, he visited a cousin in Utica, New York, and during the journey was especially attracted by the railroad bridge over the Hudson River at Albany. As an adolescent and a young man he was to find himself equally absorbed by the construction of the Eads Bridge at St. Louis and the railway bridge at Dixville, Kentucky. He tells us that at about the time of the Utica trip he learned that bridges were designed by men and that he then decided once and for all to become an architect.

Although his parents moved to Chicago in 1869, Louis remained in Boston, where he entered the English High School in 1870. He enrolled in the architectural school of the Massachusetts Institute of Technology in 1872.

[9] Sullivan's feeling for bridges is of crucial importance for the understanding of his personality and his art. For further discussion of this interest, see pp. 168–71.

He called the course there "architectural theology." To him it was mechanical, empty, and repetitious, made up of a succession of styles, orders, and details drawn from historical handbooks. Even if we discount Sullivan's characteristic exaggeration, we can understand why some of the best architects of the Chicago school either studied engineering or had no higher education at all. Sullivan stood M. I. T. for one year (or might it have been the other way around?), then left with the intention of studying at the École des Beaux-Arts.

Instead of Paris, however, he went to Philadelphia to live with his grandparents. There, having decided to try his hand at architecture, he entered the firm of Furness and Hewitt as an apprentice draftsman. Sullivan chose Furness partly because of the superior quality of his buildings and partly because he had heartily damned M. I. T. Frank Furness and his partners enjoyed a number of large commissions in Philadelphia—among them Broad Street Station—and treated all of them with a kind of personal and reckless eclecticism stamped with a peculiarly original, forceful, and ugly ornament. Sullivan's early ornamental detail shows a marked debt to Furness, as his personal development may show the influence of the powerful individualism of the older man. What Sullivan took from Philadelphia, however, may have been far more decisive than anything he derived from Furness. The city contained a number of commercial buildings erected around mid-century whose architects had taken a long forward step in the transmutation of vernacular utility into a new commercial architecture. Some of these buildings show anticipations of certain forms that Sullivan later developed in the succession of "vertical" façades from the Rothschild to the Guaranty Building.[10]

The panic and consequent depression of 1873 and 1874 proved disastrous for the business of Furness and Hewitt, and Sullivan had to leave after a year at the drawing board. He went to Chicago in 1873. The city as he saw it was a mass of ashes, dirty ruins, dilapidated shacks, and scores of buildings newly or half-finished amid the chaos. The crudeness and the violence of the first immense efforts of reconstruction impressed Sullivan deeply. He loved the city for its sheer power and decided to stay.

His method of getting a job consisted of walking about the city, picking a building he liked, discovering the name of the architect, then requesting that he be taken on as a draftsman. By this process and an extraordinary intuition, he landed in the office of William Le Baron Jenney. The building that had impressed him was the Portland Block.[11] In Jenney's office he shortly found

[10] For specific Philadelphia buildings and their relation to Sullivan's skyscrapers, see pp. 38–39.

[11] For a description of the Portland, see pp. 30–31.

himself in the company of William Holabird, Martin Roche, and Daniel Burnham. It was at this time that he acquired his love of music, in good part through his close and affectionate friendship with John Edelman. The composer he most admired was, characteristically, Richard Wagner.

But the experience in Jenney's office was not enough for the restless Sullivan. He finally realized his earlier intention when he went to Paris in 1874 and enrolled at the École des Beaux-Arts. It was here that an obscure teacher of descriptive geometry, a M. Clopet, achieved some immortality by uttering a sentence that Sullivan made famous. Referring to the text in his course, Clopet once remarked to his student, "I suggest you place the book in the waste-basket; we shall have no need of it here; *for here our demonstrations shall be so broad as to admit of* NO EXCEPTION."[12] Sullivan afterward tossed all the textbooks in the wastebasket and devoted his life as an architect to a search for the rule that shall admit of no exceptions.

Outside the school, at the atelier of Émile Vaudremer in Paris, Sullivan was given two projects that required him to execute a decorative border for a ceiling. In both cases he designed an intricate, flowing floral pattern that foreshadowed many of his mature ornamental systems. The second design was based on a thistle-like motive that was to appear twenty-five years later in the Carson Pirie Scott Store.

For the most part, what the École des Beaux-Arts could offer him Sullivan thought he had already learned at M. I. T. Believing that the French institution carefully avoided the acceptance of any real architectural problem, he found it equally sterile and academic. To study architecture as a series of styles seemed to Sullivan superficial and unrealistic, for it never penetrated to the heart of design and construction. Sullivan's criticism was not strictly fair, but whatever the case, he felt that he had to return to Chicago in 1875 to refresh himself once more through direct contact with the constituent facts in the structural art of his time. Through his friendship with John Edelman, he was offered the job of draftsman in the office of Johnston and Edelman, which is otherwise undistinguished in the history of American architecture.

In 1876 the firm received the commission for the interior decoration of Moody's Tabernacle and turned the job over to Sullivan to provide the young apprentice with his first professional opportunity. The resulting ornamental design was the elaborate, interlaced floral and foliate pattern that was to distinguish his mature work. A remarkably acute architectural critic on the staff of the *Chicago Times* discerned the true inner nature of Sullivan's system of ornament and its proper role in the whole architectural composition: he was trying to express not only organic nature in its phenomenal sense but

[12] Sullivan, *op. cit.*, p. 221.

also the underlying dynamic principle of movement, growth, and evolution-ary change.

The idea underlying these frescoes is botanical; the anatomy of plants is geologi-cally treated—the structural growth is carried throughout the forms, and the leaves and flowers are seen geometrically—that is, without perspective—as one sees their lines when pressed in the herbarium. . . . The principle of the forms is botanical, and the forms themselves are not the end of the decoration, but the means of illustrating the surfaces they cover, and of uniting into a consistent whole the structural features of the interior. . . . The conception is, therefore, purely architectural and scientific, and, when completed, its dignity and richness will first bewilder, next astonish, and finally charm. . . . Mr. Sullivan brings to architecture and architectural decoration a thorough and fine culture, an enthusi-asm and persistence which give glowing promise, and a taste founded upon classical principles and inspired by artistic imagination. Leading architects of the city have bestowed upon his work the highest encomium, and some of them char-acterize his invention and power as wonderful.[13]

Sullivan's experiences in Chicago, his reading, and his association with John Edelman soon brought him to realize that much of the most vital struc-tural art of his age was the work of engineers. They became Sullivan's he-roes, along with the supermen Wagner and Michelangelo. His favorites were James B. Eads of St. Louis, C. Shaler Smith, who built the bridge at Dixville, Kentucky, and Frederick Baumann of Chicago. The last was an expert on foundations, and his book, *A Theory of Isolated Pier Foundations*, published in 1873, became the basis of many innovations made by the Chicago build-ers. Sullivan's interest in engineering developed rapidly into an enthusiasm for science. It centered mainly in biology, from which his organic theory of architecture stemmed in part. He read Darwin, Huxley, Spencer, and Tyndall at length. Thus his philosophy of architecture lay in the mainstream of nineteenth-century thought on the subject, not only as it could be inferred from the new science, but as it was developed by men like Greenough in the United States and Semper and Viollet-le-Duc in Europe.

Sullivan was often inconsistent; yet the philosophy which matured with his growing powers as an architect was original and profound. More than any other artist of his time, he understood the social basis, the responsibility, and the problem of art in a technical and industrial culture. He felt that he had discovered the rule with no exceptions in the concept "form follows function." The idea was first stated by Plato as a logical correlative to his

[13] *Chicago Times*, May 21, 1876, as quoted in Willard Connely, *Louis Sullivan as He Lived* (New York: Horizon Press, Inc., 1960), pp. 83–85. This review provides another illustration of the extent to which Chicago was receptive to new ideas and imaginative artis-tic achievements. The *Times* critic appears to have been familiar with the new literature of biological science as well as with the principles of good architectural ornament.

metaphysical system and has appeared in various forms throughout the history of aesthetic theory, but it remained for Sullivan to give it its systematic concrete demonstration in terms of a contemporary building art.[14] The proper understanding of the word "function" is the key to his whole philosophy. An organic architecture, he believed, is one that grows naturally or organically out of the social and technical factors among which the architect lives and with which he must work. These factors embrace not only the technical and utilitarian problems of building but also the aspirations, values, ideals, and spiritual needs of human beings. Thus *functionalism* involved for him something far wider and deeper than utilitarian and structural considerations, as important as these are.

To Sullivan the creation of a genuine style of architecture was not a matter of historical styles or of dipping into a vocabulary of modern forms and details in order to secure a style that the architect might feel to be consonant with modern culture. The architect must first recognize the importance of aesthetic expression for the harmonization and emotional enrichment of the many practical and intellectual elements of contemporary civilization. In American society such an art would have to start with the fundamentals—technology, industry, and the commercial urban milieu. It is the task of the architect, as Sullivan conceived it, to take the products of technics, on the one hand, and the logic and order of mechanical processes, on the other, and mold them into a form uniting both in a single, unified aesthetic expression. An architecture so developed means the humanization through aesthetic and symbolic statement of the non-human facts of industrial techniques.

The style of a building would thus become in part whatever the materials, utilitarian demands, and structural solutions might make it. It would have to be equally determined by the spiritual needs of the people who give the architect his commission. Thus a modern style would be a matter not of one form or another but rather of an organic whole taking shape from the physical, intellectual, and emotional milieu in which it exists. Consciously or unconsciously, the architects of the Chicago school approached their task in this way, and their achievement must be measured against these criteria.[15]

Sullivan entered Adler's office in 1879, becoming a partner in 1880, and the two men established the firm on an equal basis in 1881. The first building which Sullivan designed with Adler was the Borden Block, built between 1879 and 1880 at the northwest corner of Randolph and Dearborn streets

[14] To cite one Platonic formulation of the basic idea, Socrates says in the *Republic:* "The excellence or beauty or truth of every structure, animate or inanimate, and of every action of man, is relative to the use for which nature or the artist has intended them" (X, 601 C).

[15] For further discussion of Sullivan's theory in view of his ultimate achievement as an architect, see pp. 167–73.

(Fig. 5). It was demolished in 1916 to make way for the original Woods Theater, now gone with its predecessor. The Borden revealed a radical departure from most of the previous works of masonry architecture. Except for Jenney's first Leiter Building, which is almost a completely framed structure, and the Nixon, it was the first office block to break away from heavy pier or solid-wall construction.[16]

In order to gain the maximum amount of light in the interior of the building the architects sharply narrowed the piers and thus widened the open span of the bay. The strength of the pier was maintained by increasing its depth. Isolated stone footings carried the piers and interior columns—apparently the first use of such footings for wall piers. Two large windows separated by a cast-iron mullion filled each bay. Except for the horizontal divisions and the semicircular panels, or lunettes, surmounting the bays at the top story, the elevations formed a remarkably clear and open pattern of relatively narrow piers and spandrels. The simple slab or cornice at the top provided an appropriate termination to the unambiguous statement of function and construction.

The vigorous articulation which the Borden revealed was not duplicated by Sullivan for seven years. His capriciously experimental temperament in ornamentation prevented his following its obvious implications. The next important commission of the firm, the building at 210 West Monroe Street, shows a new departure (Fig. 6). This structure was the Rothschild Store when it was completed in 1881, but it has changed hands repeatedly since its construction. Here Sullivan first turned to the vertical emphasis that culminated in his so-called skyscraper designs of the 1890's.

There is now reasonable evidence that Sullivan was influenced in the design of the Rothschild and its successors by several remarkable buildings erected in Philadelphia during the decade of 1850's. These obscure structures reveal the same formal treatment that appears in the hesitant and awkward essays of the early 1880's and that reaches its brilliant climax in the skyscrapers of the next decade. The major elements in this treatment are continuous piers, recessed spandrels, or complete suppression of the spandrel, and unbroken surface planes with ornamental detail subordinated to the main structural and functional elements. Among the Philadelphia buildings that stand closest to the Rothschild are the eight-story Jayne Building (1849–50), designed by William Johnston and Thomas U. Walter; the store at 241 Chestnut Street, erected in 1852; and the Leland Building, at 39 South Third Street, completed in 1855. The latter two, both five-story structures, were designed by the Philadelphia architect Stephen D. Button and are characterized by highly articulated cellular façades of large windows

[16] For Jenney's first Leiter Building, see pp. 79–80.

and narrow recessed spandrels. Fundamentally similar but with a more sober utilitarian quality are the factories designed by Joseph C. Hoxie for William H. Horstman and Sons and the Cornelius Baker Company (both completed in 1853). The last two were probably influential in the design of the Selz, Schwab and Company factory (1886–87), one of the few industrial commissions of Adler and Sullivan. It is reasonable to suppose that Sullivan was aware of these Philadelphia buildings, since they were within easy walking distance of Furness and Hewitt's office.

In the case of the Rothschild building, three continuous piers of masonry divide the main elevation into two 25-foot bays and carry the outer floor and roof loads. The narrow continuous mullions and recessed spandrels are of cast iron. The large glass area points to the mature work of the Chicago school, but the restless and exotic ornament, however original, obscures the essential form of the building and produces an effect of shallowness and indecisiveness.

The former Jewelers Building, constructed between 1881 and 1882 at 15–19 South Wabash Avenue, is free of the spiky ornament of the previous building, but the variety of openings and details in the façade betrays the absence of a clear goal in Sullivan's mind (Fig. 7). The over-all pattern of the main elevation, however, is derived from the system of construction: two brick piers close to the end walls divide the building into two narrow bays and one wide bay at the center.[17] The original Revell Building (1881–83), at the northeast corner of Wabash and Adams, shows progress in its greater clarity and directness, but the irregularity of the openings is pointless and confusing (Figs. 8, 9). This building, still standing, was extensively modernized in 1929 chiefly through the application on the two lower stories of a smooth stone envelope surrounding casement windows set flush with the wall surface. The spacing of these windows betrays the fact that the piers do not occur in pairs, as Sullivan has them in his street elevations. This is the first case of his arbitrary addition of false piers for aesthetic effect. The piers of the Revell are brick, the interior bearing members and mullions being of iron. False piers—two for each bay—are used in a surer and more direct way in the façade of the six-story Kennedy Bakery, now the Pettibone Printing Company, at 27 North Des Plaines Avenue (1883–84). The closely ranked piers strongly suggest the work of the nineties, although the familiar and inharmonious semicircular windows at the top story indicate that Sullivan was still in the early phase of his search.

Progress toward greater openness and stronger articulation is revealed

[17] Shortly after the opening of the Jewelers Building, Sullivan was commissioned to design the exhibition cases and background partitions for a silver exhibit in Chicago. The ornamental pattern was the subject of a laudatory notice in the *Revue des Arts Décoratifs* (Paris, 1883) and thus brought Sullivan his first international recognition.

in the Knisely Building (1884), at 551 West Monroe Street, and the Ryerson Building, erected in the same year at 16–20 East Randolph. The latter structure was demolished for the bus terminal at this location. The Knisely is unusually straightforward for Sullivan, virtually a simplified and refined vernacular essay like the Philadelphia buildings of the fifties. Plain brick piers extend continuously from ground to roof. Solid masonry walls are presented as a simple fact, without adornment. Despite its exotic and vaguely derivative ornament, the Ryerson was important for the introduction of a great area of glass carried on an iron armature between masonry piers. The openings were disposed in the form of shallow bow windows.[18]

The steppingstone from the Central Music Hall to the Auditorium was the third McVickers Theater, completed in 1885 at 25 West Madison Street (Fig. 10). This century-old institution in the theatrical life of the city has suffered an unhappy and baffling history. The original was built in 1857 and burned in the great fire. It was reconstructed in 1872 and again in 1883 and was remodeled between 1884 and 1885. Fire destroyed the interior in 1890, but it was replaced the following year. The new structure lasted until 1922, when it was finally demolished to make way for the present movie theater. Adler and Sullivan designed the interior facilities and ornament for both the 1885 and the 1891 remodelings, but it is questionable whether they made any changes in the exterior of the building. The ornamental lions' heads and the cornice are naïve relics of the 1872 or 1883 structure. Yet the unusually open wall, light and simple in construction and effect, is a greatly refined example of the glass and cast-iron construction that often represented the highest expression of nineteenth-century structural art before the technical revolution of the eighties.

Like the Central Music Hall, the McVickers was a shell of offices surrounding a theater. The offices of the top story were added between 1890 and 1891. They were carried on six steel trusses spanning the theater and supported by open latticework columns that were carried on foundations independent of those of the walls. Many advancements were introduced in lighting, heating, and arrangement of mechanical facilities, and fireproofing was complete. The rich interior ornament and the airy façade of the building were its most important features. Both foreshadow Sullivan's great achievements of the century's final decade.

Two identical small buildings of 1886 that lie outside the mainstream of Sullivan's development were the suburban stations of the Illinois Central

---

[18] A building much like the Ryerson that still survives (1963) is the Garden City Warehouse, at 320 West Jackson Boulevard, built in 1880 (see p. 58). For illustrations of the Knisely and the Ryerson, see Hugh Morrison, *Louis Sullivan: Prophet of Modern Architecture* (New York: W. W. Norton & Co., 1935), Pl. 3 (p. 323) and Pl. 6 (p. 325). The negatives were apparently lost.

Railroad at Thirty-ninth (Fig. 11) and Forty-third streets, which were demolished in 1934 and 1942 respectively. The architects undoubtedly secured these commissions through the influence of Sullivan's brother, Albert, who was at that time superintendent of the railroad's Chicago Division. The two stations had the essential features of plan and elevation of the conventional railroad way station, the basic elements of which have remained unchanged for over a century. The formal treatment of the elevations, especially the grouped windows and the gables, suggests a vaguely Tudor character, but the smooth wall planes of brick and the sharp-edged reveals were to appear later in the work of Sullivan and those who followed in his footsteps.

The building originally known as the Wirt Dexter, with the present address of 630 South Wabash Avenue, was constructed in 1887. It is another work of extreme simplicity, frankly relying on the structure of stone and brick piers and iron mullions for the effect of its façade (Fig. 12). Sullivan eliminated the fantastic and redundant ornament of the earlier buildings, thereby achieving a geometric harmony while increasing dignity and force. For Sullivan it was the culmination of the old vernacular tradition in masonry architecture and close in feeling to the expression of iron and steel framing. Although the alterations in bay span in the symmetrical façade weaken the general effect, the wide central bay and the narrow flanking bays made such a treatment necessary.

The influence of Richardson's Marshall Field Wholesale Store began to manifest itself in the Standard Club (1887–88), at the southwest corner of Michigan Avenue and Twenty-fourth Street (Fig. 13).[19] The Romanesque details, the rusticated limestone facing, the simplicity of the wall treatment, the horizontal division of the elevations, the sense of mass together with a rich plastic quality—all reveal Sullivan's debt to the eastern architect. The interior surfaces were covered with the characteristic ornament that Sullivan had introduced in Moody's Tabernacle a decade earlier. The Standard Club, demolished in 1910, was a fine work of architecture in its own right but was less in the mainstream of the Chicago development than the Marshall Field Wholesale Store.

A much more important work in the Richardsonian manner was the Walker Warehouse (1888–89), at 210–14 South Market Street (Fig. 14). Like the Standard Club and the Marshall Field building, the Walker Warehouse represented the deliberate following of a certain form of architecture appropriate to masonry bearing walls and interior iron framing rather than a logical step in the development of the commercial style. It was important, however, as an assimilation of the Richardsonian form in a way that pointed

[19] For the Marshall Field Wholesale Store, see pp. 60–63.

more clearly in the new direction. The warehouse was a geometric volume, with no rustication or other detail to interrupt its sharp-edged rectangular profile or its smooth planes. The arches and the various openings were firmly and positively integrated and heightened the sense of volume through the virtual absence of moldings. For all its intrinsic excellence, however, it stood at a considerable distance from Sullivan's later work, which shows so skilful a mastery of the new techniques. The warehouse was demolished in 1953 to make way for the southward extension of Wacker Drive, which now occupies the site of old Market Street.

The Auditorium is the triumph in the traditional materials of masonry and iron and the structural forms appropriate to them. But because of its complexity and the multitude of paths it opened to the structural art, as well as its debt to Richardson's Marshall Field building, it is best treated separately at the end of the present chapter. Moreover, the careers and early achievements of two other architects, D. H. Burnham and John Wellborn Root, largely parallel those of Adler and Sullivan and consequently require our consideration at this point.[20]

If Daniel Hudson Burnham had lived anywhere except in the city of Chicago, he would not have had the architectural reputation that he now enjoys. He was an organizer and a merchant of work often designed by others. The great designs that came from the office of Burnham and Root were either the work of the latter or of men trained by him and designing under his direction. After Root's death in 1891, as long as original architecture flourished in Chicago, the work of Burnham's office continued in the commercial style. As soon as the powerful effect of the classical taste touched him, however, he willingly embraced the new fashion. He enjoyed the greatest success of the Chicago architects, but he did so by increasingly turning against what they stood for. Yet his presence was necessary, and his contribution during the Chicago renaissance was valuable.

[20] Adler and Sullivan enjoyed many more commissions than those I have discussed here. The most important for the evolution of the Chicago school are the following: Rosenfeld Building, 1881–82, Washington and Halsted streets; Brunswick and Balke factory and warehouse, 1881–83, Orleans, Huron, Sedgwick, and Superior streets; Hammond Library (later Union Theological College), 1882, 44 North Ashland Avenue (demolished); Frankenthal Building, 1882, 141 South Wells Street (demolished); apartment building, 1882, 3200 South Prairie Avenue; Scoville Building, 1884–85, 619–31 West Washington Boulevard; Selz, Schwab and Company factory, 1886–87, Superior and Roberts streets. This last structure is one of the few architecturally worthwhile factories of the latter part of the nineteenth century and strongly suggests the Philadelphia buildings of Button, Hoxie, and others. The continuous piers, carried without break to the top of the parapet, dominate the severely simple façade. The extreme architectonic economy reflects the structural economy: the factory cost only five and one-half cents per cubic foot. For descriptions and illustrations of these and other commissions of Adler and Sullivan up to the Auditorium, see Morrison, *op. cit.*, pp. 52–78, 111–16, 294–300, 321–27.

Daniel Burnham was born in Henderson, New York, in 1846, and came to Chicago with his family in 1855. He studied at Snow's Swedenborgian Academy and at Central High School. He managed to graduate in 1865 with an extremely poor record, distinguishing himself only in freehand drawing. He failed the entrance examinations for Harvard and Yale—badly enough, apparently, to discourage him from trying any other university. All his life, he once said, he felt the lack of mental training at college age, a defect that may have been partly responsible for his pliability in the hands of educated eastern architects. But it must be recorded that Burnham was a man of genuine vision and originality. His failure in schoolwork was a personal matter; his failure, however, to maintain the standards that produced the Chicago Plan of 1909 was in large part the failure of a national culture.

Burnham started his career in 1868 as a clerk in a retail store, but he hated the work and was convinced that he had no ability to insure progress in it. He had felt a bent for architecture when he graduated from high school, and as a consequence, he entered the office of William Le Baron Jenney in the same year that he gave up the retail business. But a curious restlessness drove him out in a short time. He went to Nevada with a mining expedition that failed. He returned to Chicago, ran for state senator, and was defeated. He tried architecture again, establishing a partnership with Gustave Laureau in 1871. The fire ruined them, and Laureau left town.

Finally, Burnham's father took a hand in this disordered and pointless career. In 1872 he placed him as a draftsman in the firm of Carter, Drake and Wight, widely known and successful Chicago architects. He came to admire Peter B. Wight, an eminent Gothic Revivalist, who taught him the practical work of building design and aroused in him an appreciation for scholarship. There is every possibility that Wight may have had a strong and lasting influence on him, which later appeared in the insistence on his designers' meticulous fidelity to the origins of ornamental detail.

The opportunity and the association that Burnham needed came in 1872, when he met John Wellborn Root. The partnership that they formed in 1873 proved to be another highly productive example of architectural symbiosis. Root possessed a creative technical and artistic talent of the highest order. Burnham, an affable and friendly man, proved an excellent salesman and organizer. When the new office started business, it had one draftsman. The second one the partners hired was William Holabird, and the third, Clinton J. Warren.

Burnham rapidly developed into a good executive, and the new business began to grow. He did little designing, but he thoroughly mastered the technical, utilitarian, and financial aspects of building. "Uncle Dan was an impresario"—such was Frank Lloyd Wright's sharp but friendly summation of his ability. But his sense for business was a valuable factor, so long as there was creative talent to give it aesthetic expression. "He considered it was his highest duty," A. N. Rebori wrote, "to permit the structure to serve in the most economical manner possible the functions for which it was intended."[21]

The organizing and business ability that Burnham demonstrated in the amazing rise of his firm brought about his election as chief of construction for the Columbian Exposition of 1893, and after Root's death, chief consulting architect. During the work on the fair most of the business of Burnham's office was handled by Dwight Perkins, who was later to make valuable contributions in his own right to the Chicago movement.[22] Before the end of the century Burnham saw the enormous business possibilities of the Renaissance Revival and confidently expected the day when all the cities of America would be rebuilt in the classical mode. He tried to persuade Wright to join him in the exploitation of this fashion. It was fortunate for architecture all over the world that Wright was able to give the answer that he did—"I'm afraid it's too late now, Uncle Dan."

Richardson, Sullivan, and Wright are always regarded as the great triumvirate of American architecture. If a fourth were to be added, the choice would be difficult, but it would certainly have to give serious consideration to John Wellborn Root. His death as the age of forty-one was a calamity. In addition to his talent as a designer, he knew where the structural art ought to be going, and he had the courage, idealism, and conviction to keep it to its path. As a philosopher of the new movement in architecture, he was second only to Sullivan, but he often spoke with greater force and clarity than his more widely read colleague.

Root was born in Lumpkin, Georgia, in 1850. His youth, like his talent, was the perfect opposite of Burnham's. He was destined from childhood for some kind of artistic career: he started the serious study of drawing at the age of seven and of the piano at the age of twelve. When Sherman's army captured his native town the family was driven out. John was sent to England with Robert T. Wilson, a business associate of his father, Sidney Root. At the age of fourteen he began to attend a school in Liverpool, where he took special courses in architecture and music. His precocity expanded: a lively interest in nature was followed by an enthusiasm for the whole domain of the arts. The breadth and depth of Root's interests seem to have been fully established at high-school age.

[21] A. N. Rebori, "The Architecture of Burnham and Root," *Architectural Record*, XXXVIII (July, 1915), 62, as quoted in Charles H. Moore, *Daniel Hudson Burnham, Architect, Planner of Cities* (Boston: Houghton Mifflin Co., 1921), I, 26.

[22] For Perkins' work as an independent architect, see pp. 159, 200–203.

In 1866 he returned to New York and entered New York University in the same year. His record as a student was superior, and he distinguished himself outside the classroom in drawing, playing the piano and organ, and composing music. He graduated in 1869 with the degree of Bachelor of Science in civil engineering—the best education in the nineteenth century for an architect who had Root's highly trained aesthetic sense. He was a draftsman in the office of James Renwick during the years 1869 and 1870. The influence of Renwick lasted, for Gothic details appeared in some of Root's buildings up to his death. He moved to the office of John B. Snook in 1870, staying for about a year.

Root went to Chicago in 1871 and entered the office of Carter, Drake, and Wight, who hired him on the basis of a large portfolio of his plans, sketches, and renderings. It was in this office that he met Daniel Burnham. The latter, always ambitious, had now become energetic and practical. Root was lazy, something of a dreamer, the "artistic" soul who loved money because it enabled him to live the hedonistic life he enjoyed but who always managed to get the job done. The two men complemented each other professionally, but their partnership was equally based on a strong mutual affection. Burnham's influence saved Root from dilettantism and kept him purposeful and confident.

For Root, existence in Chicago was divided between the exacting routine of keeping a new office going during the depression of 1873 to 1874 and a lively plunge into the musical and theatrical life of the community. He was constantly involved in amateur play-producing, concerts, and recitals. He achieved a semiprofessional status in his avocation by reviewing concerts and operas for the *Chicago Tribune*. Meanwhile, the number of commissions slowly increased. For the first eight years the work of the new firm consisted largely of residences. Commercial work came with the Montauk Block (1881–82), their first big commission. After that the office was flooded and success was assured.

In 1882 Root married Dora Louise Monroe, his second wife and the sister of Harriet Monroe, who was to become one of the most important figures in the development of the American poetic renaissance. Her biography of her brother-in-law is excessively adulatory, but it is an accurate and comprehensive source of information about the life and thought of one of America's greatest architects. Root's architectural philosophy is almost as important as the buildings he designed; yet there has been no adequate examination of it since Harriet Monroe's biography was published in 1896. Along with Sullivan, he was one of the few architects in the late nineteenth century who clearly and fully understood the necessary character, importance, and purpose of the structural art in an age of mechanized industry.

Although Root sometimes indulged a taste for derivative forms and details, he considered it fortunate that America had no native artistic precedents comparable to those of Europe. She was free, he thought, to create her own architecture, and he believed steadfastly that she would. He aligned himself with the growing movement in the nineteenth century toward honesty and realism in the expression of an organic form. The basic ideas of modern architecture are extensively anticipated in Root's papers and addresses, a number of which were unpublished before their appearance in Harriet Monroe's biography.

On the subject of style and its relation to the whole cultural milieu, he discovered the important truth early in his Chicago career.

To rightly estimate an essentially modern building, it must not be viewed solely from an archaeological standpoint. . . . Whenever in the world there was a period or style of architecture worth preserving, its inner spirit so closely fitted to the age wherein it flourished, that the style could not be fully preserved, either by the people who immediately succeeded it, or by us after many years. . . . Our architecture if it is good will fit us. . . . The object of all this study of architectural styles must be to acquire from former times the spirit in which our predecessors worked; not to copy what they did. . . . Where architects faithfully follow out the logic of a predetermined theory of their building, they have purity of style.[23]

Root demanded a rational and empirical attitude toward the structural art. He was deeply opposed to the literal use of historical styles, since he was convinced that sound formal solutions could come only from the inherent elements of the structural-utilitarian-human complex with which the architect has to deal in the process of design. In this respect he believed that reason plays a greater part in architecture than in any other art but that imagination is essential after reason has defined the problem and determined its practical solution. Style, in the best sense of the word, could arise only in this way. In his own words:

Styles grow by the careful study of all the conditions which lie about each architectural problem, and thus while each will have its distinct differentiation from all the others, broad influences of climate, of national habits and institutions will in time create the type, and this is the only style worth considering. . . . The particular thing chosen for the given purpose shall be the best fitted for that purpose—shall in short grow out of it. This is as obvious as to say that a man's exterior form shall be the result of his interior structure.[24]

One could hardly find a closer parallel than this to Sullivan's organic theory.

Root insisted on a fully functional approach to the structural art. The

[23] Quoted in Harriet Monroe, *John Wellborn Root* (Boston: Houghton Mifflin Co., 1896), pp. 63–64.

[24] *Ibid.*, p. 69.

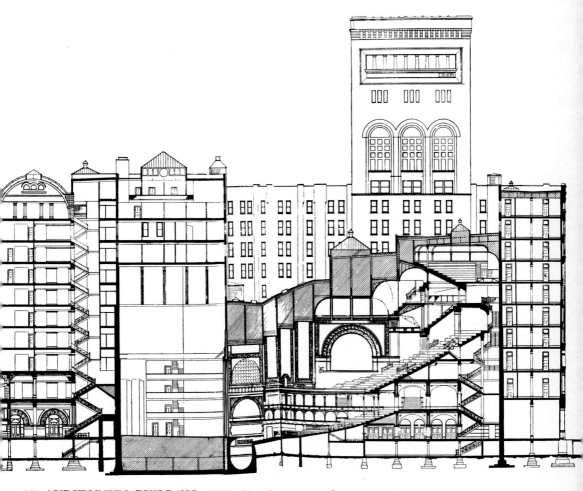

33. AUDITORIUM BUILDING, 1887–89   ADLER AND SULLIVAN

Longitudinal section, a view of interior spaces, looking south.
(From *Inland Architect and News Record*.)

34. AUDITORIUM HOTEL, 1887–89 Adler and Sullivan

Main lobby. (*Chicago Architectural Photographing Co.*)

35. AUDITORIUM HOTEL, 1887–89   ADLER AND SULLIVAN

Restaurant and bar. (*Chicago Architectural Photographing Co.*)

36. AUDITORIUM HOTEL, 1887–89 ADLER AND SULLIVAN

Second-floor lobby. (*Chicago Architectural Photographing Co.*)

37. AUDITORIUM HOTEL, 1887–89 ADLER AND SULLIVAN

Main dining room. (*Chicago Architectural Photographing Co.*)

38. AUDITORIUM THEATER, 1887–89 ADLER AND SULLIVAN

Orchestra floor and balcony. (*Chicago Architectural Photographing Co.*)

39. AUDITORIUM THEATER, 1887–89   ADLER AND SULLIVAN

View toward the stage. (*Chicago Architectural Photographing Co.*)

40. FIRST LEITER BUILDING, 1879   William Le Baron Jenney

Now the Morris Building, at the northwest corner of Wells and
Monroe streets. (*J. W. Taylor.*)

41. FIRST LEITER BUILDING, 1879   William Le Baron Jenney

The Monroe Street elevation as it now appears. (*William Malm.*)

42. TROESCHER BUILDING, 1884   ADLER AND SULLIVAN

Now the Chicago Joint Board Building, at 15 South Wacker Drive.
(*Commercial Photographic Co.*)

43. WILLOUGHBY BUILDING, 1887 Leroy Buffington

Northwest corner of Jackson Boulevard and Franklin Street.
(*Kaufmann & Fabry Co.*)

44. HOME INSURANCE BUILDING, 1884–85
WILLIAM LE BARON JENNEY

Formerly at the northeast corner of La Salle and Adams streets;
demolished in 1931. (From Frank A. Randall, *History
of the Development of Building Construction in Chicago*
[Urbana: University of Illinois Press, 1949].)

45. HOME INSURANCE BUILDING, 1884–85
WILLIAM LE BARON JENNEY

Detail of a column at the third-story spandrel girder.
(From T. E. Tallmadge, *Architecture in Old Chicago*
[Chicago: University of Chicago Press, 1941].)

46. CHAMBER OF COMMERCE BUILDING, 1888–89
  BAUMANN AND HUEHL

Formerly at the southeast corner of La Salle and Washington streets;
demolished in 1928. (From *Industrial Chicago*
[Chicago: Goodspeed Publishing Co., 1891].)

47. CHAMBER OF COMMERCE BUILDING, 1888–89
BAUMANN AND HUEHL

Interior light court. (*Commercial Photographic Co.*)

48. SECOND LEITER BUILDING, 1889–91
WILLIAM LE BARON JENNEY

Now the Sears Roebuck Store, at the southeast corner of State and Van Buren streets. (*Commercial Photographic Co.*)

49. FAIR STORE, 1890–91   William Le Baron Jenney

North side of Adams Street from State to Dearborn.
(*Commercial Photographic Co.*)

50. FAIR STORE, 1890–91 WILLIAM LE BARON JENNEY

The steel frame during construction. (From *Industrial Chicago* [Chicago: Goodspeed Publishing Co., 1891].)

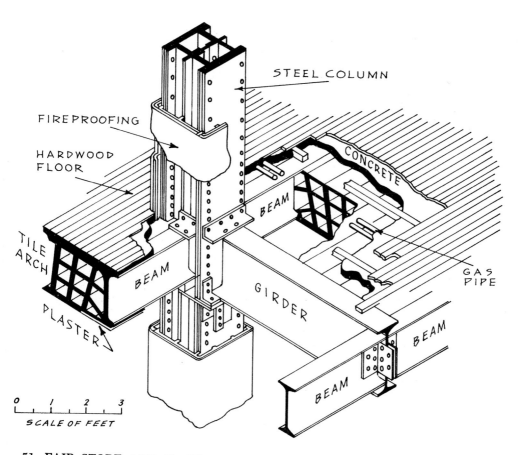

STEEL COLUMN

FIREPROOFING

HARDWOOD FLOOR

CONCRETE

BEAM

TILE ARCH

BEAM

GAS PIPE

PLASTER

GIRDER

BEAM

BEAM

0 1 2 3
SCALE OF FEET

51. FAIR STORE, 1890–91 WILLIAM LE BARON JENNEY

Detail of a typical column-and-beam joint. (From *Industrial Chicago* [Chicago: Goodspeed Publishing Co., 1891].)

52. MANHATTAN BUILDING, 1889–91
William Le Baron Jenney

431 South Dearborn Street.
(*Chicago Architectural Photographing Co.*)

53. South Dearborn Street near Van Buren, looking north.
The tall structures (*from right to left*) are the Manhattan, Old Colony,
and Fisher buildings. (*Commercial Photographic Co.*)

54. Plymouth Street near Van Buren, looking north. The view shows
(*from left to right*) the Manhattan, Old Colony, and Fisher buildings
and a portion of the Great Northern Hotel in the background. The
correlation of the huge blocklike forms is striking.
(*Commercial Photographic Co.*)

55. UNITY BUILDING, 1891–92 CLINTON J. WARREN

Now known by its address, 127 North Dearborn Street. The
iron and steel frame during construction. (From *Industrial Chicago*
[Chicago: Goodspeed Publishing Co., 1891].)

56. LUDINGTON BUILDING, 1891   JENNEY AND MUNDIE

1104 South Wabash Avenue. (*Kaufmann & Fabry Co.*)

57. MORTON BUILDING, 1896　Jenney and Mundie

538 South Dearborn Street. (*Commercial Photographic Co.*)

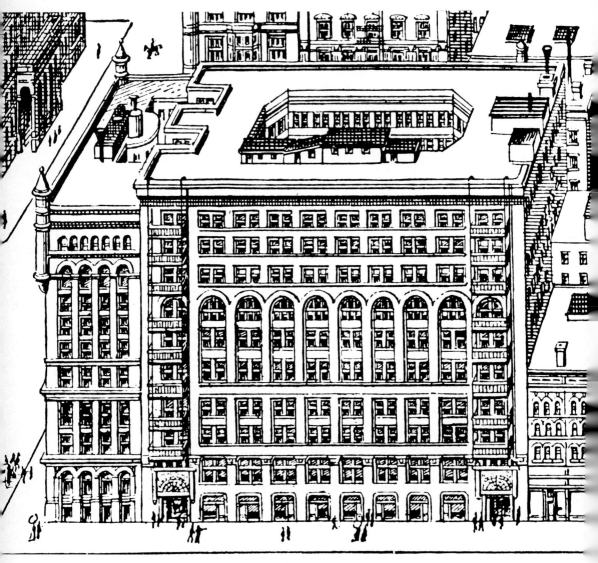

58. INSURANCE EXCHANGE, 1884–85 BURNHAM AND ROOT
SECOND RAND McNALLY BUILDING, 1889–90 BURNHAM AND ROOT

The Insurance Exchange (*left*) stood on the west side of La Salle Street
between Adams and Quincy before its demolition in 1912. The
Rand McNally (*right*) faced Adams Street midway between La Salle
and Wells; it was demolished in 1911. (From Frank A. Randall,
History of the Development of Building Construction in Chicago
[Urbana: University of Illinois Press, 1949].)

59. SECOND RAND McNALLY BUILDING, 1889–90
   BURNHAM AND ROOT

Detail of the east entrance. (From Harriet Monroe,
John Wellborn Root [Boston: Houghton Mifflin Co., 1896].)

60. GREAT NORTHERN HOTEL, 1890–92   Burnham and Root

Formerly at the northeast corner of Dearborn Street
and Jackson Boulevard; demolished in 1940.
(*Commercial Photographic Co.*)

61. ASHLAND BLOCK, 1891–92   Burnham and Root

Formerly at the northeast corner of Clark and
Randolph streets; demolished in 1949.
(*Commercial Photographic Co.*)

62. ASHLAND BLOCK, 1891–92   BURNHAM AND ROOT

A later view showing the parapet that replaced
the original cornice. (*William Malm.*)

63. WOMAN'S TEMPLE, 1891–92   Burnham and Root

Formerly at the southwest corner of La Salle
and Monroe streets; demolished in 1926.
(*Commercial Photographic Co.*)

64. MASONIC TEMPLE, 1891–92 Burnham and Root

Formerly at the northeast corner of State and
Randolph streets; demolished in 1939.
(*Commercial Photographic Co.*)

architect must deal rationally and analytically with a large number of physical, economic, social, and psychological factors: the town, the community, the nature and location of the street, climate, orientation, quality of the air, available materials, and supply of labor; and, if a residence, the personalities, habits, activities, and vocations of those who will live in it. And finally, there was the necessity—which we have yet to recognize—of correlating the form of the building with those around it. But after all the functional and practical considerations, it was an act of creative imagination that turned building into the *art* of architecture. What resulted was not this style or that; it was *style*, if we must use the term.

In describing the aesthetic qualities of a finished building, Root employed an ingenious metaphor. He compared the characteristics of a fine building with those of a cultivated man. The criteria by which he tested both were Repose, Refinement, Self-containment, Sympathy (that is, an organic and unified relationship to the milieu), Discretion, Knowledge (the reflection of its designer's practical knowledge and aesthetic intuition), Urbanity, and Modesty.[25] They are abstractions, but the buildings themselves as well as subsequent papers show that Root understood them well in their concrete dimensions.

Root was very much aware of the confusion of architecture in the latter half of the nineteenth century, and he consequently realized that freedom from idolatry of the past was a primary condition for renewed order and significance.

Architecture [he wrote in 1888] devotes itself to sensation making. Renaissance follows Renaissance so fast that the new birth never gets past the teething age, and dies before we know the color of its eyes or what its form and complexion would have been. . . . Within the memory of the youngest of us, architectural creations have twice over embodied the whole history of architectural development from Hiram to Norman Shaw.[26]

But a genuine American art can grow up and flourish only if we can discover what art, and particularly architecture, truly is.

Every work of fine art is the expression of one dominating idea. . . . It is the dominance of one leading quality over others which is the absolute test of the merit of any work, as it is the law which creates what we call "style." . . . The style . . . must not be understood to be . . . a thing of exterior form alone. It lies far deeper. It is the life and existence of the work. As far as material conditions permit it to be possible, a building designated for a particular purpose should express that purpose in every part. The purpose may not be revealed by conventional means,

[25] "Style," *Inland Architect and Builder*, VIII (January, 1887), 99–101, as quoted in Monroe, *op. cit.*, p. 79.

[26] "Broad Art Criticism," *Inland Architect and News Record*, XI (February, 1888), 3.

but it must be so plainly revealed that it can be escaped by no appreciative student. . . . The great work of art is that which expresses the same intention by less obvious but more inherently significant means—means vital in themselves—the sweep of roof lines—the general repose of mass—the delicacy and grace of ornament—the generosity and openness of aspect. What has just been said indicated another essential characteristic of all true art work—moderation.[27]

Thus the true expression of functionalism lies in simplicity, directness, and moderation.

The great architectural problem, as Root saw it, was to develop a continuous architectural expression through mass and structure of the age of machinery, steam power, and large-scale industry. With surprising acuteness he saw the problem of the arts in a mechanized industrial society and how they would have to meet the challenge of the machine. But he also saw that the development of a modern style would not occur as the result of some arbitrary fiat.

We must grant that . . . architecture must normally express the conditions of life about and within it, not in a fragmentary and spasmodic way, but in the mass and structure; the life of the building in large and comprehensive type. As yet the search for a national or new architectural style is absolutely useless for this purpose. Architectural styles . . . were never discovered by human prospectors. . . . Styles are found truly at the appointed time, but solely by those who, with intelligence and soberness, are working out their ends with the best means at hand, and with scarce a thought of the coming new or national style.[28]

Root not only posed the problem but also presented in detail the best solution the century had developed. In a masterful technical and aesthetic analysis of the modern office building, he summed up the best that his age had said on the structural art. He began with the statement that the culture of his time was predominantly pragmatic and scientific, that its approach to building, then, would be rational, empirical, and systematic rather than intuitive. The technical process of design he outlined in nine steps. (1) Cost: the aim is to produce the most efficient and spacious building within the allowance, which includes the price of land. (2) Floor plan for maximum light: the L-shaped plan with narrow wings makes it possible for all offices to have at least one exposure to natural light. (3) Elevators: for easiest access the elevators are concentrated in two central areas flanking the entrance hall. (4) Service facilities: heating and ventilating equipment, electrical conduits and outlets (or gas lines), and storage space are located for ease of use, maintenance, and alteration. (5) Optimum height per story: 10 feet 6 inches. (6) Framing: framing and fireproofing of framing members are

[27] *Ibid.*, p. 5.

[28] "A Great Architectural Problem," *Inland Architect and News Record*, XV (June, 1890), 68.

determined not only by loads but also by conditions of soil. (7) Foundation: the conditions of Chicago soil (that is, any wet, sandy, or spongy soil) require the use of Root's chief structural innovation, a floating raft of concrete reinforced with steel rails, stepped up to receive the wall or the bearing plate at the column foot. (8) Wall construction: the walls should be as open as possible, and their construction involves, among other factors, the temporary support of flanking party walls. (9) Settlement: construction of all parts of the building proceeds simultaneously to avoid unequal settlement. When this complex of technical problems has been adequately dealt with, the architect then turns to his final aesthetic expression.

All that has been written relates to those portions of the building with which the public at large can have but little interest, but which are the inner and significant principle about which every external aspect must arrange itself. The truest and best forms which this external aspect is to present will be found by a reasonable application of conditions of our civilization, of our social and business life and of our climatic conditions. Even a slight appreciation of these would seem to make it evident . . . that all conditions, climatic, atmospheric, commercial and social, demand for this external aspect the simplest and most straightforward expression. Bearing in mind that our building is a business building, we must fully realize what this means. Bearing also in mind . . . that dust and soot are the main ingredients of our native air, we must realize what this means. Both point the same way. Every material used to enclose the structure we have raised must be, first, of the most enduring kind, and, second, it must be wrought into the simplest forms.

These buildings, standing in the midst of hurrying, busy thousands of men, may not appeal to them through the more subtle means of architectural expression, for such an appeal would be unheeded; and the appeal which is constantly made to unheeding eyes loses in time its power to attract. In them should be carried out the ideas of modern life—simplicity, stability, breadth, dignity. To lavish upon them profusion of delicate ornament is worse than useless, for this would better be preserved for the place and hour of contemplation and repose. Rather should they by their mass and proportion convey in some large elemental sense an idea of the great, stable, conserving forces of modern civilization.

Enough has been said to suggest how radically new in type such edifices are, how essential is the difference between the modern and any of the preceding recognized architectural types.

One result of methods such as I have indicated will be the resolution of our architectural designs into their essential elements. So vital has the underlying structure of these buildings become, that it must dictate absolutely the general departure of external forms; and so imperative are all the commercial and constructive demands, that all architectural detail employed in expressing them must become modified by them. Under these conditions we are compelled to work definitely with definite aims, permeating ourselves with the full spirit of the age, that we may give its architecture true art forms.

To other and older types of architecture these new problems are related as the poetry of Darwin's evolution is to other poetry. They destroy, indeed, many of the most admirable and inspiring of architectural forms, but they create forms adapted to the expression of new ideas and new aspects of life. Here, vagaries of fashion and temporary fancies should have no influence; here, the arbitrary dicta of self-constituted architectural prophets should have no voice. Every one of these problems should be rationally worked out alone, and each should express the character and aims of the people related to it. I do not believe it is possible to exaggerate the importance of the influence which may be exerted for good or evil by these distinctively modern buildings. Hedged about by many unavoidable conditions, they are either gross and self-asserting shams, untrue both in the material realization of their aims, and in their art function as expressions of the deeper spirit of the age; or they are sincere, noble and enduring monuments to the broad and beneficent commerce of the age.[29]

Root's concern with the theory of architecture and of art in general led to an interest in some of the metaphysical aspects of the subject. In an unpublished paper entitled "A Utilitarian Theory of Beauty," he tried with very questionable success to relate art and science in a logical unity by going to the biological basis of color and form as the basis for the "utility" of the arts to mankind. The idea was certainly organic in a narrow Darwinian sense, but it was a case of stretching the Darwinian theory even beyond the limits of Spencer. This naïve attempt to find a basis for aesthetic values in natural phenomena or external reality, however, lay in the mainstream of contemporary thought, finally culminating in Whitehead's impressive synthesis, a systematic and comprehensive organic metaphysics. Other and more fruitful investigations by Root along the same line appeared in a paper entitled "Art of Pure Color." Root had some useful if undistinguished things to say about the importance of color in interior architecture. He also pointed out what had then come to be a subject of much interest in the visual arts: the importance to graphic representation of the new work in optics of Young, Helmholz, Tyndall, and others.[30]

As a designer directly involved in the preparation of building plans, Root was a qualified engineer as well as an architect. He was constantly required to make decisions and to propose novel solutions in the new technical areas of iron framing, column and wall footings for high buildings, and problems of settlement of party walls. He had been trained as an engineer, but he worked primarily from practical experience and intuition, in the pragmatic tradition that most American engineers followed until about 1875, when progress in the sciences of structure and structural materials rapidly began

[29] *Ibid.*, pp. 68–71, as quoted in Monroe, *op. cit.*, pp. 106–8.

[30] See "Art of Pure Color," *Inland Architect and Builder*, I (July, 1883), 80–82, and II (August, 1883), 89.

to transform the building art into a scientific technology. But the growing volume of business that flowed into the office made it increasingly difficult for Root to keep abreast of the new developments in structural science that poured out at an accelerating rate. He had to rely more and more on specialists as his own detailed engineering knowledge declined. His brother, Walter C. Root, who was a member of the office staff from 1879 to 1886, accurately described John Root's dilemma and, indeed, that of most architects after him.

In a technical and narrow sense, John's mathematical and engineering abilities were deficient. He had not time to learn and keep up the many branches of constructional detail. He was rusty in his calculus and his trigonometry, ditto much of his applied mathematics. I do not believe he would have cared to test himself to calculate an important truss; it was not necessary nor desirable that he should. With the increasing press of work in his office, the custom developed rapidly of having specialists work out the various problems; for example, after an idea like the steel-rail footings had been developed, engineers were consulted as to the best methods of execution [the reference is to the Montauk footings, discussed below]. But John had such a quick perception that he could suggest to a specialist an idea which would illuminate him, and enable him to work out a solution of a hard problem in a new and brilliant manner.[31]

The first important commercial structure designed by Burnham and Root was the Montauk Block, located at 64 West Monroe Street, near the northwest corner of Monroe and Dearborn (Fig. 15). It was built in 1882 (a record year—3,113 buildings!) and, for no structural but rather some economic reason, demolished in 1902. The Montauk was an epoch-making building, not only because of its intrinsic characteristics but equally because of its genesis and its architects' method of dealing with the problems it presented. It was the first large commercial project that came into being as the result of a painstaking investigation in the new scientific spirit of all the factors involved: the economic need, the costs, the financial possibilities, and the utilitarian requirements associated with the urban office building, and the technical means by which such requirements could be met and the possibilities realized.

The Montauk was commissioned by Peter and Shepard Brooks, Boston entrepreneurs who had grown wealthy in the shipping business and who were looking for profitable investments in the rapidly expanding economy of Chicago. Their agent in these operations was the lawyer and real estate

---

[31] Quoted in Monroe, *op. cit.*, pp. 117–18. The division of labor described by Walter Root has now reached the extreme, with as much as 50 per cent of the cost and the designing effort of a large commercial building being devoted to structural details and mechanical and electrical utilities. The union of architecture and engineering demanded by the philosophy of the modern movement has achieved the ironic result of contracting the architect's role to a minority status in the creation of a finished building.

expert Owen F. Aldis. The unprecedented and prophetic qualities of the Montauk were the consequence of Root's translation of Brooks's and Aldis' shrewd, daring, and original ideas into the design and construction of the skyscraper office building. It was an extraordinary union of talents, in which Peter Brooks issued the commands with the expectation of immediate and exact obedience. He awarded the commission to Burnham and Root in February, 1881. His first letter to Aldis, dated February 5, laid down the basic principles.

Having thought over a building on the 89½-foot lot on Monroe Street next west of the First National Bank, I think, by utilizing all of the space on the main floor and by building up eight stories with also a basement—if the earth can support it in the opinion of the architects—that it may be large enough to support an elevator. If you can get this lot for $100,000 cash I am rather inclined to purchase it.[32]

Brooks's letter of March 22, 1881, contains a prophetic sentence that simply and clearly indicates his primary motive for commissioning the building: "Tall buildings will pay well in Chicago hereafter, and sooner or later a way will be found to erect them." It is the letter of March 25, however, that contains the classic description of the functional purpose and the necessary utilitarian features of the new multistory office block. Brooks knew precisely what he wanted and he laid down an exact prescription for his architects.

Enclosed are rough plans but sufficient to express my idea of the ground floor of a building for the lot on Monroe Street. The architect can improve on them or submit better, giving also an idea of cost. Let his preliminary plans be on a small scale and not expensive.

I prefer to have a plain structure of face brick, eight stories and also a basement, with flat roof to be as massive as the architect chooses and well braced with iron rods if needed. The building throughout is to be for use and not for ornament. Its beauty will be in its all-adaptation to its use.

Windows as well as doors should be all worked in brick with as little stone and terra cotta to be introduced as possible consistent with not absolute plainness. No projections on the front (which catch dirt). The brick arch over the main entrance might be carried in several feet over the vestibule and inside steps to show in face brick and to convey the idea of strength. Indeed all the entries might be of face brick with red or black mortar (if as cheap as plaster) which would convey the idea of "fireproof" to the whole structure—a valuable idea in a building of eight stories. The first floor entry ought to be of tile. For all the other entries there is no better and cheaper flooring probably than good face brick.

Have a fire escape and a standpipe on the outside at the southeast corner. Let the plastering in the rooms be directly on the interior brick walls wherever prac-

---

[32] This and the subsequent letters from Brooks to Aldis are now in the possession of Graham Aldis, nephew of Owen Aldis and president of Aldis and Company. All quotations from these letters are made with his kind permission.

tical. The outer walls may require an intermediate air space between the footing and the walls and therefore furring off. Have a picture molding all around the walls near the ceilings for picture hooks to avoid defacing with nails. At each floor let the space between the furring and the outer walls where the floor rafters rest be carefully filled with mortar and be made air tight to cut off the draft. This is important in case of fire. In case of a serious fire the draft up the elevator shaft would be violent and dangerous. There is space enough to have a brick wall on the east side of the shaft as well as on all the others if the architect thinks advisable; if simply a wire network, light would be obtained from it in the shaft, but if of brick there should be windows along the outer walls of the shaft for light. These would be inaccessible and hard to keep clean and repaired. Windows may possibly be introduced in the upper stories on the west but must not be depended on permanently, for the adjoining building may be razed and a new one erected. Let the elevator car be as light as possible, with a seat that can be removed.

There should be fireplaces in each room for ventilation as well as heat, but if the Holley System [of hot air control] is introduced, giving ventilation, no doubt many fireplaces and chimneys can be dispensed with.

The less plumbing the less trouble. It should be concentrated as much as possible, all pipes to show and be accessible, including gas pipes. It might also be advisable to put in wire for future electric lights. It is not uncommon to do it in Boston now. The two soil pipes on the upper floors are supposed to join into one in the ceiling of the first floor. The water closet in Suite 7 and similar rooms above it is introduced to make these suites on the corners more desirable. It may be as well to omit this water closet and have nothing of the sort except in the room for the purpose.[33]

Burnham and Root completed the plans of the Montauk in July, 1881. In the course of design they increased the number of full floors from eight to ten and apparently introduced a variety of visual improvements beyond Brooks's rather spare proposals. When he saw the completed plans, his Boston conscience was outraged and he raised strenuous objections to the result. Yet the character of these objections shows with what extraordinary thoroughness Peter Brooks had grasped all the details of a large office building and how valuable such a grasp was for the subsequent development of commercial architecture.

The most is certainly made of the lot, to the credit of the architects, but I have no idea it can be built well for the sum proposed. The building is a much more extravagant one than my original design although much on the same plan. The architects are of course indifferent to the future cost of repairs and care, an item worthy of much consideration. Tile is expensive and bothersome to keep clean, it

[33] Letter of Peter Brooks, March 25, 1881, in Aldis and Company papers. It is clear from the letter that Brooks had not entirely resolved the conflicting ambitions between having a first-class building and having the least expensive one he could get. This is a prevision of the fundamental dilemma of all modern commercial architecture.

is good on the first floor only—nowhere else. A cast iron floor is the thing for the galleries with holes in it to keep it rough, no noisier than tile, indestructible and simply requires sweeping to clean it.

There is a needless amount of plate glass and the panes should be divided horizontally in halves. In the size of the sashes I regret to say, as usual, the architect has had his own way. For use and comfort I regard this as the chief defect of the building. Colored glass is mere nonsense, a passing fashion, inappropriate in a mercantile building and worse than all, it obstructs the light. Strike it all out.

What is the object in glass at the front of the urinals? The best I see here are made of slate with trickling water and a simple slate gutter at the bottom, the floor of slate sloping towards it—thirty years old in the streets of Paris.

I notice all the wash bowls are to be boarded up with a door underneath, a good receptacle for dirt, mice too. Expose the pipes below, traps and all, they do not look badly and ought not to leak. This covering up of pipes is all a mistake, they should be exposed everywhere, if necessary painted well and handsomely. If the w. c. seats could be exposed underneath it would be much better, there is no need of covers to them, they are never used. . . .

Is this Montauk Block—or Montauk Building? M. Block sounds best but it is not a block. M. Building is more appropriate and this I think it must be.[34]

The Montauk exerted a considerable influence not only in Chicago but in other cities as well. The building excited a good deal of attention as a structural and architectural novelty and must have seemed to less enterprising men a daring experiment. In the matter of its appearance, Brooks's prescription was well filled. There was some Romanesque detail in the arched entranceway and in the rough, battered masonry of the base, but the general treatment was strikingly original with little precedent behind it.

The unique element among all its unusual technical and aesthetic characteristics was the foundation. The stone masonry of the base and the interior iron columns rested directly on a "floating-raft" foundation, developed by Root and used here for the first time, to reduce the height of the individual stepped-up footings under walls and columns and to reduce the unit pressure delivered by the footing to the soil. The raft did not extend continuously under the area of the building but was divided into the traditional independent wall and column footings, although these were of much greater area than those previously used. Root personally calculated the dimensions of the footings and the quantity of reinforcing and supervised the preparation of the construction drawings. The foundation was designed expressly for the soft and compressible soil of the Chicago area, which consists almost entirely of sand and clay interspersed with water pockets. The raft consisted of a slab

[34] Letter of Peter Brooks, July 23, 1881, in Aldis and Company papers. The cast-iron flooring specified by Brooks would not be tolerated today: exposed metal flooring or stairways are outlawed by fire codes.

of concrete about 20 inches thick reinforced with layers of steel rails to withstand shearing and bending forces. By means of it the load of the building could be distributed over a relatively large area rather than concentrated on the narrow strip or square beneath the wall or column footing. Unit pressures were thus materially reduced, and reasonable uniformity of settlement was assured. Root and Owen Aldis thought of the raft as a steel foundation with a concrete envelope to prevent rusting.

When the Montauk was under construction in the early part of 1882, Peter Brooks found that he was satisfied, although he saw the crucial nature of the foundation problem for tall buildings in Chicago.

I am well pleased with the construction of [the] Montauk Block in comparison with the New York buildings—from your description; for its situation it could not be better. . . . For the future I should never build but of brick and terra cotta with iron and wood covered with fireproof tile—but I think hereafter I should, like the New York people, build ten stories high—the Chicago foundations with care will stand it, if broad enough—but there must be a limit to the cost of foundations beyond which it will not pay to go.[35]

The Montauk Block in its finished form was a completely fireproof, ten-story prism of stone and brick, each story above the first identical with every other. Fireproofing was achieved through hollow-tile subflooring and tile envelopes around the cast-iron columns and wrought-iron floor beams. The use of a continuous terra-cotta band at the sill line of each story heightened the appearance of a rectangular block composed of similar horizontal elements. The windows formed the most striking feature of the building. They were conventional in details of sash and frame but unusually wide and high and closely ranked. Each was capped by a brick lintel in the form of a flattened arch. The Montauk was a perfectly functional structure, well proportioned, simple and dignified, with an almost monastic austerity. It evolved in part from the vernacular propensity for flat, unadorned wall surfaces, which Brooks must have known well in the warehouses and markets of his native city.

There were functional defects, however, and one was serious enough to shorten the Montauk's potential life. The building had two "first" floors, which had been achieved by setting the ground floor three feet below grade level at the sidewalk. This proved to be a mistake: it left insufficient headroom in the basement for boilers and machinery, which had to be located in an annex at the rear of the building; and the elevators had to be started at the upper "first" floor, with the consequence that tenants were forced to walk up a long flight of stairs to reach them. Partly offsetting this defect,

[35] Letter of Peter Brooks, February 5, 1882, in Aldis and Company papers.

however, was the high standard of mechanical equipment and the centralization of all heating and plumbing facilities in a single utility shaft. The chief factor in the early demolition of this otherwise carefully designed building was the use of fixed interior partitions of brick, which made it impossible to subdivide and rearrange office space. But Brooks closed his investment with a handsome profit: he sold the land and the building to the First National Bank for $500,000, against a total expenditure on his part of $325,000. The bank demolished the structure in 1902 to make way for its own office building.[36]

Root, with his characteristic flair for waggish irony, made the final comment on the Montauk. Five days before his death on January 15, 1891, an unnamed man entered the office to offer the architect his last commission. Harriet Monroe recorded the conversation.

It was a very polite gentleman who came in to offer it. "Now, Mr. Root," he said, after their talk, "you will give me a beautiful building, won't you?"

"We shall try to, Mr. X.," replied the architect.

"Much of your work I like very much," continued the polite gentlemen, "but— you will permit me to be quite frank?"

"I desire it above all things."

"Many of your buildings are remarkably successful; but—there are one or two I do not like quite so well."

"Very natural, I am sure," said Root.

"I suppose my taste is at fault, but—may I venture upon a criticism?"

"You could not do me a greater favor."

"Well then, Mr. Root,"—it was diffcult for so polite a gentleman to confess his trouble,—"I like most of your buildings immensely, but—I do not like the Montauk Block."

Root put his hand on his critic's shoulder and shocked him black and blue by exclaiming, "My dear Mr. X., who in h[ell] does?"[37]

The technical excellence of the Montauk was not improved on until the construction of The Rookery three years later. After the earlier building the work of Burnham and Root took a somewhat different turn, chiefly in the direction of a more open wall and a more pronounced emphasis on revealing the structural characteristics. The exception was a non-commercial building, the Chicago Club, at Michigan Avenue and Van Buren Street, erected in 1882 and demolished following its partial collapse during remodeling

[36] For a number of years one of the Montauk's major tenants was the Hartford Fire Insurance Company. Nearly sixty years after the demolition, this company built its own office building at Monroe Street and Wacker Drive (1960–61), a contemporary example of realistic architecture based on the direct statement of column and flat-slab framing (see p. 218).

[37] Monroe, *op. cit.*, pp. 259–60.

in 1929. In this building the architects turned to a bold Romanesque with little modification.

The irregular progress that culminated in The Rookery and the Monadnock began with the Calumet Building, constructed from 1883 to 1884 on La Salle Street near Adams and demolished in 1913. Although in part a duplication of the Montauk, it represented in one respect an important departure from it. The walls were smooth planes except for narrow projecting courses at certain stories. But the windows, instead of being separate openings, as in the Montauk, were grouped together in pairs between the piers. The solidity and gravitational thrust of masonry construction were reflected in the breadth and massiveness of the piers and spandrels.

The Counselman Building, at the northwest corner of La Salle Street and Jackson Boulevard, and the Insurance Exchange (later Continental Bank), at 208 South La Salle Street, were completed in 1884 and 1885, respectively. The Counselman was demolished in 1920, and the Insurance Exchange in 1912. The first looked toward the Montauk in its flat walls and its absence of ornament. The second, typical of the financial and banking structures designed by Burnham and Root, revealed the continuous piers and grouped openings of the Calumet Building (Fig. 58, *left*). The Insurance Exchange was the largest of the early group of Burnham and Root's commissions. Nine stories high and covering an area 60 by 165 feet, its floor and roof loads were again divided between masonry bearing walls and interior framing of cast-iron columns and wrought-iron beams. The street elevations were simplified versions of the forms so skilfully developed in The Rookery: the verticalism of the continuous piers was interrupted by five horizontal courses to provide a composition of long narrow rectangles which reflected the slab-like form of the building.

The Austin Building, at 111 West Jackson Boulevard, originally known as the Phoenix and later the Western Union, was completed in 1886. It was a tall, narrow structure, eleven stories in height, with windows paired between slim piers. It was richly ornamented but badly organized. Its profusion suggested The Rookery, but it lacked the latter's unity, clarity, and firm articulation. The Phoenix Building was particularly distinguished by its monumental and highly ornamented entrance, a part of the elevation that Root particularly liked and on which he lavished much of his decorative genius. The building survived longer than most of its contemporaries; it was demolished in 1959 to make way for the Union Tank Car Building (1960–61). The Illinois Bank on La Salle Street (*ca.* 1886) involved a long step in the direction of The Rookery. Again the windows were grouped in pairs between the masonry piers, but in this case the piers and spandrels were quite narrow, giving much greater openness and sharper articulation to the wall. Low, flattened arches spanned the bays at the first and third stories, and the ever present projecting courses stretched across the main elevation at the first, third, and fifth stories.

The Rookery and the Monadnock Building join the Marshall Field Wholesale Store and the Auditorium as the final monuments of the art of masonry architecture. Many individual buildings by lesser men, however, show us that other architects were moving in the same direction as Richardson, Sullivan, Burnham, and Root. Three of these built during the early eighties are particularly good examples of the vernacular tradition in urban architecture, and two of the three are still standing to remind us of it. One is the former Garden City Warehouse, a little six-story building at 320 West Jackson Boulevard (1880), with its remarkably open façade of glass carried on a cast-iron armature. Another is the big warehouse of Hiram Sibley and Company, designed by George H. Edbrooke and built between 1882 and 1883 at 315 North Clark Street (Fig. 16). The warehouse stands along the north bank of the river and is apparently the first structure in Chicago other than grain elevators to rest on wood piling. The footing of the river wall is supported by three longitudinal rows of oak piles 30 feet long and spaced 3 feet on centers. The wall itself is of brick bearing masonry and rests on an open base of narrow piers and glass-filled bays. The wide grouped windows of the second and third stories preserve the open character, but the narrower windows above increase the mass of the wall and intensify the inversion of the usual order in masonry building. As a whole, the wall is an effective composition of flat planes and shallow reveals, although this is marred by the curious feature of continuous corbels at the third, fifth, sixth, and attic stories that extend progressively outward the higher they are located.

The third is the Dexter Building, 39 West Adams Street, erected in 1883 (Fig. 17). The commission went to Burnham and Root, but the design seems to have been intrusted entirely to Clinton J. Warren, a young member of the firm who early exhibited one of the major talents of the Chicago school. Warren was the school's leading architect of hotels and apartment buildings, reaching his full stature in this field around 1890.[38] He was born in 1860 and came to Chicago in 1879. He entered the office of Burnham and Root in 1880, remained for six years, and founded his own business in 1886. His name disappears from the role of the Chicago architects around 1893, but in seven years he was remarkably productive in his chosen specialty.

The Dexter Building revealed Warren's adaptation of Root's predilection for continuous piers, windows grouped in pairs between them, and semicircular or full-centered arches. The doubling of the rhythm in the upper two stories was a variation on a common feature of masonry buildings in

[38] For Warren's hotels and apartments, see pp. 152–56.

Chicago. Two characteristics, however, distinguished the Dexter from other comparable work. One was the nearly smooth, uninterrupted plane of the façade up to the seventh story. This, together with the extensive area of glass, took the main elevation close to the curtain wall of iron or steel framing. The other distinguishing characteristic was the use of shallow reveals and the very slight projection of the piers beyond the plane of the spandrels. The result was a nearly impartial expression of horizontal beams and narrow piers and columns, further revealing the tendency toward the neutral wall pattern of a framed building. The Dexter was demolished in 1961 as part of the site cleared for the new Federal Office Building (1961–64).

The Mallers Building, built in 1884 to 1885 after the plans of John J. Flanders, was an early skyscraper of some structural importance in its day. The first twelve-story building in Chicago and the highest masonry building at the time of its completion, it stood until 1920 on the southwest corner of La Salle and Quincy streets. Its designer, Flanders, the only architect of the school who was a native of the city, was born in Chicago in 1848. After a few years in Edward Burling's office, he established an independent practice in 1874. He formed the partnership of Flanders and Zimmerman in the late eighties but terminated it in 1898. He continued to practice architecture in Chicago until his death in 1914.

Architecturally, the Mallers was disfigured by a profusion of ornament— clustered pilasters at the top story, corbels, arches, elaborately decorated spandrels—but it pointed in the right direction. The windows were grouped between continuous piers separating narrow bays, a treatment that gave the building a pronounced vertical accent suggestive of Sullivan's approach to the tall office block. A considerable area of glass was the chief characteristic, aside from its highly functional interior, that made it a recognizable example of the commercial style.

One of the triumphs of the early period was the Chicago Opera House, designed by Henry Ives Cobb (1859–1931) and Charles S. Frost (1856– 1932). It was constructed between 1884 and 1885 at the southwest corner of Clark and Washington streets, where it stood until 1912 (Fig. 18). The two designers were partners for only a few years, from about 1884 until 1888. Frost's later reputation rested chiefly on the Chicago and North Western Railway Station in Milwaukee, which satisfied the company well enough to secure for him and Alfred Granger the enviable commission for the great North Western terminal at Canal and Madison streets (1906–11). Cobb was one of the best-known and most successful architects in Chicago during the eighties and nineties. He enjoyed an astounding number of commissions from virtually every part of the United States. Aside from the Opera House, his most important work in Chicago is the Newberry Library and the first group of buildings of the University of Chicago. The Opera House was another combined theater and office block, with the theater in the interior surrounded by a shell of offices. Information about the structural character of this building is entirely lacking, except for the fact that its exterior walls were of masonry construction. The illustrations, however, would seem to suggest precisely the opposite. Exterior bearing members appear to be non-existent at the first two stories, where there is a floor-to-ceiling envelope of glass divided by narrow mullions. The effect is astonishing and suggests the most advanced contemporary design, in which an uninterrupted sweep of glass surrounds the columns of framed construction. But an analysis of the probable structure shows that the architect could have achieved this effect even within the stringent limitations imposed by masonry and iron construction.

The street elevations throughout the upper eight stories of the Opera House were composed of a succession of alternately wide and narrow piers. The narrow piers obviously had no bearing function. The wide piers, on the other hand, must have been carried to the foundations either by cast-iron columns the outer edges of which projected into the glass curtain of the base or by deep, narrow piers set behind the panes of glass. The great area of glass, the shallow reveals, and the general light, open, regular quality of the elevations save the structure from a top-heavy appearance. The clarity, sharpness, and rectangularity of the walls and over-all profile place the Opera House close to the front rank of Chicago buildings in the 1880's.

None of the local architects had such a profound and pervasive effect on Chicago building in the decade of the eighties as Henry Hobson Richardson. Every important architect in the city except Jenney took something from him. His dominance was broken by the general adoption of iron and steel framing, a structural technique for which he offered no architectonic solution. Of Richardson's four commissions in Chicago, two were commercial buildings and two were residences. One of the residences, built in 1886 to 1887 for J. J. Glessner, still stands at the southwest corner of Prairie Avenue and Eighteenth Street, a blackened but perfectly sound revelation not only of the architect's power in handling massive stone masonry for an urban residence but equally of the remarkable homogeneity of his domestic and commercial designs (Fig. 19).[39] Richardson's greatest achievement and the basis of his influence was the Marshall Field Wholesale Store, which was constructed between 1885 and 1887 on the block bounded by Adams, Wells, Quincy, and Franklin streets (Fig. 20). The store was demolished in 1930 for no discernible reason, economic or structural, to make way for a parking lot. It would have lasted for more than a century. The building replaced the earlier Field

[39] The Glessner house, formerly owned and used by the Lithographers Research Association, is now for sale (1963). For the American Express Company building, see pp. 22–23.

wholesale establishment, which was originally known as the Field and Leiter Wholesale Building, constructed in 1872 on the northeast corner of Madison Street and Market (now Wacker Drive). It was replaced in turn by the Merchandise Mart.

The significance of the Marshall Field building has both a positive and a negative aspect. It was an immense block with a total area in plan of 61,750 square feet. It was Richardson's genius that he was able to master so effectively this huge bulk. Yet his mastery was appropriate only to masonry building. "This store," Giedion wrote, "showed Chicago architects how unobtrusively a great volume could be integrated. Richardson injected into this building something of the vitality of the rising city, in a treatment which was full of dignity. The dominance of the windows is emphasized . . . but the construction is rather conservative. Richardson's massive stone walls belong to an earlier period."[40]

All his life Richardson wanted to design a great commercial structure that would reflect the power and organization and boldness of modern commerce. He came closest to it in the Marshall Field building. In the daring simplicity and directness of its huge rectangular prism, in the massive granite and sandstone walls with their severe economy of detail, in the subtle rhythms of its fenestration, it was a forerunner of the new architecture of industry and commerce, where volume and surface texture and the free expression of structure determine aesthetic effect. Although in part derived from Romanesque forms, the plain and massive stone walls reflected a basic element of American vernacular building for over a century. Thus it can be regarded as indigenous, as "an artistic transmutation of elements which had grown out of American life," in Giedion's words.[41] The construction of the store followed that of the typical elevator building: floor and roof loads were carried for the most part on interior cast-iron columns and wrought-iron beams; the outer walls were bearing elements of solid masonry, red granite at the base and sandstone above.

The elevations of the Marshall Field store were simple, but the simplicity is deceptive, for it seems to deny the care which Richardson lavished on this powerful and harmonious composition. Henry-Russell Hitchcock caught the high quality of its design in his detailed description.

The rhythm of the first four stories is absolutely even except for the wide corner piers. These assure the solid massive appearance of the building in spite of the very large proportion of window space. These broad corners entail some sacrifice in the interior, but they give the building unity of effect. . . . The rhythm of the two upper floors is doubled and that of the attic quadrupled. By providing a

[40] Giedion, *op. cit.*, p. 294.
[41] *Ibid.*, p. 285.

low basement story with segmental arches, and by subdividing the windows of the main floors with stone pilasters to support the intermediate stone floor spandrels, the weight of the design at each level of the composition is exactly proportioned. The plain corners and the heavy cornice frame the whole design and emphasize the solidity of the total block, which needs no visible roof. Here Richardson finally escaped from the picturesque and achieved the highest type of formal design.[42]

The deep impression made by Richardson's building is best reflected in the ironic and impressionistic metaphors of Sullivan's *Kindergarten Chats*.

Let us pause, my son, at this oasis in the desert. . . .

You mean, I suppose, that here is a good piece of architecture for me to look at—and I quite agree with you.

No; I mean, here is a *man* for you to look at. A man that walks on two legs instead of four, has active muscles, heart, lungs and other viscera; a man that lives and breathes, that has red blood; a real man, a manly man; a virile force—broad, vigorous and with a whelm of energy—an entire male.

I mean that stone and mortar, here, spring into life, and are no more material and sordid things, but . . . become the very diapason of a mind rich-stored with harmony. . . .

Four square and brown, it stands, in physical fact, a monument to trade, to the organized commercial spirit, to the power and progress of the age, to the strength and resource of individuality and force of character; spiritually, it stands as the index of a mind, large enough, courageous enough to cope with these things, master them, absorb them and give them forth again, impressed with the stamp of large and forceful personality; artistically, it stands as the oration of one who knows well how to choose his words, who has somewhat to say and says it—and says it as the outpouring of a copious, direct, large and simple mind.[43]

The lesson for Sullivan in Richardson's great building was exactly the one that the younger architect needed to free him from his preoccupation with irrelevant details and give direction to his inchoate powers. The historians Burchard and Bush-Brown described what the Marshall Field Wholesale Store could teach him.

We know that Sullivan learned from it how to express what was really central in architectural composition, and that this pulled him out of the morass of minor themes and decorative touches in which he was floundering. Here in the sight of this building, Sullivan found what others would find later, a way of form so that the technical need not be ugly and the aesthetic would be neither borrowed nor

[42] Henry-Russell Hitchcock, *The Architecture of H. H. Richardson and His Times* (New York: Museum of Modern Art, 1936 [copyright now held by the Shoe String Press, Hamden, Conn.]), pp. 275–76.

[43] Louis Sullivan, *Kindergarten Chats* (New York: Wittenborn, Schultz, Inc., 1947), pp. 28–30.

flimsy. Richardson gave to many architects a goal of quality, an index of scale, a sense of stateliness possible in architecture for an industrial civilization.[44]

A livelier and richer essay in the architecture of commerce than Richardson's store is The Rookery, which stands today in sound condition and full occupancy, little altered over the years of its long and useful life (Fig. 21). Like the Montauk, the building was commissioned by Peter and Shepard Brooks of Boston, who again employed Owen Aldis as their agent and Burnham and Root as their architects. The location of The Rookery, at 209 South La Salle Street, was the site of the temporary city hall and water tank from 1872 to 1884. Half the pigeons in Chicago seem to have selected these structures as a roost; consequently, they came to be known popularly as "The Rookery." When the building was completed in 1886, the owners, in a moment of practical and humorous good sense, decided to retain the name. It seems likely that the idea was a product of Root's irrepressible sense of humor.

In plan The Rookery is a hollow square surrounding an interior court. Bounded by Quincy Street and an alley on the elevations opposite the thoroughfares (La Salle and Adams streets), it is thus naturally lighted on four sides and in the interior. The exterior walls along La Salle and Adams up to the top story are composed of a series of stout, widely spaced granite columns surmounted by brick piers. At the top story the window rhythm is doubled, and the piers merge with the wall surface. On the periphery of the court, however, and at the first two stories along Quincy Street and the alley, the wall load is carried on a series of cast-iron columns joined by wrought-iron spandrel beams—in short, true skeletal construction. The brick piers above the second story on the rear elevations are thus carried by the iron columns of the base. By extending the spandrel beams a few inches beyond the outer edge of the columns along these elevations, the architects were able to open the walls at the second story into continuous windows divided by extremely narrow iron mullions. This marked one of the early uses of the so-called ribbon window, which has now become a standard feature of commercial and sometimes domestic building.

The inner elevations around The Rookery court form an open, simple, nicely proportioned and articulated expression of the iron skeleton that supports them (Fig. 22). The court walls are perfectly homogeneous compositions of rectangular cells of glass, each filling the entire bay, with a single mullion dividing the opening into a pair of windows. The spandrels and piers are covered with white glazed brick, and a pronounced horizontal emphasis is

[44] John Burchard and Albert Bush-Brown, *The Architecture of America: A Social and Cultural History* (Boston: Little, Brown & Co., 1961 [© 1961, by American Institute of Architects]), p. 186.

achieved through continuous ornamental bands of tan terra cotta extending around the entire periphery of the court at the sill and lintel lines of each story. It is the same device that Root used in the street elevations of the Montauk. The Rookery court is exceptional in that seldom has an architect given so much attention to the visual satisfaction of tenants who occupy the inward-facing offices.

The glass and iron vault over the inner court and the curving iron stairways on its west side provide a remarkably impressive example of their kind of construction, which had become common in the best commercial buildings of the nineteenth century following the Crystal Palace (Figs. 23, 24). The vault and the court that it covers won high though somewhat qualified praise from Henry Van Brunt, one of the leaders of eastern architectural taste, who was seldom disposed to find anything acceptable in the advanced Chicago work.[45]

"The Rookery" is not only a noted example of great fertility of design, but there is nothing bolder, more original, or more inspiring in modern civic architecture either here or elsewhere than its glass-covered court. Where the work has been committed to such a multitude of new devices in construction and to such a prodigality of invention in ornament, it is not strange that one may find reasonable objection to certain points of detail. One may admire the audacity of the double iron staircase which, supported by ingenious cantilevers, ramps with double curvature out into open space, meeting at a landing in the sky, as it were, from which the straight second run rises soberly backward to the stories above. One may admire this and wonder whether such an obvious *tour de force* is worth the study which must have been bestowed upon it. Even the imaginative prison visions in the etchings of Piranesi, with their aerial ladders and impossible galleries, present nothing more audacious.[46]

Unfortunately, much of the beauty of the dome, with its intricate geometric pattern of translucent glass and black iron tracery, was lost when the owners of The Rookery covered the outer surface of the skylights with a waterproof membrane and painted the inner surfaces of the glass and iron a uniform gray. The present interior ornament of the court was designed by Frank Lloyd Wright and executed in 1905. The combination of Root's delicate ironwork and Wright's elaborate gold and ivory decorations provides a rich and luxurious but perfectly disciplined effect, suggesting a nineteenth-century

[45] See, for example, Van Brunt's comment on Burnham and Root's Masonic Temple, p. 106.

[46] Henry Van Brunt, "John Wellborn Root," *Inland Architect and News Record*, January, 1891, as quoted in Monroe, *op. cit.*, p. 277. On the matter of the stairway, the hangers that appear in the illustration were added in 1905, after Van Brunt wrote his description. The stair runs originally stood free and literally appeared to meet "at a landing in the sky."

counterpart to the profusion, magnificence, and delicacy of Baroque architecture.

Equally in the spirit of Piranesi—to follow Van Brunt's parallel—is the cast-iron stairway that rises continuously from the second floor to the tenth and is housed in a semicylindrical curtain of glass and bolted cast-iron panels, the whole enclosure projecting entirely beyond the plane of the west court wall (Figs. 25, 26). The whole stairway has the form of a half-helix divided along its longitudinal axis, or rather, a succession of half-turns of a helix, each of which is made by a single flight mounting between adjacent floors. The stairway functions as a fire escape reached by the broad corridor between the elevator bays.

The architectural excellence of The Rookery's outer elevations grows chiefly out of the extraordinary openness of the walls, the airy yet vigorous articulation of the elevations, precise scale and pleasing proportions, and the firm integration of many diverse elements of decorative detail. The main entrances of the building, on Adams and La Salle streets, are among the best features of the outer elevations and are expressive of Root's love of richly ornamented entranceways (Fig. 27). There is a great diversity of figures, textures, and materials, but the many details form a true architectural ornament, exactly subordinated to the main features of arch, spandrels, and surrounding wall. The entire portal complex is set in a ground of massive, rough-faced granite blocks laid with precisely made and extremely narrow joints of superb workmanship. The fan-like design in the lunette above the doorway, the floral pattern in the archivolts, and the intricate geometric pattern in the spandrels, suggesting the iron tracery of the court dome, constitute a luxurious but well-harmonized association of stone and iron. All of this work is now covered by a black patina and badly needs cleaning; only the polished granite of the columns at the base retains its original color of dark red.

At the time he designed the building Root wondered whether the profusion of ornament would stand the test of time. It has, through his sure sense of organization and his subordination of detail to mass and structure. In spite of the elaborate decorative elements on the street elevations—the arches at the seventh and tenth stories, the corner pinnacles, the five-part horizontal composition, the highly ornamented parapet—The Rookery is a sure and powerful revelation of its pier-and-lintel and pier-and-arch construction.

The Monadnock Building differs radically from the older Rookery in every respect (Fig. 28). Originally known as the Monadnock and Kearsarge, it was built between 1889 and 1891 at 53 West Jackson Boulevard. The first discussion of plans for the Monadnock appeared in a series of letters between Peter and Shepard Brooks and Owen Aldis during the period from

January to June, 1885. The initial proposal to buy the property was made by the Brooks brothers in September, 1885, but the decision to build seems to have been put off until 1888. Burnham and Root completed the working plans by the summer of the following year. The building was thought to be beyond the frontier of the commercial urban core at the time it was planned. According to the architect Edward A. Renwick's report:

When Owen Aldis put up the Monadnock on Jackson boulevard there was nothing on the south side of the street between State street and the river but cheap one-story shacks, mere hovels. Everyone thought Mr. Aldis was insane to build way out there on the ragged edge of the city. Later when he carried the building on through to Van Buren street they were sure he was.[47]

But the Monadnock was unquestionably the Brooks brothers' most profitable investment: the building was recently renovated, and its offices are fully occupied today, as they have been throughout its history. The original building extended for half a block south along Dearborn Street. In 1893 an addition was constructed after the design of Holabird and Roche, thus extending the building for the rest of the block to Van Buren Street. The addition is of steel-framed construction, and the fenestration differs sufficiently to mark it off clearly from the north half.[48]

The original block is a tremendous unadorned slab two bays wide and sixteen stories high. Its extremely narrow form makes possible an outside exposure for all offices, which are arranged on the periphery of the plan. A stairway rises continuously from ground floor to top through openings centrally located in the main corridors. It is, without question, the ultimate logical step in strictly functional construction with masonry bearing walls; it remains today the last great building in the ancient tradition of masonry architecture. The walls are of smooth-cut stone and brick at the base and brick above; cast-iron columns and wrought-iron beams support the inner floor and roof loads. The genesis of the Monadnock's design shows to what extent Root felt that the aesthetic appeal of a building lay in richness of carefully integrated detail as well as in the forceful expression of structure and function. This austere building, consequently, posed a considerable problem for Root's artistic conscience. Harriet Monroe recorded the struggle in her biography.

For this building, Mr. Aldis, who controlled the investment, kept urging upon the architects extreme simplicity, rejecting one or two of Root's sketches as too ornate. During Root's absence of a fortnight at the seashore, Mr. Burnham ordered from one of the draftsmen a design of a straight-up-and-down, uncompromising, unornamented façade. When Root returned, he was indignant at first over

---

[47] Quoted in John A. Randall, *History of the Development of Building Construction in Chicago* (Urbana: University of Illinois Press, 1949), p. 123.

[48] For the south addition of the Monadnock, see p. 119.

this project of a brick box. Gradually, however, he threw himself into the spirit of the thing, and one day he told Mr. Aldis that the heavy sloping lines of an Egyptian pyramid had gotten into his mind as the basis of this design, and that he thought he would "throw the thing up without a single ornament." At last, with a gesture whose pretense of disgust concealed a shy experimental interest, he threw on the drawing table of Mr. Dutton, then foreman of the office, "a design," says this gentleman, "shaped something like a capital I—a perfectly plain building curving outward at base and cornice." This was the germ of the final design, and it provoked much study and discussion in the office.[49]

The technical features of the Monadnock—the immense raft footings to carry the great weight of sixteen stories, the continuous bow windows to provide for the maximum admission of light, and the interior braced frame of cast and wrought iron—reveal that Root's creative powers in structural engineering were equal to his artistic conception. The engineering assistant's calculation of the footing areas, however, proved to be none too generous: although the building was set up 8 inches against settlement, it has settled slightly more than 20 inches in the seventy-two years since its completion (1891–1963). But at least the settlement was uniform, in spite of the jacking up and underpinning of the east wall during construction of the Dearborn Street subway. The most noteworthy technical feature of the Monadnock is the presence of portal framing for the windbracing of an iron-framed building, in what may be its pioneer American use. This distinction has been granted to Jenney's Manhattan Building, but the plans of the two structures were completed almost simultaneously.[50] In the framing system of the Monadnock, the portal frame consists of a deep girder of I-section the ends

[49] Monroe, *op. cit.*, p. 141.

[50] The early history of windbracing in American buildings has so far remained obscure. The origins appear to lie in the end or portal frames of truss bridges or in the iron-framed train shed or both. Windbracing was introduced in England by Charles Fowler when he built the Hungerford Fish Market at London in 1835. In this case the bracing consisted of deep girders rigidly connected to the columns by means of spandrel brackets. Bracing girders in the form of trusses rigidly connected to columns were used in Paxton's Crystal Palace (1851), a building that attracted a great deal of attention in Europe and the United States. The modern type of bracing in the form of solid-web girders rigidly connected throughout their depth to the column was introduced by G. T. Greene in the Boat Store at Sheerness, England (1858–60). Windbracing in the form of iron rods extending across the two diagonals of each bay was included in Clarke and Reeves' project for a 1,000-foot wrought-iron tower to be erected at the Centennial Exposition in Philadelphia in 1876. The Statue of Liberty (1883–86) appears to have been the first American structure other than a bridge to be systematically wind-braced throughout the frame, although in this case the bracing was achieved by means of a complex of diagonal braces and struts. The reference to bracing with iron rods in one of Peter Brooks's letters on the Montauk, on the other hand, suggests the existence of diagonal rods for windbracing as early as 1881 (see p. 52). For windbracing in the Manhattan Building, see pp. 91–92; for still another form, see the discussion of the Old Colony Building, pp. 123–24.

of which are riveted throughout the depth of the web to the supporting columns. The maximum girder depth is 15 inches. The projecting bays are carried on peripheral beams supported in turn by brackets cantilevered from the spandrel girders.

The general appearance of the Monadnock building almost belies its masonry construction. The projecting bays of the walls with their large glass area give the structure a light and open appearance in spite of its great mass and the relatively small size of the windows (Figs. 29, 30). Stripped of every vestige of ornament, its rigorous geometry softened only by the slight inward curve of the wall at the top of the first story, the outward flare of the parapet, and the progressive rounding of the corners from bottom to top, subtly proportioned and scaled, the Monadnock is a severe yet powerfully expressive composition in horizontal and vertical lines. It presents in its relentless exactitude the formal beauty latent in the commercial style, but at the same time it demonstrates the limitations of the old method of construction. "Its expression," Giedion wrote, "derives more from architectonic refinement than from the new potentialities. And heavy masonry walls were not the solution to the problem of the many-storied building. The rather small dimensions of the windows indicate the extent to which they hampered the architect."[51]

As odd as the Monadnock must have looked at the time of its construction, it was acceptable enough in Chicago, where the expression of power and utility seemed appropriate. Its meaning was not wholly lost in the East, however, for one of the most eloquent tributes to Root's audacity came from Robert D. Andrews, then president of the Boston Architectural Club.

It was the evident purpose of the designers of this building to simply solve the problem and let the result stand. The integrity of mind through which this decision was made and carried out relates this work to the product of the greatest men everywhere who have advanced the things they stood for and gained the honor of mankind. It took prodigious courage to do this thing. It is an achievement unsurpassed in the architectural history of our country. . . . What I want to dwell upon is the dignity and worth of this simple statement of fact. Most of us seem to apologize for being forced to state the truth. Here were men who rejoiced in it, and, far from apologizing for it, emphasized it. . . . The results arrived at are, therefore, not gotten haphazardly, but with a deliberate and conscious intention. This building has no precedent in architecture. It is itself a precedent. Yet it has a precedent outside of architecture; it comes up to an ideal, and by virtue of its correspondence with this ideal it becomes a work of art.[52]

[51] Sigfried Giedion, op. cit., p. 296.
[52] Robert D. Andrews, "The Broadest Use of Precedent," Architectural Review, II (May 15, 1893), 34–35.

The only other eastern critic of the time who appreciated the Monadnock's unique beauty was Montgomery Schuyler.

The Monadnock may not be the embodiment of a new technical-artistic synthesis, as the architecture of iron and steel framing was then struggling to become. Yet Root's building is a great work in its own right, and it offers one of the most exciting aesthetic experiences our commercial architecture can show. The precisely logical relationship between form and function has the appeal of mathematical rigor: it is the widest generalization free of contradiction, the nearest thing, perhaps, to Sullivan's rule without exceptions. In this respect Walter Behrendt, an early historian of the modern movement, found the building highly significant.

In its rigid functionalism, demonstrating a new conception, it became a landmark of modern building: the architect, as an artistic personality, steps back behind the commission given him by society. In an act of self-denial, he puts his individual forces into service for common needs, arising from the new social evolution. In this attitude is manifested the truth that building is a social art. The consequence of this conception . . . is to bring building again into a reasonable organic relation to the actual social and economic world, thereby re-establishing that indispensable identity between the content and the form of life, which is missed in the works of those who have turned their backs on their time.[53]

While Root was discovering the full reach of his powers in the Monadnock, Sullivan was well on the way to finding the extent of his own in the Auditorium (Fig. 31). Indeed, the reputation of Adler and Sullivan, and for that matter, of Chicago itself, was made and secured by the Auditorium Building. One of the largest and most complex buildings in the country at the time of its construction, matched only by the great railroad terminals, it was built more from civic and aesthetic than from commercial motives. The sheer size of the building makes even more impressive the extraordinary architectural and technical skill that entered into its design and construction. Ten stories in height, it extends for the entire block along Congress Parkway from Michigan to Wabash Avenue. Its total area in plan is 63,350 square feet; the substructure required 28,000 cubic yards of excavation; the foundation contains 22,000 linear feet of steel rail; the total weight of the finished structure is 101,000 tons. Nearly three years, 1887 to 1889, were needed to complete the construction, the final cost of which was $3,145,291 (or about $29,250,-000 at the current price level). The whole country could show nothing grander.

The building embraces much more than a theater. The auditorium proper, with a seating capacity of 4,237, occupies the center portion of the enclosure;

[53] Walter C. Behrendt, *Modern Building* (New York: Harcourt, Brace & Co., 1937), p. 120.

the west, or Wabash Avenue, end is a typical commercial office block; the east, or Michigan Avenue, end is a hotel; at the center of the south elevation is a tower that provides additional high-rent office space (Figs. 32, 33). The problem of integrating this complex of separate and diversified elements within uniform elevations taxed the ingenuity of Adler and Sullivan to the utmost. That they succeeded is attested not only by the appearance of the building but by the fact that except for the theater it is in good condition and in active use today.

The forerunner of this extraordinary venture into the presentation of dramatic and musical performances was the Chicago Opera Festival, whose productions were given in the auditorium of the Grant Park Exposition Building, erected in 1873 after the plans of W. W. Boyington.[54] In 1885 Ferdinand W. Peck, sponsor of the opera festivals at the Exposition, projected the idea of a permanent opera house that would include a civic center for musical festivals, symphony concerts, dance programs, balls and other social functions, and political conventions. To make the large investment financially possible, Peck proposed the addition of office and hotel space around the theater. To prosecute this ambitious program the Chicago Opera Association was founded in 1886. The commission for the design of its building went to Adler and Sullivan in the same year.

The first projects were more ornate than the final design, and they were constantly modified at conferences with Peck and the directors.[55] The decisive change in the plans of the Auditorium came as the result of the influence of Richardson's Marshall Field Store. Both Sullivan and Peck had a profound admiration for the earlier building; in addition, the board of the Opera Association saw many possible economies in the adoption of its simplicity. Fortunately for architecture everywhere, Sullivan abandoned his propensity for elaborate exterior ornament and concentrated on the architectonic effect of mass, texture, and the proportioning and scaling of large and simple elements. The final over-all plans were completed early in 1887, and construction began immediately. Often the building gangs worked in shifts, continuing through the night under electric floodlights.

The exterior walls of the Auditorium and all partitions dividing the theater from offices and hotel are load-bearing members of solid masonry. Brick was used throughout, with granite facing at the first three stories and lime-

---

[54] William W. Boyington (1818–98) was a prolific if undistinguished architect and the leading designer of Chicago railroad stations during his life. He was the author of the first and second La Salle Street stations, the first Union Station, and the North Western's Wells Street Station.

[55] For earlier designs of the Auditorium, see Morrison, *op. cit.*, Pls. 12 and 13 (p. 328). The greater part of my discussion of the interior formal design of the building is based on Morrison's clear, detailed, and comprehensive analysis (*ibid.*, pp. 85–110).

stone above. The wall load on the foundations is continuous rather than distributed over separate footings. The foundations, concrete reinforced with timbers and steel rails, deliver a unit pressure of 4,000 pounds per square foot to the soil beneath them. The total settlement of the building under full load was 18 inches, which necessitated the use of lead-pipe connections to absorb the strain on iron pipe and conduit. Between structural walls the interior load falls on isolated spread footings of the typical pyramidal shape. The great problem in the design of foundations was occasioned by the tower on the Congress Street side, which weighs 15,000 tons; its area in plan of 2,870 square feet is carried on a foundation 6,700 square feet in area. Thus unit pressure under the tower was increased to 4,480 pounds per square foot. Adler supported the load on a massive raft five feet thick, reinforced with two layers of timbers, three of rails, and three of I-beams.

To avoid increased settlement of the tower after construction Adler used what amounted to a kind of crude prestressing of the supporting soil. He forced artificial settlement of the tower foundation by loading it with brick and pig iron to the extent necessary to secure maximum settlement. As construction progressed, he constantly decreased the artificial load by an amount equal to the weight of the portion of the tower just completed. This Gargantuan effort was later rendered unnecessary by the introduction of caisson foundations for the Stock Exchange Building in 1893.

But the tower foundation was not the end of Adler's special worries over the Auditorium. The basement floor below the stage lies about seven feet below mean water level in Lake Michigan. Waterproofing concrete by means of a bituminous covering had been achieved before, but waterproofing it against considerable pressure was an unprecedented difficulty. Adler met the problem in his characteristic way, which was direct, ingenious, and highly empirical. He designed a laminated floor made up of alternate layers of concrete, asphalt, and asphalt-saturated felt, counterweighted with additional concrete and rails to offset the upward-acting hydraulic pressure.

Although the exterior walls of the Auditorium Building follow the traditional technique of construction in masonry piers, the interior floor, vault, and roof loads are carried on a remarkably complex system of cast- and wrought-iron framing. Indeed, Adler virtually exhausted all the forms of iron construction that his age had developed. The chief problem was the support of the great elliptical vault over the orchestra floor of the theater. Adler's solution consisted in a system of truss-framing adopted from the forms of contemporary railroad truss bridges. The flat roof above the theater vault is carried on six transverse trusses with flat parallel chords extending for a maximum span of 117 feet. These trusses together carry a total load of 660 tons. From them are hung a series of elliptical arched trusses with a maximum span between springing points of 116 feet 11 inches. The vault itself is suspended from the underside of the arched trusses. At approximately the halfway point between the proscenium arch and the west wall of the theater, the elliptical vault gives way to a flat ceiling at the height of the vault crown to make room for the balconies. This ceiling is hung from three transverse trusses with parallel chords that are supported at their ends and mid-points, each half spanning 46 feet clear. At the forward edge of the upper gallery, the roof steps up above the rehearsal hall. The east edge of this high roof (toward the stage) is carried on still another transverse truss; the west edge rests on the brick wall separating the theater from the office block. The roof is supported throughout its area by a series of longitudinal trusses spanning between the brick wall and the transverse truss. The primary framing members under the orchestra floor, balcony, and two galleries are sloping wrought-iron girders resting on cast-iron columns. A closely spaced array of smaller beams span between the floor girders and act as joists. Nowhere is this elaborate system of framing visible except for the columns supporting the galleries, but it was the most efficient way in which the vast interior space could be inclosed while preserving uninterrupted sight lines and the acoustical perfection for which the theater is famous.

As in the Central Music Hall and the Chicago Opera House, the theater of the Auditorium at no point projects to the streets, being surrounded on the three open sides (east, south, and west) by a continuous volume of offices, hotel rooms, and public facilities (Fig. 33). The fenestration of the building is thus determined by the hotel and office blocks. The entrance to the theater is marked by a triple arch on the Congress Parkway elevation close to Wabash Avenue. It is relatively subdued in treatment and hardly as impressive as the hotel entrance on the Michigan Avenue side, with the heavy balcony on corbels above it. Elsewhere on the street elevations the base is a succession of massive piers of huge, rough-cut granite blocks. The full size of these masonry supports can now be clearly seen, since the base of the Congress elevation has been arcaded by placing the sidewalk within the area of the outer bays along this side. The same change was made in the north bays of the Congress Hotel, on the other side of the street, both operations having been required by the widening of old Congress Street clear to the building lines on either side.

The general design of the Auditorium walls was derived in part from the Marshall Field Wholesale Store. The heavy stonework of the three-story base, the stout piers, narrow windows, and massive lintels together convey a sense of great strength and stability. The four middle stories fall under semicircular arches, each of which spans the whole bay. The next two stories are under arches of half the span of the lower, and the openings of the top story are rectangular. The wall above the base rises in a rhythmic succession of continuous stone piers of smooth limestone blocks, relatively narrow compared with the bay span. The rhythm developed by piers and arches is doubled at the ninth story, then tripled at the top. A simple belt course brings the whole upward motion to a clean stop at the same time that it helps to assert the great horizontal dimensions of the building. The elevations form a beautiful illustration of Sullivan's unique feeling for harmony, scale, and proportion. The subdued texture of the masonry and the alternating accents of pier and opening have the quality of a musical composition: there are four basic, repetitive rhythms, each representing a slight variation on the other, but all positively integrated into a harmonious whole.

As in all his buildings except for the factories and warehouses, Sullivan treated the elevations of the Auditorium as plastic elements, to be molded according to his feeling about the structure. Hugh Morrison wrote of it that

the disposition of the elements in the façade is . . . a formal and artificial one, and it certainly does not correspond to the internal functional divisions . . . of the building. On the other hand, the exterior design admirably expresses the heavy masonry construction, and in its large simplicity, its absence from merely trivial or "picturesque" outbreaks of surface ornament or irregularities of silhouette, it goes far beyond the building of its era in achieving a truly monumental form.[56]

The only interruption to the uniformity of the elevations is the tower on the Congress Parkway side (Fig. 32). It stands seventeen stories high above grade, its south elevation nearly flush with the main wall of the building. The projecting course that marks the top of the main parapet cuts across the tower, thus detaching the upper portion from the main mass. The result is that the tower is partly separated from and partly merged with the building proper. The presence of the recessed balcony, or loggia, with its little colonnade, a feature Sullivan was to use again in the Schiller Building, further differentiates the tower from the long elevation below it. It is not a completely satisfactory treatment of the difficult problem of mastering a functional necessity. The tower was constructed primarily to house the hydraulic machinery for the stage and to provide choice, high-rent office space. Within it for twenty prosperous years were the offices of Adler and Sullivan and briefly of Sullivan alone.

The space once occupied by the Auditorium Hotel incloses the theater on the Michigan Avenue and Congress Parkway sides. The average depth of this L-shaped honeycomb of rooms and facilities is only 45 feet; yet it contained a lobby, smoking room, parlor, restaurant, dining room, banquet

[56] Morrison, op. cit., p. 95.

hall, four hundred guest rooms, kitchens, and service rooms.[57] The entrance on Michigan Avenue opened into a rich lobby with a marble mosaic floor and a dado of Mexican onyx (Fig. 34). The decoration on the structural details consisted of gilded plaster relief of an intricate foliate pattern. (The relief still remains but has been painted over.) With respect to ornament, the bar was an excellent example of Sullivan's originality: it reflected his rebellion against tradition, his fertility of invention, and his astonishing fluency in trying to develop a new ornamental vocabulary (Fig. 35).

The second floor of the hotel contained another lobby and the main lounge, reached by a stairway with onyx paneling, gilded plaster relief, and wrought-iron stair rails (Fig. 36). The mosaic floors of the landings were composed of an intricate profusion of detail and a great richness of color, all thoroughly disciplined and harmonized. It was the lyrical and romantic element of nineteenth-century architecture developed almost to the point of Baroque lavishness.

The main dining hall on the tenth floor ran the whole length of the Michigan Avenue front, with a view of Grant Park and the lake to the east (Fig. 37). The area is covered with a curved vault that springs directly from the floor level. The vault is carried on five arched trusses covered by panels decorated in plaster relief centered around electric light bulbs.[58] Smaller dining rooms at the ends were separated from the main room by columns carrying a rich frieze. The tympana of the arches over the frieze were adorned by mural paintings chosen, like the rest in the building, with unqualified bad taste.

What was formerly the hotel kitchen is a remarkable feat of construction. It is structurally independent of the main building, being carried on wrought-iron trusses spanning the theater stage. Bridges connected it with the dining

[57] Since the purchase of the Auditorium Building by Roosevelt University in 1946, the old hotel facilities have been progressively transformed into classrooms, laboratories, offices, lounges, and a library. The former private dining room and second-floor lounge have been completely restored to their original color and condition. On the problem of the theater, see pp. 77–78.

[58] The extensive use of elliptical vaulting in the Auditorium Building does not seem to have been dictated by any utilitarian or structural necessities, except in the case of the theater vault. Although the form has many masonry precedents extending back to classical antiquity, it is more likely that it was derived from the all-covering balloon train shed, which was then appearing with growing frequency in the big metropolitan terminals and exciting great popular enthusiasm. Sullivan, who was profoundly moved by the new engineering works, undoubtedly chose the floor-level elliptical vault because it possessed the same inherent power and grace. At the same time, the engineers of the train shed provided Adler with the necessary structural precedents. Until 1963, when the vault was replaced by a flat ceiling, the main waiting room of Central Station at Michigan Avenue and Roosevelt Road (1892–93), designed by the New York architect Bradford Gilbert, was a good example of a large vaulted room with the vault springing from the floor level.

rooms. The special banquet hall was handled in the same way, its ceiling being supported by a similar system of trusses. Again, Sullivan's use of decorative electric lighting showed his power of integrating utilitarian necessities into a formal architectural whole.

The office block on Wabash Avenue, still much as it was when completed, contains 136 offices. This section is separated from the theater by a thick masonry bearing wall. The sixth-floor corridor, however, was used as an auxiliary entrance and exit for the upper galleries of the theater, to which it is joined by iron bridges. The recital hall above the upper galleries was reached from the seventh-floor corridor. Elevators serve all the offices and the upper galleries of the theater.

But the offices and hotel of the Auditorium Building are incidentals; the theater is the main element of the inclosure. Its over-all area, including foyers, vestibules, stage, and facilities, is nearly half the area in plan of the whole structure. The box-office vestibule on Congress Parkway leads to the ground-floor foyer, from which tunnels lead to the front rows of the orchestra floor. The rear rows of the orchestra floor are reached from the second-floor foyer. The same arrangement of tunnels and foyers at two levels serves the balcony.

The main floor of the the theater was designed according to acoustical principles rather than sight lines, the total rise of 17 feet from front to rear being more than necessary for unobstructed vision (Fig. 38). This stepped-up floor, together with the elliptical vault of the theater ceiling and the lateral breaks in the ceiling, provides virtual acoustical perfection. The lateral breaks cover the lower chords of the arched trusses and house the ventilating ducts. The general form of the vault is that of a succession of four elliptical cylinders whose axes become progressively longer toward the rear. The breaks or steps divide the successive vaults from each other. Most of the reflected waves can thus be diffused over the whole theater, while the waves that have traveled farthest are interrupted by the breaks, which thus prevent annoying echoes at the rear of the theater. But the elimination of echoes and reverberation is chiefly a matter of the height of the vault, which Adler carefully calculated to this end. The architects of the Chicago Civic Opera House (1928–29), Graham, Anderson, Probst and White, followed the design of the Auditorium as the acoustical standard. Adler was forty years ahead of his time in this respect.

The balcony is somewhat longer than the main floor. The vertical height of the balcony floor, amounting to 40 feet, was determined by the same acoustical principles followed in the design of the orchestra level. The two galleries above the balcony are reached by stairways from the rear balcony, from the sixth-floor office corridor, and by means of bridges and tunnels in the case of the second gallery. The galleries are supported on cast-iron columns and wrought-iron trusses so located as not to interfere with sight lines.

The proscenium arch of the stage rises in an elliptical curve bordered by murals on a gold ground (Fig. 39). The proscenium wings, which spread out at angles from the plane of the curtain, are decorated with fan-like trellises and gilded plaster relief. The organ grill opens at the left of the proscenium, the organ itself standing in a separate enclosure north of the stage. It was described as the most complete instrument in the world at the time of its installation. The grill opposite the organ was originally used to admit fresh air cooled by roof sprays—a feature which made the Auditorium the first air-conditioned theater. Although the stage is the center of attraction, the great arches of the vault form the dominant architecural motive. Their grand sweep is covered with intricate ornament and studded with electric lights. "Rarely has there been such a wedding of large and majestic simplicity with refined and subtle detail"—in Morrison's words.[59]

Adler developed an ingenious method for reducing the seating capacity for recitals and other programs likely to appeal to a smaller audience. On the advice of Augustin Daly, he devised a means of closing off the galleries and the rear third of the balcony by making the ceilings above these areas a series of hinged panels which could be dropped by windlasses into the position of partitions. But this device resulted in a deterioration of the acoustical properties, and shortly after the initial use of the technique, performers said that they preferred to sing or play to the whole theater volume even with the galleries empty.

The mechanical equipment of the stage was the most complete and refined at the time of its installation. Adler went to Europe to study the best facilities on the Continent, but he introduced radical changes into European techniques to suit American practice. An important innovation was the construction of the stage in sections that could be lifted by hydraulic machinery. In this way the stage could be banked for choral concerts and the like. Lowered flat, overlaid with hardwood, and opened to its fullest extent, it became a ballroom capable of accommodating eight thousand people. There is a great amount of mechanical and hydraulic equipment above and below the stage, which is still one of the largest and best equipped in the country. With few exceptions, there is nothing like it in theaters devoted to opera and drama.

There were no consulting engineers on the Auditorium. Except for minor details, Adler did the whole job. He belongs, on the merit of this building, with the great engineers of the nineteenth century—world figures—Eiffel,

[59] Morrison, *op. cit.*, p. 104.

Roebling, Eads, Paxton. On the Auditorium, the later success of Adler and Sullivan was built and, in good measure, the later fame of the Chicago school and of the city itself. Like the Monadnock, it was the high point of masonry and iron construction in the new age of mechanized industrial techniques. It brought the old system of construction to a close and at the same time substantially advanced the new structural technique growing up around it.

For forty years after their completion the Auditorium Theater and the associated hotel and office block continued in full and profitable use. The theater housed not only the performances of the Chicago Opera Company, but symphonic concerts, recitals, lectures, religious meetings, charity balls and other social gatherings, and sports events. On the completion of the Civic Opera Building in 1929, however, the brilliant life of the magnificent theater was mortally threatened. The departure of the highly successful opera company meant the loss of a major tenant, and the depression of the 1930's proved disastrous to the revenues of the aging hotel. The building could not long survive as a going concern: bankruptcy came in 1940, when the theater closed its doors, and the movable contents of the structure were sold at auction in 1941. Parts of the hotel and the orchestra floor of the theater were used as the Chicago center of the United Service Organization during the war years of 1942 to 1945. In the following year the entire property was purchased by Roosevelt University and the hotel space was progressively transformed into the classrooms and other facilities of an educational institution.

The theater, dark and fast deteriorating, was at least spared from demolition, but there seemed no answer to the question of what to do with this vast inclosure. There was no lack of good will toward the idea of its preservation and restoration, but neither the university nor any other civic institution could offer a viable plan for its use. On December 31, 1957, the City Council of Chicago established the Commission on Architectural Landmarks to select and mark significant buildings and "to prepare recommendations for a policy and for a permanent organization for preserving such landmarks." In 1960 the Commission designated the Auditorium Building as an architectural landmark and thereby officially lent its sanction to the idea of restoration, but it could provide no funds for the work. The decision to undertake restoration lay with Roosevelt University, and accordingly, late in 1960 the institution sponsored the founding of the Auditorium Theater Council, which was established to raise funds to restore the theater. Its first meeting was held on December 14 of that year. The problem was formidable enough to discourage the most ardent civic enthusiast: the cost of restoration had risen to $3,000,000; the possible uses of a 4,200-seat theater were difficult to imagine; and the completion in 1960 of the 5,000-seat auditorium of the new Metropolitan Fair and Exposition Building (McCormick Place) offered still another facility for conventions, public gatherings, and the musical and dramatic arts. Although the university and the council remained undaunted, there seemed to be little possibility of success. The fundamental problem in this situation arises from the failure of American culture to develop a mature architectural taste. Had we done so, the Auditorium would have been preserved as a matter of national policy.[60]

[60] For further discussion of the problem of building preservation, see the discussion of the Schiller or Garrick Theater Building, pp. 130–35.

65. Looking east on Randolph Street: the Ashland, Schiller, and Masonic Temple buildings. (*Kaufmann & Fabry Co.*)

66. MAJESTIC HOTEL, 1892–93   D. H. BURNHAM AND COMPANY

Formerly at 29 West Quincy Street; demolished in 1961.
(*Commercial Photographic Co.*)

67. RELIANCE BUILDING, 1894–95   D. H. BURNHAM AND COMPANY

Now known by its address, 32 North State Street.
(*Commercial Photographic Co.*)

68. FISHER BUILDING, 1895–96   D. H. BURNHAM AND COMPANY
343 South Dearborn Street. (*Commercial Photographic Co.*)

69. RAILWAY EXCHANGE BUILDING, 1903–4
 D. H. BURNHAM AND COMPANY

Northwest corner of Michigan Avenue and Jackson Boulevard.
(*Commercial Photographic Co.*)

70. TACOMA BUILDING, 1887–89 HOLABIRD AND ROCHE

Formerly at the northeast corner of La Salle and Madison streets; demolished in 1929. (*Chicago Architectural Photographing Co.*)

71. CAXTON BUILDING, 1889–90   HOLABIRD AND ROCHE

Formerly at 508 South Dearborn Street; demolished in 1947.
(*Commercial Photographic Co.*)

72. MONADNOCK BUILDING, SOUTH ADDITION, 1893
HOLABIRD AND ROCHE

Northwest corner of Dearborn and Van Buren streets.
(*Commercial Photographic Co.*)

73. PONTIAC BUILDING, 1891 HOLABIRD AND ROCHE

542 South Dearborn Street. (*Commercial Photographic Co.*)

74. MARQUETTE BUILDING, 1893–94   HOLABIRD AND ROCHE

140 South Dearborn Street. (*Commercial Photographic Co.*)

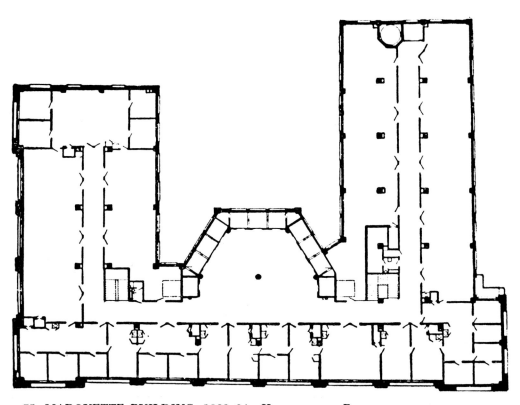

75. MARQUETTE BUILDING, 1893–94   HOLABIRD AND ROCHE

Typical floor plan. (From J. K. Freitag, *Architectural Engineering*
[2d ed.; New York: John Wiley & Sons, 1901].)

76. OLD COLONY BUILDING, 1893–94   Holabird and Roche
407 South Dearborn Street. (*Commercial Photographic Co.*)

77. OLD COLONY BUILDING, 1893–94   HOLABIRD AND ROCHE

North elevation. (*Chicago Architectural Photographing Co.*)

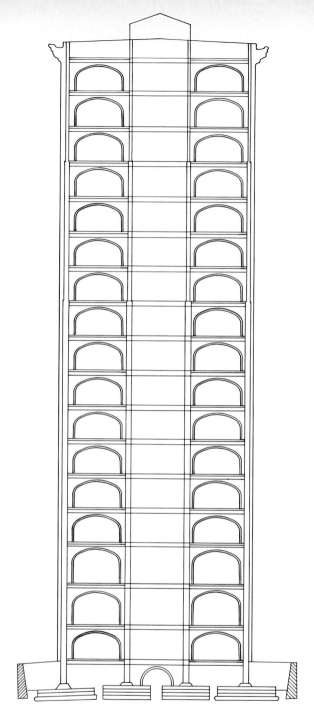

78. OLD COLONY BUILDING, 1893–94
Holabird and Roche

End elevation of the steel frame showing
the portal bracing. (From J. K. Freitag,
Architectural Engineering [2d ed.; New York:
John Wiley & Sons, 1901].)

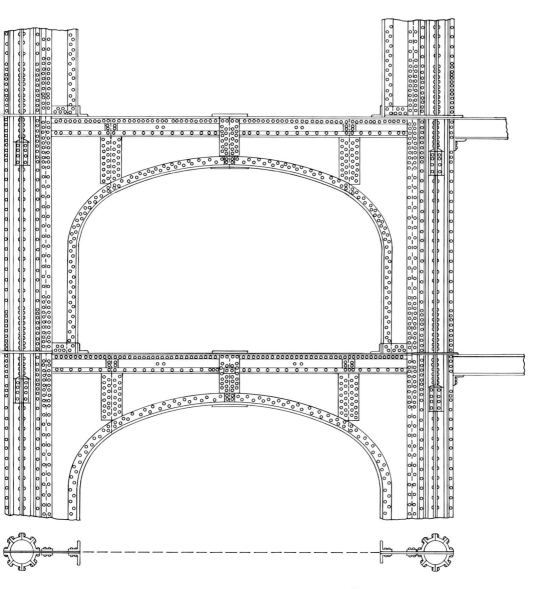

79. OLD COLONY BUILDING, 1893–94   HOLABIRD AND ROCHE

Elevation of an end bay of the frame showing details of a typical arch.
Cross sections of two Phoenix columns are shown at the bottom
of the drawing. (From J. K. Freitag, *Architectural Engineering*
[2d ed.; New York: John Wiley & Sons, 1901].)

80. The buildings of the Gage group. 30 and 24 South Michigan Avenue
(*left*), 1898   HOLABIRD AND ROCHE; 18 South Michigan Avenue (*right*),
1898–99   LOUIS SULLIVAN. (*Chicago Architectural Photographing Co.*)

81. The buildings of the Gage group
showing later alterations. (*Chicago Architectural
Photographing Co.*)

82. WILLIAMS BUILDING, 1898   HOLABIRD AND ROCHE

205 West Monroe Street. (*Kaufmann & Fabry Co.*)

83. CABLE BUILDING, 1898–99 HOLABIRD AND ROCHE

Later the Hoops Building, it stood at the southeast corner
of Wabash Avenue and Jackson Boulevard until its demolition
in 1961. (*Commercial Photographic Co.*)

84. CABLE BUILDING, 1898–99   HOLABIRD AND ROCHE

Detail of the ornament at the second story.
(*Richard Nickel, for the Chicago Commission
on Architectural Landmarks.*)

85. McCLURG BUILDING, 1899–1900   HOLABIRD AND ROCHE

Now the Crown Building, at 218 South Wabash Avenue.
(*Commercial Photographic Co.*)

86. WAINWRIGHT BUILDING, 1890–91   ADLER AND SULLIVAN

Northwest corner of Seventh and Chestnut streets,
St. Louis, Missouri. (*Keystone View Co.*)

87. SCHILLER BUILDING, 1891–92   Adler and Sullivan

The upper stories of the tower after removal
of the original cornice. (*Ralph M. Line.*)

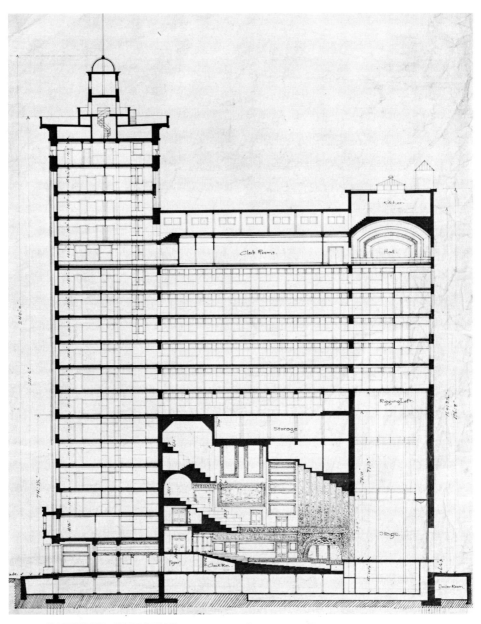

88. SCHILLER BUILDING, 1891–92   ADLER AND SULLIVAN

Longitudinal section. (*Photocopy of original tracing
by Richard Nickel.*)

89. SCHILLER BUILDING, 1891–92   ADLER AND SULLIVAN

Vault over the orchestra floor of the theater. (*Richard Nickel.*)

90. SCHILLER BUILDING, 1891–92   Adler and Sullivan

Detail of ornament on the vault, interior wall of the orchestra floor,
and forward edge of the balcony. (*Richard Nickel.*)

91. VICTORIA HOTEL, 1892–93 ADLER AND SULLIVAN

Formerly in Chicago Heights, Illinois; partially destroyed by fire
and the remainder demolished in 1961.
(Chicago Architectural Photographing Co.)

92. MEYER BUILDING, 1893   ADLER AND SULLIVAN

Southwest corner of Franklin and Van Buren streets.
(*Chicago Architectural Photographing Co.*)

93. TRANSPORTATION BUILDING, WORLD'S COLUMBIAN
   EXPOSITION, 1893   Adler and Sullivan

(*Chicago Architectural Photographing Co.*)

94. TRANSPORTATION BUILDING, 1893 ADLER AND SULLIVAN

Main entrance, known as "The Golden Door."
(*Chicago Architectural Photographing Co.*)

95. STOCK EXCHANGE BUILDING, 1893–94 ADLER AND SULLIVAN

Now known by its address, 30 North La Salle Street.
(*Commercial Photographic Co.*)

96. STOCK EXCHANGE BUILDING, 1893–94   ADLER AND SULLIVAN
East elevation of the first three stories. (*Richard Nickel.*)

JENNEY AND THE NEW STRUCTURAL TECHNIQUE

The step that completed the most radical transformation in the structural art since the development of the Gothic system of construction in the twelfth century was the invention of complete iron framing or skeletal construction. To continue the account of the evolution of the internal iron frame in Chicago takes us back ten years before the completion of the Auditorium. In 1879 the first Leiter Building of William Le Baron Jenney was erected at the northwest corner of Wells and Monroe streets (Fig. 40). It was originally five stories in height, but two more were added in 1888. Now the Morris Building, with a base spoiled by "modernization," it still stands in good condition (Fig. 41). The little building embodies a special kind of mill construction that marks an intermediate step between James Bogardus' timber and cast-iron factory of 1848 and Jenney's establishment of full framing between 1883 and 1885.

The first Leiter is very nearly a glass box. The interior floor and roof loads are carried on timber joists and girders supported in turn by cast-iron columns. It has brick piers, which, however, are not essential bearing members. The outer floor beams are carried to iron columns immediately inside the piers, thus freeing the latter from interior loads and reducing them to fireproof envelopes. The piers support only themselves and serve chiefly to inclose the predominantly glass envelope of the building. Since they are not bearing members, Jenney was able to reduce them to a very narrow width. "Had the wall columns been inserted in the piers," Randall wrote, "and had three more columns been added, the construction would have been essentially skeleton construction."[1]

In appearance the Leiter Building is a series of slender, widely spaced piers and spandrels forming a continuous pattern from base to roof. Each of

[1] Frank A. Randall, *History of the Development of Building Construction in Chicago* (Urbana: University of Illinois Press, 1949), p. 89. The construction of the first Leiter Building is a peculiarly complex mixture of the new and the primitive; for a full description, see *ibid.*

the large rectangular panels enframed by the brickwork is filled with three windows extending from floor to ceiling and separated by cast-iron mullions that extend between successive spandrels and have no bearing function. The wide openings of glass anticipate the big "Chicago windows" of the next decade. Devoid of ornament except for an unobtrusive cornice, happily free from the frequent horizontal composition reminiscent of the base-shaft-capital treatment of the column, with fine proportions, the Leiter Building exhibits one motive from top to bottom, that of a simple, open, glass-inclosed cage. In some respects the little building is structurally more advanced than even the Monadnock, though hardly comparable to it in formal treatment.

Adler and Sullivan's small building at 15 South Wacker Drive (originally Market Street), constructed in 1884 and named the Troescher, is a variation on Jenney's achievement in the first Leiter (Fig. 42). The piers are masonry, but the lintels are 8-inch wrought-iron I-beams, which carry the spandrels and the sashes of the bay above. Thus they anticipate the wall-supporting spandrel beam of skeletal construction. The lunettes at the top story of the Troescher represent some of the worst that Sullivan did in the ornamental tradition of Frank Furness, and they spoil an otherwise graceful and open façade.[2]

The Willoughby Building (1887), at the northwest corner of Jackson Boulevard and Franklin Street, is an advanced example of the cast-iron frames of the kind that Daniel Badger and James Bogardus had begun to construct forty years earlier (Fig. 43). This building was probably designed by Leroy Buffington, who took out a patent on skeletal construction in 1888.[3] The street elevations of the Willoughby are composed almost entirely of glass set between cast-iron columns and wrought-iron spandrel beams. The heavy ornament detracts from what is otherwise a lively and open pattern of closely spaced, slender piers and large windows.

The development of cast- and wrought-iron framing shows that skeletal construction had been virtually achieved in several buildings prior to the completion of Jenney's Home Insurance Building. The decisive step for the tall office building, however, remained to be taken. This was the reduction of the exterior wall to a mere curtain or envelope that is supported throughout by the interior framing and nowhere supports itself or any part of the building load. In a framed building the curtain wall has only a protective function. A finished building of skeletal construction can be reduced to nothing more than a framework covered with glass, as many today are. Actually a

---

[2] The building at 15 South Wacker has had many names, among them the Troescher, the Chicago Journal, the Louis Sullivan, and the Chicago Joint Board Building. It now bears the last one, and is the office of the International Ladies Garment Workers Union. It stood as a belated memorial to its architect for a short time around 1945, when it carried his name.

[3] On Buffington's patent and associated claims, see p. 82.

structure such as Jenney developed has no wall in the usual sense of the word but only a succession of vertical and horizontal bands of masonry or other weatherproof and fireproof material covering the outermost columns and beams.

The Home Insurance Building represented the decisive step in the evolution of iron and steel framing, and a century of experiment and practical achievement lay behind its creation. Indeed, Jenney himself held the view that his building was the product of the gradual evolution of construction with iron columns and beams. A number of specific buildings, American and European, clearly constituted precedents for the structural system of the Home Insurance, although the question of how far Jenney was directly and consciously influenced by them is a matter of speculation. William B. Mundie, who was Jenney's partner from 1891 to the latter's death, offered the suggestion that the older architect was first impressed by the possibilities of framed construction when he spent three months in Manila, in the Philippines, following a voyage on one of his father's whaling ships. The Filipinos constructed houses by using whole tree trunks as columns and split trunks as beams, joists, and diagonal braces in a complete framing system. (Framed construction of this kind has Neolithic origins.) A less exotic source, however, would have been the traditional New England braced frame or its derivative, the balloon frame, both of which would have been familiar to Jenney.

Iron-framed buildings were likely to be more impressive, and they were becoming common in the major eastern cities around the middle of the century. Perhaps the most advanced structure among those pointing toward the Home Insurance was the shot tower built by James Bogardus in 1855 for the McCullough Shot and Lead Company of New York. The tower embodied a true if primitive system of skyscraper construction: the brick panels of the octagonal wall were carried entirely by cast-iron beams spanning between the eight iron posts that constituted the primary bearing members. Jenney may have learned of the McCullough tower through George H. Johnson, who worked in the office of Daniel Badger, Bogardus' closest New York competitor, and who made two visits to Chicago in the 1870's.[4]

But Johnson's own work as a builder may have been equally important in its influence on Jenney. Johnson himself designed the next two structures after Bogardus' shot towers to be built with iron framing and brick curtain walls. The earlier was the grain elevator of the United States Warehousing Company at Brooklyn, New York (1860 or 1861). Again, the contact for Jenney may have been Johnson, or in this case Peter B. Wight, who knew the

---

[4] For Johnson's fireproof tile and the occasions of his Chicago visits, see p. 24.

elevator and who manufactured the fireproof tile for the Home Insurance Building. Another grain elevator designed by Johnson and constructed in the same way was built for the Pennsylvania Railroad in Philadelphia in 1862.

A vastly more impressive work involving similar structural techniques is the warehouse of the St. Ouen docks in Paris, designed by Hippolyte Fontaine and built from 1864 to 1865. This building combines the curtain wall of Johnson's elevators with the interior iron frame that had by then become well developed in England, France, and the eastern United States. The warehouse excited wide interest and could hardly have escaped Jenney's attention. England's leading historian of early iron framing, A. W. Skempton, places the St. Ouen warehouse on the same level in Europe as is generally accorded the Home Insurance Building in America. In the warehouse, he wrote, "the multi-storey iron-framed building with incombustible walls and floors had been achieved. It led, finally, to the creation of the first masterpieces of modern architecture in Chicago in the 1890's."[5]

Still another foreign source of ideas on iron framing was Viollet-le-Duc's *Lectures on Architecture,* which was translated by Benjamin Bucknail and published in the United States in the fall of 1881. In this work the French historian and theorist proposed a system of skeletal construction for a vaulted enclosure with all structural members of iron. This project, however, could not be interpreted as a system of framing appropriate to a multistory building, although it was claimed by the Minneapolis architect Leroy S. Buffington as the basis for his proposals of 1886 to 1887 for a series of fantastic skyscrapers supported on iron frames. Buffington secured a patent on this design in 1888, but his claim of earlier invention and application has now been demonstrated to be fraudulent.[6]

[5] A. W. Skempton, "The Boat Store, Sheerness (1858–60), and Its Place in Structural History," *Transactions of the Newcomen Society,* XXXII (1959–60), 72.
The sheer size of the St. Ouen warehouse could have convinced the imaginative builder of the wide adaptability of the new structural system. The building is six stories high and 680 feet long; its 15-inch brick panels rest on cast-iron spandrel beams carried in turn by cast-iron columns. The floors rest on hollow-tile arches set between joists spanning 13 feet between wrought-iron plate girders with a 20-inch depth. (Skempton, *op. cit.*) The only element in the warehouse that belongs to a day that was rapidly passing is the use of cast-rather than wrought-iron for the spandrel beams.

[6] Buffington claimed that he was the author of three projects in 1881 and 1882 for sky-scrapers that were, respectively, 425, 600, and 1,320 feet in height and that he used Jenney's later system of shelf angles to support parts of the brick piers in the lobby of the West Hotel, Minneapolis, constructed in 1882. The truth is that he knew very little of skeletal construction until he read Jenney's article on the structural system of the Home Insurance Building published in the December 10, 1885, issue of the *Sanitary Engineer.* He actually designed his projects and his own version of internal framing during 1886 and 1887, applied for a patent on November 14 of the latter year, and received it on May 22, 1888. The patent design shows a relatively thorough mastery of skeletal construction that was well in advance

Closer to home for Jenney was the proposal advanced by the Chicago engineer Frederick Baumann in his pamphlet, *Improvement in the Construction of Tall Buildings*, printed in 1884. Baumann advocated what he called his "Concealed Iron Construction of Tall Buildings" for rigidity, light, and speed and economy of construction. He wrote the essay during the preparation of plans for the Home Insurance Building, but since Jenney knew Baumann, there may very well have been an earlier interchange of ideas between them.

Whatever the source, the major step in the conversion of a building from a crustacean with its armor of stone to a vertebrate clothed only in a light skin occurred in the two years following 1883, when Jenney received the commission for the Chicago office of the Home Insurance Company. Construction began in 1884 and was completed in the following year. The building stood on the northeast corner of La Salle and Adams streets until its demolition in 1931. It was the major progenitor of the true skyscraper, the first adequate solution to the problem of large-scale urban construction (Fig. 44). This achievement alone would have secured a lasting reputation for Jenney, but it is equally to his credit that he went far toward developing a valid architectonic expression of his great technical innovation. His accomplishment ultimately came to be both structural and aesthetic, although the latter aspect did not emerge in its potential clarity and vigor until the completion of the second Leiter Building in 1890.[7] The structural system of the Home Insurance was in some of its details the work of Jenney's engineering assistant, George B. Whitney.

The construction and functional arrangement of the building were relatively simple and grew directly out of already well-tested techniques. The frame consisted of a serial column-and-beam system made up of cylindrical cast-iron columns, wrought-iron box columns of built-up section, and wrought-iron and steel I-beams joining them to receive the floor loads (Fig. 45). Lintels and mullions were cast iron. The spandrel beams and girders above the sixth floor were Bessemer steel members and thus marked the first use of the material for a building. It had previously been used in the United States only in three bridges, of which the Eads Bridge at St. Louis (1868–74) was most influential among the Chicago builders. The framing members of the Home Insurance were bolted together by means of angles, webs, and gusset plates. The columns were carried on isolated spread footings designed

---

of Jenney's understanding as revealed in the Home Insurance. Buffington's publicizing and patenting of the principles of the new system constitute a valuable contribution to the advancement of the building art, although vitiated by his extravagant and baseless claims of priority.

7 For the second Leiter Building, see pp. 89–90.

to transmit a unit pressure of 4,000 pounds per square foot to the soil. The footings in turn rested on reinforced concrete rafts supported by hardpan clay at an average depth of 12 feet 6 inches below grade level. The exterior envelope was granite at the first story and brick with sandstone trim above. The building was originally nine full stories high, with two more being added in 1890. The granite envelope of the columns at the base carried 18 per cent of the total column load on the periphery, a deviation from full framing that made possible the addition of the two top stories. Above the base all portions of the exterior wall, which was not self-supporting, were carried on shelf angles fixed to the spandrel beams. Thus the outermost floor girder carried not only its part of the floor load but also one bay of the exterior wall up to the beam next above it. This method of supporting the outer envelope remains the standard practice for tall steel- or concrete-framed structures. Without this technique, as a matter of fact, the skyscraper as we know it would have been an impossibility.[8]

In its total architectural treatment the Home Insurance can hardly be said to have lived up to its great technical promise. The street elevations were in general appearance impartial revelations of the iron and steel frame. One sees that the formerly characteristic gravitational thrust of the masonry bearing wall here gave way to the balanced tension and compression of the internal cage, which is neither predominantly horizontal nor vertical but simply a honeycomb of rectangular cells. But Jenney obscured and distorted the powerful impression his building could have made by covering it with ornamental detail that was unattractive in itself as well as confused and badly scaled for the cellular curtain wall. The elevations revealed a six-part horizontal composition undoubtedly employed to interrupt what was thought to be the monotony of a nine-story wall. The corner piers and the continuations of those flanking the entranceway were wide, the rest relatively narrow. All piers carried elaborate capitals at the third, sixth, eighth, and ninth stories. A balcony on corbels over each entrance and a complicated parapet added to the inappropriate excess of other details. The whole composition showed a characteristic weakness in Jenney: his inability to free himself in the design of a big and expensive building from derivative systems of ornamentation that the specialists in his offices imported from the German schools. It was a curious mixture of great structural vigor and redundant decorative details. It appeared again in much worse taste in the Fair Store and to a lesser extent in the Manhattan Building, but it was greatly refined in the second Leiter.

The utilitarian advantages of iron and steel framing were enormous and immediately obvious to architects, builders, and owners. First was the possi-

[8] For a detailed structural analysis of the Home Insurance, see Randall, *op. cit.*, pp. 105–7.

bility of getting rid of a supporting wall, with a consequent reduction in weight and an immense increase in height. The steel necessary to carry a tall building weighs only one-third as much as bearing masonry for an equal number of stories. The virtually unlimited increase in glass area, up to 100 per cent of coverage, allowed the maximum admission of natural light. The slender columns and wide bays offered greatly increased freedom in the disposition of interior partitions. Economy in the cost of materials together with speed and efficiency of construction convinced even the most skeptical builders of the superiority of steel and iron framing. In the case of the Home Insurance Building, the deciding factor seems to have been the admission of the greatest quantity of natural light available on a narrow, closely built street.

The interesting question for students of building history concerns the extent to which Jenney consciously sought to develop a new architectural form or the basis of a new style. The answer appears to be that, although he was aware of the new aesthetic possibilities, he was little concerned with such matters. Elmer C. Jensen, a member of Jenney's office from 1885 until the latter's death in 1907, thought that Jenney's approach was strictly utilitarian.

While he felt he was contributing to the making of new architectural forms, that was not his motive. His main purpose was the development of more efficient structural features. My personal opinion is that while he was fully conscious that his ideas and buildings were developing new forms, his main purpose was to create structural features which increased the effective floor areas and made it possible to secure more daylight within the buildings. . . . I do not recollect that he made any remarks about creating new forms although he did remark that skeleton construction would bring about a revolution in the design of office buildings.[9]

The question of the exact place of the Home Insurance Building in the total formal, structural, and economic development of the skyscraper must rest on a statement of the criteria against which we would measure the success of a particular achievement in the evolution of this building type. The art historian J. Carson Webster has provided the most complete formulation of the factors that the fully developed skyscraper must embody.

1. Essential characteristics (the end).
   a. Great height (relative to buildings).
   b. Arrangement (interior) in stories.
   c. Utmost space and light (potentially) in each story.
2. Necessary means
   a. A structural system adequate to achieving the essential characteristics taken together. To date this means skeleton construction. [This must be amended to include flat-slab and box framing, which are not framing systems in the strict sense of serial column-and-beam construction.]

[9] Letter to the author from Elmer C. Jensen, April 13, 1949.

    b. Materials necessary to the structural system, above all steel (iron and rein-forced concrete as possible alternatives), and fireproofing, heat-resisting material

    c. Passenger elevators.

3. Favoring conditions

    a. Economic—such as high value of land; availability of labor and capital; etc.

    b. Social—such as living in large groups; enterprise; organization of work; publicity; etc.

    c. Technological—such as availability of suitable tools, processes, and sources of power; development of plumbing, heating, etc.; growth of engineering; development of the craft of building to a certain point; etc.

    d. Psychological—desires (conscious or unconscious) which a tall form can express.

    e. Aesthetic—liking for height; preference for the effect of towers related to lower buildings; etc.[10]

If we seek to establish the place of the Home Insurance Building according to this comprehensive scheme, we may immediately conclude that all the favoring conditions were present and that the building embodies all the essential characteristics, its "great height," of course, being understood as relative to the buildings of its time. With respect to technological and architectural factors, however, we would be forced to admit that the Home Insurance fell far short of maturity in the development of the skyscraper. The most obvious feature in this respect was the fact that a portion of the total load was carried on the granite piers of the base and the brick party walls. In the latter instance the decision was required by the building commissioner and was thus not in the architect's hands. Equally important was the total absence of windbracing, a defect arising either from Jenney's and Whitney's belief that the large amount of masonry offered sufficient rigidity or from the fact that at the time they may have been largely ignorant of the matter. The presence of steel beams in the upper stories represents a vital step in the direction of full maturity, but their limited use indicates that the cost was prohibitive, which it was to remain until the mid-nineties.

A crucial question for determining whether Jenney contributed to the potential development of skyscraper construction is, To what extent were the new and rapidly progressing sciences of structure and materials available to him? In the light of designing practices then current, we can argue that the architect was somewhat in advance of his time, but this does not mean that the structural system of the Home Insurance Building was the product of scientific investigation and calculation. Although samples of the ferrous

[10] J. Carson Webster, "The Skyscraper: Logical and Historical Considerations," *Journal of the Society of Architectural Historians*, XVIII (December, 1959), 127.

materials in the frame were undoubtedly tested by the manufacturers, since the practice had been established on a systematic basis in the previous decade, Jenney and Whitney relied to a great extent on the empirical and pragmatic approach of the traditional building crafts. The frame of the Home Insurance seems crude indeed compared with the great bridges that had been opened or were to be completed within the decade—most notably the railroad cantilever spans at Poughkeepsie, Niagara Falls, and Memphis—which were products of a thorough scientific analysis. On the other hand, the Home Insurance as a finished structure was the result of a careful, quasi-scientific consideration of the utilitarian demands and the functional necessities for meeting them. In this respect the building belongs to the new tradition established by the Montauk Block in 1882.

By any standard the architectural quality of the Home Insurance can hardly be judged a success. Leaving the ornamental detail aside, we may ask whether the cellular façade provides the best aesthetic revelation of skyscraper construction. The answer depends on whether the more powerful visual effect comes from the expression of structure or from the more plastic and formal approach that springs from and seeks to intensify the sense of great height. Most of the Chicago architects, who tended toward the empirical and utilitarian view of such matters, generally preferred the former approach. The exception, of course, was Sullivan, whose highly emotional and subjective approach to design led to an intensification of height and the plastic treatment of elevations. In the last analysis, the Home Insurance must be considered as a long step on the way—as a "proto-skyscraper," in Carson Webster's words—whereas Sullivan's Guaranty Building in Buffalo may be regarded as a mature skyscraper in structure, utility, and form.

For a building whose length exceeds its height, the cellular wall of the Home Insurance seems more appropriate than Sullivan's verticalism. In this respect the second Leiter Building is a more vigorous revelation of the new construction; however, an intermediate step in the development of the new structural system lies between it and the Home Insurance. The third Chamber of Commerce Building was another proto-skyscraper, but it represented the next logical advance after Jenney's work. It was designed by Edward Baumann (1838–89) and Harris W. Huehl (1862–1919) and was erected on the southeast corner of La Salle and Washington streets between 1888 and 1889 (Fig. 46). Its design was obviously influenced by the Home Insurance, and it stood as a greatly refined expression of what Jenney was seeking in the earlier building. It was demolished in 1928 to make way for the present American National Bank Building. The Chamber of Commerce replaced not only its outmoded predecessor but also the old Board of Trade Building, constructed immediately after the fire. Thus it had an important symbolic function as well as a utilitarian purpose. It was the proudest and most advanced work of structural art at the time of its completion.

The Chamber of Commerce was almost a fully framed building: a small proportion of the total load fell on the masonry piers in which the peripheral columns were inserted. Its bolted wrought-iron and steel skeleton rested on a raft foundation made up of the usual grillage of steel rails imbedded in concrete. The total weight of the frame of this thirteen-story structure was 32,000 tons, of which 3,300 tons were steel. The frame was covered with an exterior envelope of marble at the base and brick above. The articulation of the wall was remarkable for its clarity and precision. The two-story base was a radical departure from the traditional massive stonework and piers, a characteristic even of the Home Insurance. The architects reduced the base to a succession of narrow piers of smooth-faced marble enframing large areas of glass that filled the entire bay. Except for the arbitrary horizontal division produced by means of continuous courses at the top of the second, fifth, eighth, and twelfth stories, the dominant accent was vertical, the result of continuous piers and slightly recessed spandrels. Aside from these details and the awkward and heavy-handed ornamentation at the thirteenth story and the parapet, the walls were incisive statements of the neutral cage that lay within them. There were other questionable elements—the banded columns at the main entrance, the capricious alteration of the pier width, the capitals on the wide piers at the top of the fifth story—but the over-all treatment of the street elevations revealed a surer mastery of the means of expression than Jenney's building could show.

The striking feature of the Chamber of Commerce Building was the interior light court extending the entire height of the building and roofed by a glass and iron skylight at the top (Fig. 47). Like The Rookery, the building was a hollow rectangle in plan. The offices formed a shell or honeycomb around the court, and the corridors were in reality balconies carried on cantilevered beams fixed to the columns on the periphery of the court. The elaborate ironwork of the railings was entirely in keeping with the rich character of the whole structure, with its unusual quantity of costly marble veneer on both interior and exterior. Open light courts such as this were a common feature of the high office and apartment buildings of the time. Although they were dictated by the practical necessity of admitting light to the interior of the building, their exuberant formal treatment revealed the popular delight excited by the many-storied building and the enthusiasm for making the most of it. The Chamber of Commerce justly made a great impression in its day. The authors of *Industrial Chicago* were perfectly clear about its position in their own city. "In the matter of light and live air," they wrote, "it is

83

superior to all other buildings, and in strength, equipment, and decoration equal to any of them except the Auditorium."[11]

The great block-long structure generally known historically as the second Leiter Building was Jenney's triumph. Although it was originally built for Siegel, Cooper and Company, it must have remained in their hands for no more than seven years, since by 1898 it had come to be known as the Leiter Building. From the time of the Civil War until the end of the century the dry-goods and department store business of Chicago was dominated by the partnership of Levi Z. Leiter and Marshall Field. The first Field and Leiter Store was built in 1868 at the northeast corner of State and Washington streets, only to fall before the fire three years later. The second store, on the same site, was opened in 1873, to be followed by a larger building in 1878. Up to the turn of the century, this building continued to be known as the Field and Leiter Store, although the partnership was dissolved before that time and Leiter moved his business to a newer building on what was shortly to be the south edge of the Loop.[12] The latter building still retains the name Levi Z. Leiter on the State Street face of the parapet, although it is now the main store of Sears, Roebuck and Company, founded in 1886 by Alvah Roebuck and Richard Sears. The building stands on the southeast corner of State and Van Buren streets, where it was erected between 1889 and 1891 (Fig. 48). In its boldness, vigor, and originality it remains one of the most impressive works of commercial architecture in the empirical spirit that the nation can show. Jenney knew exactly what he was doing, and he never wavered in the execution of his plan.

The Sears Roebuck Store is a huge rectangular prism 402 feet long, eight stories high, and 57,900 square feet in area of plan. The exterior surfacing of columns and spandrels is white Maine granite, with no outbreaks or ornamental detail to interrupt its smooth planes. The building is of straight warehouse construction. The interior at any point reveals a great sweep of open space divided into broad avenues marked off by the ranks of high, slender columns. The extraordinarily wide bays and the unusual story height of 16 feet combine with the slender steel columns to produce this dynamic impression of open and airy spaciousness. Only the Carson Pirie Scott Store can match the Sears Roebuck in this respect. Typical of warehouse construction, the plan is a closed rectangle up the sixth story. Above this level there is a

[11] *Industrial Chicago* (Chicago: Goodspeed Publishing Co., 1891), I, 204.

[12] After Leiter left the business, Marshall Field replaced the 1878 store with a larger building in 1902. Successive expansions eventually filled the whole block bounded by State, Randolph, Wabash, and Washington with the present department store of Marshall Field and Company. D. H. Burnham and Company were the architects of the 1902 building and its various additions.

shallow indentation one bay deep along the alley that flanks the rear elevation.

The chief importance of the Sears Roebuck Store lies in its formal character. The structural problems that it posed were solved by Jenney and his engineering assistants with a mature grasp of the technical means now available for the fully developed skyscraper. What is essential is that for the first time the steel and wrought-iron skeleton became fully and unambiguously the means of architectonic expression. The interior frame furnishes the dominant accent of the street elevations—the pattern of large, open rectangles into which the outer walls are divided. These panels or cells are filled with glass divided into either two or four large windows separated by thin wrought-iron mullions. The long west elevation is developed directly out of the structural system behind it, much as the isolated buttresses of the Gothic cathedral serve as primary visual elements in its indissoluble unity of structure and form. In the Sears Roebuck Store the impartial equilibrium of the steel cage takes the place of the gravitational thrust of the bearing wall. The unbroken horizontal lines of the spandrels at every third story and the continuous vertical bands of the piers provide a simple revelation of the construction of steel and wrought-iron framing. All ornamental details are reduced to the point of austerity. Only the uneven rhythm of the wide and narrow piers (the latter being deliberately obscured) mars the purity of the street elevations.

The Sears Roebuck Store was the work of a man of unusual courage and imagination. In the language of *Industrial Chicago:*

It has been constructed with the same science and all the careful inspection and superintendence that would be used in the construction of a steel railway bridge of the first order. . . . Designed for space, light, ventilation, and security, the Leiter Building meets the object sought in every particular. . . . A giant structure . . . healthy to look at, lightsome and airy while substantial, was added to the great houses of a great city . . . a commercial pile in a style undreamed of when Buonarotti erected the greatest temple of Christianity.[13]

The union of science, techniques, and art in this structure still represents a synthesis that is refreshing and healthy. Yet Jenney, as most of his later buildings show, seems not to have realized the soundness of his own intuition.

Three large buildings designed by Jenney were completed in 1891, the year he formed a partnership with William B. Mundie (1863–1939), and all three stand today. The first and largest is the Fair Store, extending along the north side of Adams Street from State to Dearborn (Fig. 49). The big Loop store and its suburban offspring are now owned by Montgomery Ward and Company. Construction of the building began in 1890 and was com-

[13] *Industrial Chicago*, I, 205.

pleted in a year and a half (the total cost was $3,000,000). The Fair is considerably greater in volume than the Sears Roebuck Store, being eleven stories high and having an area in plan of 55,000 square feet. Like the Sears Store, it is of warehouse construction, a closed rectangle in plan and a completely framed and fireproof structure. In spite of its great size and its profusion of tasteless ornament, it is light and open in appearance. The elevations, though lacking clarity, are direct expressions of the wide-bayed steel and wrought-iron frame that supports them (Fig. 50).

On the basis of concrete raft foundations reinforced with rails, the frame of the Fair rises in a series of built-up box columns and deep I-beams. The finished flooring is laid on a subfloor of concrete, which in turn is carried on fireproof tile arches set between the joists. A tile envelope provides fireproofing for the columns. The construction is typical of the large commercial building with a bolted iron frame (Fig. 51). The basic structural element of the Fair is revealed in the continuous piers and narrow spandrels of the street elevations, but the revelation is again distorted and obscured by incredibly heavy-handed details. Two massive courses at the top of the fifth and sixth stories, respectively, divide the street elevations into three parts in a clumsy 5-1-5 ratio. The rustication at the sixth story and the huge pier capitals at the fifth and eleventh detract still further from the validity of the design. The windows, as in all of Jenney's designs, are relatively small as a result of the division of the bay into three parts separated by slender mullions. These are so thin, however, that the total area of glass is very large.

The permit for the Manhattan Building was issued on June 7, 1889, by which date the plans had been substantially completed. The building was opened at 431 South Dearborn Street early in 1891 (Figs. 52, 53, 54). The frame of this structure is carried on the usual spread footings of concrete reinforced with steel rails. The unit load transmitted by the footing to hardpan is 3,000 pounds per square foot. The exterior facing of the front and rear elevations is gray granite up to the fifth story and pressed brick and terra cotta above. The building originally consisted of a central block twelve stories high flanked by two nine-story wings. Four additional stories were added a few years after completion, making it the first sixteen-story building in the world.

The framing system of the Manhattan, designed by the engineer Louis E. Ritter, contains an unusual combination of advanced innovations and traditional materials. The continuing high cost of steel led to the adoption of cast iron for the columns and wrought iron for many of the secondary girders and beams. Steel was restricted to the main girders and joists and to the channels used for the spandrel beams. According to William B. Mundie, the Manhattan frame was the first for which an American designer recognized windbracing as a necessity.[14] The engineer employed both diagonal and portal bracing for wind resistance. The columns at the basement floor level, where the shearing forces and bending moments induced by wind are at a maximum, are joined by double diagonals extending across the bays in the form of wrought-iron rods fitted with turnbuckles to maintain tension. Above the first floor windbracing is secured through deep girders riveted throughout the depth of the web to the angle fixed to the columns (the maximum depth of the girders is 15 inches). In certain places in the first and second floor framing systems, the girders are doubled. The framing of the numerous projecting bays is similar to that of the Monadnock: short cantilevers carry the peripheral channels of the projecting area (see the skeleton of the Unity Building, Fig. 55).

Another important structural innovation characterizes the Manhattan Building. Jenney and Ritter had to face the problem of dangerously overloading the party walls and footings of the two low buildings that originally flanked the Manhattan.[15] Ritter solved it by carrying the floors along the outer bays of the side elevations on cantilever beams anchored to the columns located on the second column line inside the planes of the party walls. Variations on this method of cantilevering the floor slab beyond the outermost line of columns came to be common in buildings with continuous or ribbon openings.

What immediately strikes the observer of the Manhattan is the variety of window openings in the street elevations. There are large undivided areas of glass set flush with the pier surface at the base, conventional paired windows in the second and third stories, trapezoidal bow windows in the middle three bays above the third story, and bow windows forming triangular projections above rounded spandrels in the wings. Above the twelfth story standard openings in the wall plane are paired under arches, as they were in any number of Chicago buildings erected during the eighties. The tripling of the rhythm in the top story may be a late relic of Richardson's treatment of the walls in the Marshall Field Wholesale Store. This curious mixture of sizes and types of window openings in the Manhattan is not entirely a matter of caprice. Jenney sought to admit as much light as possible along narrow, densely built streets, which was especially necessary for the rear elevation along Plymouth Street. Where the Manhattan rises above its neighbors, the windows sink back into the primary wall plane.

The most crisp and elegant treatment of the elevations in all of Jenney's designs appears in the Ludington Building, 1104 South Wabash Avenue,

[14] For the validity of this claim, see the discussion of the Monadnock Building, pp. 67–68.

[15] The building on the north side of the Manhattan still stands, but the one on the south was removed when Congress Street was widened into Congress Parkway.

also erected in 1891 (Fig. 56). The building was commissioned by Nelson Ludington, a lumberman of Escanaba, Michigan, and was retained by his family until 1960, when it was sold to Warshawsky and Company, dealers in automobile accessories. Through its regularity and harmony, and its unusually slim piers and spandrels, the light and open and graceful wall that is possible with steel framing is given full expression. The disfiguring elements of earlier buildings—the heavy capitals, the rustication, the stout piers, and the uneven rhythm of wide and narrow members—are here reduced to a minimum. The derivative ornament of the surface is still evident, as in the little classical pilasters that decorate the piers at the end and center bays, but they are well subordinated and only noticeable when sunlight falling at a sharp angle picks them out. The base of the Ludington is unusually fine: the narrow piers and the wide, undivided window panes set flush show how far Jenney could exploit the steel frame for lively architectonic effect.

Two buildings completed shortly before the panic and depression of 1893 maintain the standard that Jenney reached around 1890. The Isabella Building (1892–93), commissioned by the Daughters of Isabella and built at 21 East Van Buren Street, is an eleven-story steel-framed structure on the common raft footings reinforced with rails. An unusual feature of the framing system is windbracing in the form of knee braces: short diagonal members at the connections between girders and columns. The Isabella may be the first American building to be braced in this way. In the main (Van Buren Street) elevation, the first seven stories form a cellular curtain with continuous piers rising above the belt course at the second-floor line. The windows at the eighth and ninth stories are grouped in pairs under arches, and the tenth and eleventh stories lie under a high hipped roof topped by a central gabled skylight.

The Association, or Central Y.M.C.A., Building, at 19 South La Salle Street, was built at the same time and is structurally similar to the Isabella, although it rises to a height of sixteen stories. With the exception of the Sears Roebuck Store, this is Jenney's most uncompromising façade: the strict rectangularity of the cellular wall is interrupted only by continuous horizontal courses at the eleventh and twelfth stories. The Association is an elongated L in plan, fronting 54 feet on La Salle Street and 187 feet along the alley on the south side.

The Morton Building, at 538 South Dearborn Street, marks a decline from the vigorous work of the early nineties (Fig. 57). Erected in 1896, the building is a compromise between the fresh architectural spirit of the Sears Roebuck Store and the classical traditions of the Columbian Exposition, in which Jenney had a major hand. The excessive ornamental details of the Morton frustrate the potential vigor of the commercial style that Jenney had reached in earlier essays. The last of his buildings to maintain the bold spirit is the Chicago Garment Center (1904–5), at the northeast corner of Franklin and Van Buren streets. A ten-story steel-framed building, it retains the articulated wall of the older structures, but its clarity and strength are softened by extremely wide brick piers and the flattened arches that span the bays at the top story. In the year that the Garment Center was completed Jenney founded the short-lived partnership of Jenney, Mundie and Jensen, which was terminated by his death in 1907. The historian cannot admire Jenney without qualification, but neither can he deny that he has a great and permanent place in American building art.

CHAPTER V

BURNHAM AND ROOT

The last decade of the nineteenth century saw an extraordinary flowering of the civic and cultural spirit in Chicago. It was marked by creative public enterprise on the highest and most effective level, and it led to an intellectual and civic renaissance unparalleled in the history of American municipalities. The initial step was an engineering project conceived and executed on the grandest scale. The Chicago Sanitary District was established in 1889 by authority of an act passed by the State Legislature at Springfield. The substance of this act was drawn up by Bernard A. Eckhart, owner of the Eckhart Milling Company, director of the Chicago Board of Trade, and chairman of the West Park Commission. The fundamental purpose of the project was to end pollution of the lake along the Chicago shore in order to maintain a supply of pure drinking water and to open the lake front to its full recreational and aesthetic possibilities. The secondary intention was the creation of a modern transportation waterway to parallel the outmoded Illinois and Michigan Canal and thus to join Lake Michigan with the Illinois River through the lower reach of the Des Plaines River. The implementation of this plan initially required the construction of the Chicago Sanitary and Ship Canal (1891–1900), which was designed to maintain flow out of the lake and into the Illinois tributary system. The ultimate realization of the program required even more extensive construction—the present sewage disposal plant, which is constantly enlarged as the population of the metropolitan area expands, the system of dams in the Illinois River (completed 1933), North Shore Channel (1911), and Calumet-Sag Channel (1922). The two subsidiary canals completed the reversal of the entire drainage pattern of the Chicago metropolitan region.

We might suppose that an engineering work of this magnitude was sufficient to absorb the attention and energies of the municipality, but in fact, it proved to be only a beginning. A major forward step in the development of an adequate system of public transportation came in 1892 with the inauguration of the elevated railway network. The preliminary planning for the World's Columbian Exposition began in 1891 and preparation of the site and construction of the physical facilities were completed by the spring of

1893. The site-planner of the fair, Frederick Law Olmsted, simultaneously planned and supervised the layout of Jackson Park. The chief of construction was Daniel Burnham. The most extraordinary project for the fair was unfortunately never executed: the bridge engineer George S. Morison proposed a steel tower 1,050 feet high on the model of the recently completed Eiffel Tower in Paris. Morison's design would have materially advanced the structural arts, but the idea was too radically at odds with the character of the fair buildings to win the approval of the Board of Architects.

For civic and educational institutions the year 1892 was climactic: the cultural life of the entire nation was enriched by the simultaneous establishment of the Public Library, the Newberry Library, and the University of Chicago, and by the construction of the present building of the Art Institute.[1] The initial group of public museums in Chicago was rounded out with the construction in 1893 of the present building of the Chicago Academy of Sciences and the founding in the same year of the Museum of Natural History, which was housed until 1921 in the Fine Arts Building of the Columbian Exposition.[2] The city's pre-eminence as a library center was further advanced with the establishment of the John Crerar Library of science, technology, and medicine in 1894.[3] At the same time, the musical life of the community shared in this spiritual regeneration with the founding of the Chicago Symphony Orchestra in 1891.

Out of the influence and the spirit of the World's Fair eventually came the Burnham Plan of 1909 and with it the great lake-front development, the Forest Preserve District, and Jens Jensen's landscaping masterpieces of the West Park District—Humboldt, Garfield, and Columbus parks. The initial proposal for the lake-front project centered on what was later to be Grant Park, which was discussed as early as February, 1897, in letters between Owen Aldis and Daniel Burnham. The actual filling of the park site began in 1904. Before this powerful impetus spent itself in the 1920's, it had led to the creation of Wacker Drive and the huge ring system of the interior

[1] The architects of the Public Library and the main building of the Art Institute were Shepley, Rutan and Coolidge, who followed Renaissance precedents for both buildings. The Romanesque Newberry Library and the Tudor forms of the original University of Chicago group were the work of Henry Ives Cobb.

[2] The Fine Arts Building of the Fair, designed by Charles B. Atwood, was reconstructed as a permanent building in 1932, when it became the home of the Museum of Science and Industry. The building housing the Museum of Natural History (formerly the Field Museum) was designed by Graham, Burnham and Company and Graham, Anderson, Probst and White and was constructed between 1911 and 1919.

[3] For a number of years the Crerar Library was housed on the upper floors of the Marshall Field Store. Its own building, at the northwest corner of Michigan Avenue and Randolph Street, was completed in 1920 after the plans of Holabird and Roche. The collection was moved for the fourth time in 1963, when it was merged with the new library of the Illinois Institute of Technology.

boulevards. The lessons for civic design and civic art embodied in these projects have a permanent and basic validity for the whole domain of urban planning.

Chicago was equally advanced in the intellectual life and the literary arts. The University of Chicago quickly rose to the front rank in the new currents of thought in social theory and philosophy. Thorstein Veblen taught at the University from 1892 to 1906, and John Dewey from 1894 to 1904. Between them they brought the pragmatic theories of social organization, ethics, and rational inquiry to their mature levels.[4] Along with the rise of indigenous philosophical and social theories came the emancipation of American historiography from its European antecedents with the delivery by Frederick Jackson Turner of his classic paper, "The Significance of the Frontier in American History," at the University of Chicago in the summer of 1893. Among the Chicago faculty was Abraham Michelson, co-author of the celebrated Michelson-Morley experiment, which laid the empirical foundations for the special theory of relativity. Shortly after the turn of the century Harriet Monroe, John Root's sister-in-law and biographer, founded the magazine *Poetry* and was soon publishing the work of the new midwestern poets, among them Carl Sandburg, Edgar Lee Masters, and Vachel Lindsay. At the same time Theodore Dreiser began the composition of his Chicago novels. The dissemination of new ideas of European origin was vigorously prosecuted by a number of Chicago publishers. Chief of these, perhaps, was the Open Court Publishing Company, which was founded before the turn of the century and shortly brought out several works with revolutionary implications in the philosophical and scientific movements of the twentieth century—books such as Ernst Mach's *Science of Mechanics*, Hugo de Vries' *Mutation Theory*, and Bertrand Russell's *Scientific Method in Philosophy*.

With this vigorous intellectual ferment it is little wonder that the new architectural theories of Europe found a congenial atmosphere in Chicago. The organic theory of architecture that was rising in Germany under the influence of Darwinism came to be known originally through Root's translation in 1889 of Gottfried Semper's "Development of Architectural Style." For this essay, Semper drew on various biological concepts—chiefly the

[4] Veblen is usually associated strictly with the pragmatic tradition. Yet one of his most lasting contributions, which forms the fundamental theme of *The Theory of the Leisure Class*, is the idea that the primary inner motive to the accumulation of wealth is totally irrational and bears no logical relation to the recognized functional needs or conscious wishes of the human being. It was Freud who independently realized the full implications of this brilliant intuition. The philosophical movement inaugurated by William James and John Dewey was carried on at the University of Chicago by George Herbert Mead. By 1910 this movement was known in Europe as well as in America as the Chicago school of philosophy.

evolutionary theory of Darwin and the theory of types of Cuvier—to develop the idea that architectural styles evolve from archetypal forms in response to needs growing out of the conditions of social life.[5] But Semper did not hold that the forms of an art arise from a deterministic context according to some quasi-biological process. The artist creates his ultimate forms, but the elements on which he draws are never spontaneously invented. They are always to a certain extent parts of a tradition that establishes the continuity and intelligibility of the visual and the building arts, as language serves to maintain the same characteristics in the literary arts.[6] The study of this original and penetrating German philosopher of art made it possible for Chicago to unite the European and the native currents of thought in aesthetics and social theory. As Burchard and Bush-Brown wrote:

In following Semper the Chicago architects put themselves in the mainstream of eighteenth and nineteenth-century thinking about adaptation. They forged a link relating themselves to Latrobe and Greenough and Emerson. They avidly read Whitman, whose *Democratic Vistas* envisioned a whole civilization unique to America. In him they felt an ally, hostile to the survival or revival of historic forms, demanding a new, modern form, expressive of American ambitions. They became conscious of living in a modern time, one that was unique in history. They followed Hegel and Taine in believing that the history of art was itself an organism, reflecting the changing natural and historical conditions that created it. Since the times had changed, it must be that a new idea was required, one related to the qualities of the new times. The Chicagoans, sensing their departure from the past, their difference from the East, determined to emphasize and preserve it, founded the Western Association of Architects. Their publications, *The Western Architect* and *The Inland Architect*, spoke of a West trying to assert its modernity. They remained in accord, however, with Populist notions and with the Sullivan-Wright theory of the identity of democracy and individuality.[7]

French contributions to the new ideas appeared in the *Inland Architect* with the translation by W. A. Otis of César Daly's "La Semaine des Constructeurs," in which Daly argued that a genuine architectural style expresses the philosophical, cosmological, and moral elements of a culture.[8] In the long run this idea proved to be more fruitful than the sometimes questionable analogies between biology and the arts. Architecture, in a fundamental sense, is the symbolic image of a cosmos, divine or natural or civic, and where

[5] Root's translation was published in *Inland Architect*, XIV (August, 1889), 76.

[6] Semper developed these ideas in an influential work, *Der Stil in den technischen und tektonischen Künsten*, the second edition of which was published at Munich in 1878.

[7] John Burchard and Albert Bush-Brown, *The Architecture of America: A Social and Cultural History* (Boston: Little, Brown & Co., 1961 [© 1961 by American Institute of Architects]), p. 247.

[8] Otis' translation of Daly's essay is in *Inland Architect*, XV (July, 1890), 5.

such a world view is lacking, architecture will find itself bound by historicism or structural necessity or will be reduced to self-expression. Among the Chicago architects, Root and Sullivan were particularly aware of this dilemma.

As for the physical character of building, the Chicago achievement stood in the front rank in the decade of the nineties. By 1890 its pre-eminence was beginning to be acknowledged in Europe and the eastern United States, as a leading editorial in *Carpentry and Building* indicated.

The character of the structures erected [in Chicago] demonstrates one notable fact—that is, that for the first time architects have risen to the plane of the highest constructive knowledge in structures. . . . In this respect Chicago is unique, and it is a common remark in Eastern and foreign cities among those actively engaged in building that Chicago today erects the best built structures ever known, and with the notable distinction that she does it with the closest economy in material and time. That is to say, that it is a fact that in Chicago buildings the quality is better, the distribution of material is more skillful, and the buildings are naturally more reliable.[9]

It was in the civic and intellectual context that we have described that John Wellborn Root led the way in bringing the building art of the nineteenth century to its maturity. What he began, Holabird and Roche were soon to complete. It was Root who took the ultimate step of freeing the big commercial building from any dependence on masonry adjuncts and creating the plan and structure of the urban office block as we know it today. Root had little time to master the architecture of steel framing before his death in January, 1891. The last two years of his life were devoted to the design of an extraordinary concentration of big commercial buildings, all of them wholly emancipated from the traditional techniques and materials so brilliantly exploited in the Monadnock. The first commission for which he and Burnham used complete skeletal construction was the second Rand McNally Building; it was the first building to be supported on an all-steel frame (Fig. 58). It was erected between 1889 and 1890 on the block bounded by Adams, La Salle, Quincy, and Wells streets to take the place of the original Rand McNally Building, a five-story structure built in 1880 at 125 West Monroe Street and demolished in 1900. The newer building survived for only two decades: it was demolished in 1911, when it was replaced by the third Rand McNally Building, designed by Holabird and Roche.[10] The 1890 structure

9 "Chicago Architecture," *Carpentry and Building*, XIII (March, 1891), 79. The periodical was edited and published in New York.

10 The third Rand McNally Building, now one of the office buildings of the Federal Government in Chicago, occupies the block bounded by Clark, Harrison, La Salle, and Polk streets. Shortly after the Second World War Rand McNally and Company moved its operations to a new printing plant and administration building in Skokie.

was a huge rectangular prism ten stories in height, which nearly filled the site bounded by the four streets. An interior court roofed by a skylight brought light to the inner portions of the floor area. In every respect the Rand McNally Building was a structural masterpiece, to a great extent the achievement of its engineering designers, the firm of Wade and Purdy and Theodore Starrett. Jenney's system of cantilever supports for carrying party walls was used in the Rand McNally to spare its lesser neighbors from the dangers of excessive or unequal settlement. The unusual feature of the steel frame was the presence of Z-bar columns, a particularly rigid form recently invented by Charles L. Strobel.[11] The external envelope of spandrel beams and wall columns was terra cotta, which marked the first use of the material for the street elevations of a building.

For the most part the elevations of the Rand McNally were well articulated, expressing with little hesitancy the frame on which they were carried. The piers and spandrels were narrow and bounded unusually large areas of glass. But the formal treatment of the elevations was somewhat restless and involved, lacking the unity of the Monadnock or even of the Rookery. The arbitrary division of the façade into separate horizontal areas was carried to an extreme. The base was relatively straightforward, although the form and proportions of the openings were not well harmonized with those above them. Above the first story ran a horizontal course that separated it from the upper nine stories. The piers at the second story terminated in capitals. A second belt course separated the third and fourth stories, which were distinguished by heavy recessed spandrels. The fifth, sixth, and seventh stories constituted another division, which was characterized by full-centered arches spanning the bays at the top of the seventh. The piers in this division were continuous, their width decreased, and the spandrels again recessed. The eighth and ninth stories were also separated from each other and from the rest of the elevation by continuous belt courses. The tenth merged with the parapet that extended around the top of the building.

This separation of the wall into horizontal areas differentiated by varia-

[11] The Z-bar column is made by riveting four Z-angles to a central plate in such a way as to give the member the following cross-sectional shape:

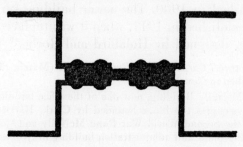

tions of detail appears capricious and inorganic. The skeleton is a perfectly regular cage that is uniform from top to bottom. Root's treatment was in no way required or suggested by internal functional arrangements, and by failing to develop a repetitive pattern expressing the internal regularity of structure and floors, he sacrificed something of the inherent power that the unadorned building possessed. It is to his credit as an architect, however, that the details were completely subordinated to the dominant expression, which was in large outline unequivocal. The natural horizontality of the large office building—it is, after all, a vertical succession of uniform horizontal planes—is a valid basis for architectonic expression. Root accomplished this in the Montauk with the simple device of thin terra-cotta bands to mark off each story. In spite of the continuity of piers in the major division of the Rand McNally façade, there is a stronger horizontal pattern that helps to emphasize the inner structural character. The entrances of the building, located in the end bays on Adams Street, were Root's finest essays in this area of design (Fig. 59). He was particularly fond of richly detailed entranceways, and in this case he achieved an ornamental pattern that is simpler and more architectural in character than the well-composed but sometimes redundant details of other large buildings.

The refinement of statement exhibited by the Monadnock was bound to appear in Root's handling of framed construction. It came with the Great Northern Hotel, which stood from 1892 to 1940 on the northeast corner of Dearborn Street and Jackson Boulevard (Fig. 60). As a hotel, the Great Northern takes its place with the work of Theodore Starrett and Clinton J. Warren, the leaders of hotel design, by virtue of the application of new structural techniques and formal ideas to a type of building other than the office block.[12] In this respect it has an additional importance in the history of architecture. It was one of the magnificent achievements of the Chicago school. If it were standing today, it would still be one of the few hotels in the United States to reveal a genuine architectural sophistication.

Burnham and Root had little preparation for the Great Northern. They had received several commissions for apartment buildings, the best of which were the Argyle and the Pickwick, both completed about 1887. Theodore Starrett's Hyde Park Hotel undoubtedly provided the major precedent for the Great Northern.[13] Aside from their having to deal with the many functional problems specifically associated with a hotel, the architects attacked the design of the Great Northern in the same way that they approached the office block. As Harriet Monroe said, "It was planned as rigorously for space

[12] For hotels and apartments, see pp. 148–59.
[13] For the Hyde Park Hotel, see pp. 150–51.

and light as an office building."[14] The many utilitarian features of the hotel followed the innovations chiefly made by Starrett and developed by Clinton Warren.

The Great Northern was a fourteen-story building originally disposed on an L-shaped plan and supported on a steel and wrought-iron frame. Its exterior envelope was nearly uniform in material, brick from top to bottom except for a small amount of terra-cotta trim. Interior fireproofing was the most extensive possible at the time of construction. The architects claimed that no fire originating in a room could spread beyond it or the suite of which it was a part. The street elevations of the building well expressed the nature and arrangement of interior facilities—a series of similar rooms or apartments along central corridors, each floor above the second planned like every other. A small portion of space on the lower floors was given to offices and stores; otherwise, the volume was devoted entirely to rooms, lobbies, service facilities, and other characteristics of a residential building.

The aesthetic excellence of the Great Northern grew out of its unity, regularity, and openness, and from the lively sense of movement provided by the undulating surfaces of the projecting bays. These projections were handled with a sure sense of function and architectonic relationship. On the Dearborn Street elevation the central bay projected in a trapezoidal plan, as did the three projecting bays on Jackson Boulevard. The rest were rounded in plan. The corner over the entrance and the northwest corner were developed into cylindrical pavilions that extended beyond the main wall planes by an amount equal to the projection of the bow windows. The primary purpose of this undulatory composition was functional—to secure the maximum admission of light—but the general treatment indicates a formal interest in handling the big structure as a plastic-utilitarian object.

The only vestige of traditional ornament in the Great Northern was at the parapet and the cornice above the thirteenth story. The flattened arches over the windows at the twelfth story and the tripling of the window rhythm of the fourteenth suggest the influence of Richardson and Romanesque forms. For the most part, however, the hotel was a great cage clothed in a thin envelope of brick and glass, the openings composed of two large windows that filled each of the bays. In the architecture of iron and steel framing, the Great Northern Hotel was undoubtedly Root at his best. The technical and aesthetic principles of Chicago construction were there adapted to the requirements of a hotel building that revealed simply and powerfully the soundness of those principles.

The formal characteristics embodied in the Great Northern appeared in one building that stood until 1949. It was the Ashland Block, opened for

[14] Harriet Monroe, *John Wellborn Root* (Boston: Houghton Mifflin Co., 1896), p. 151.

102

occupancy early in 1892 at the northeast corner of Clark and Randolph streets (Fig. 61). The original Corinthian cornice of the Ashland was removed and replaced by a plain brick parapet, which appears in the second illustration (Fig. 62). This parapet was grotesquely out of scale with the solid elements of the walls and consequently ruined the appearance of the building at the top. Aside from this clumsy alteration, however, the Ashland —in comparison with its newer neighbors—preserved the unity and lively structural expressiveness that made it one of the proudest buildings of the Chicago school. It went down after a useful life of nearly sixty years for the present Union Bus Terminal.

In construction, materials, and general exterior design, the sixteen-story Ashland was almost identical with the Great Northern Hotel. It was higher and more elongated in plan, but the over-all impression provided by major elements and details was much like that of the hotel building. Brick and terra-cotta facing formed the envelope of the steel and wrought-iron frame. Except for the full-centered arches that spanned the bays at the top of the third story and the triple openings of certain bays in the long elevation, the fenestration was close to that of the Great Northern. At alternate bays the wall projected in rounded outline, and the three street corners were developed into cylindrical pavilions. The ornamental details of the exterior were reduced to little more than the original cornice and the capitals of the piers at the third story. The horizontal division, effected by the separate treatment of the base and by the continuous courses at the seventh and fifteenth stories, was still present but reduced to an unobtrusive point.

Like Jenney, Root never opened the building wall to the full extent possible with framed construction. The Ashland contained the greatest area of glass to be found in any of his buildings, but the traditional separate openings of the Montauk and the Monadnock remained the basic unit of fenestration. It was Holabird and Roche who three years later merged the separate windows into a continuous opening extending across the width of the entire bay. The pattern of openings in the wall of the Ashland is plainly derived from the form of the skeleton. As an expression of the structural basis it lacks the homely vigor of Jenney's Sears Roebuck Store but makes up for it in the lively movement of the undulating wall. The simplicity, directness, and functionalism of Chicago construction predominate in the Ashland Building, and one can see in it, approaching maturity, the full aesthetic statement of new structural and utilitarian factors.

Of Root's last two designs one was an excursion into the romantic. The Woman's Temple, commissioned by the Women's Christian Temperance Union, was a translation of Romanesque and French Gothic details into the vocabulary of commercial architecture (Fig. 63). The building stood at the southwest corner of La Salle and Monroe streets from 1892 to 1926, when it was demolished to make way for the present office building at 120 South La Salle. In the hands of a lesser architect it might have been vulgar licentiousness. The two-story base of stonework, the steeply pitched roof, the great arches at the ninth story, the deep reveals, the dormers and pinnacles, came straight from medieval prototypes; yet Root's skill and sense of unity dominated them, and somehow out of these excessive details, the real nature of the building emerged. It was florid work—arty and feminine, perhaps— but the central portion, or shaft, stood out cleanly, and it was here that structure and function guided and informed the outer expression. The important functional characteristic of the Woman's Temple was its H-plan, representing an admirable solution to the problem of admitting sufficient light into a deep building.

Harriet Monroe tells us that the richness and exuberance of the Temple grew in part from Root's answer to the suggestion that the building ought to express the moral aspirations of the earnest crusaders who commissioned it. Yet one wonders whether it really reflected the personality of Frances Willard and her sisters in the cause. The so-called femininity of the design may well have embodied the very thing that she and her cohorts fought against and ultimately triumphed over. This is certainly the case if we consider her in the public world, where a building must have its being.

The building originally known as the Capitol and later the Masonic Temple, on the northeast corner of State and Randolph streets, was the leading skyscraper of 1892 (Fig. 64). It was the highest building in the world at the time—twenty-two stories if we include the gabled attic—and the owners boasted that it was the most expensive. It suffered the fate of much of Burnham and Root's work in being demolished in 1939 for the conglomeration of trivial buildings now occupying this site. For a building of this unprecedented height, arranged in a U-shaped plan, the engineers were concerned to erect the most rigid frame possible at the time. All structural members were steel, the foundations were deep raft footings of reinforced concrete, and the massive columns were built up of plates and channels into the box form (see the Fair Store detail, Fig. 51). The windbracing was extraordinary, although it was of a type that was beginning to be common for very high skyscrapers at the end of the century. Wrought-iron rods extended across both diagonals of a single bay in the transverse wall bays above the tenth story, and double diagonal rods running through two stories (that is, two bays, one above the other) were introduced into the transverse wall bays up to the tenth floor and into the elevator bays at the sides of the shafts throughout the height of the building. In the latter case the rods were fixed to the intermediate girder at their point of intersection. (Following is a sketch of double-bay bracing in the Masonic Temple.)

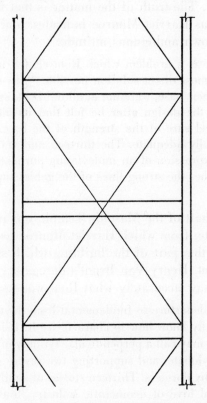

Above the sixteenth story, the Masonic was a work of traditionalism adapted to skyscraper requirements. The Venetian and Tudor windows, the steeply pitched roof planes, and the dormers and decorated gables formed the extravagant conclusion to the base-shaft-capital program. Between base and capital, however, the pressed brick and terra-cotta facing provided a simple cover for a clean and honest structure whose continuous piers imparted a strong vertical accent suggesting Sullivan's skyscraper design developed for the Wainwright and Guaranty buildings. Counteracting the vertical accent and partly preserving the neutrality of the steel cage were the wide openings of the grouped windows.

Root was not satisfied with the Masonic Temple, but at the same time he felt that he had given the problem its best aesthetic solution. As T. E. Tallmadge said, "He strove here to achieve a 'commercial style' based on the Romanesque which might be generally accepted as a formula for the expression of the skyscraper."[15] Root had come much closer to it in the Monad-nock and the Great Northern, but he was obviously searching through rich-ness of detail for what to him was a greater emotional impact than these buildings could show. The truth of the matter is that Root was not at home with the skyscraper, as Harriet Monroe indicates, and her judgment on the Masonic reflects his own ambiguous attitude.

The Masonic Temple was a problem which Root chafed under, but to which he attempted to give the most direct solution possible. "Sky-scrapers," elevated out of true proportion to their base, were not at all to his liking; and in this case, two stories were added to the design after he felt that its altitude was already too great. One does not feel sure of the strength of the base, which in most of the firm's buildings is wholly adequate. The thirteen undeviating stories which rise above it are a frank expression of an undeviating purpose, but the eye waits for its reward until it reaches the strong lines of the gables supporting the steep roof with its dormers.[16]

The bold central shaft of the Masonic Temple was not at all congenial to cultivated eastern taste, from which Harriet Monroe seems to have taken her cue, although it was this part of the building which strikes us today as its most powerful element. Henry Van Brunt's derogatory critique thus proved to be ironic; yet he saw accurately what Root was trying to do.

The [Masonic] is a departure so fundamental from the traditions of decorative architecture that I hardly know how to characterize it. It is a building absolutely committed to what one may call a perpendicular tyranny of pilasters, resting upon an inadequate open stylobate, and supporting two severe gables, connected by a steep roof and broken by dormers. Thirteen stories of similar use and importance, typical of an industrial hive of democratic industry, find themselves expressed here externally in an absolutely monotonous and unmitigated system of fenestra-tion, separated by vertical piers which rise from top to bottom without incident. It is perhaps the frankest admission of a structural and economical necessity ever expressed in architectural form. Between these pilasters, 160 feet high, rise sev-eral oriels equally vertical and equally monotonous. For the interruption of these vertical lines there would be of course only the excuse of design; none are sup-plied either by structure or use. It is probable that in this experiment, which looks like the apotheosis of the elevator in the modern social system, it was Root's desire to permit an exceptional character of structure to have the fullest and most honest architectural expression of all.[17]

[15] Thomas E. Tallmadge, *Architecture in Old Chicago* (Chicago: University of Chicago Press, 1941), p. 204.

[16] Monroe, *op. cit.*, p. 140.

[17] Henry Van Brunt, "John Wellborn Root," *Inland Architect and News Record*, January, 1891, as quoted in Monroe, *op. cit.*, pp. 278–79.

The Masonic Temple and its contemporaries were the last buildings Root was to see under construction before his death on January 15, 1891. The Ashland, the Masonic, and the Garrick Theater buildings once stood within a length of two blocks on the north side of Randolph Street, but commercial progress has now carried them all away (Fig. 65).

CHAPTER VI

D. H. BURNHAM AND COMPANY

After Root's death Burnham continued the firm under his name alone. Much of the work of design and organization in his big and prosperous office was intrusted to his lieutenants, chiefly Charles B. Atwood, Dwight Perkins, and Ernest R. Graham, the last of whom continued the corporation after Burnham's death. In the nineties Burnham's commissions grew in number and size to the point where his architectural firm was unquestionably the largest in Chicago, with offices in New York and San Francisco. Around the turn of the century his designers, engineers, and draftsmen were working on such projects as the Marshall Field Store and the First National Bank in Chicago, the Flatiron Building in New York, the Pennsylvania Station in Pittsburgh, and Washington Union Station—buildings of such magnitude and importance as to establish him as a national figure. Classical and Baroque in formal character, though always sound in functional planning and detail, these monumental works have little to do with the architecture of the Chicago school. When he chose to do so, however, he could see to it that his designers produced buildings in the very front rank of the Chicago tradition, but there were few of these after 1900.

The design in which Root's ability and point of view clearly survived was that of the Majestic Hotel, constructed from 1892 to 1893 at 29 West Quincy Street (Fig. 66). This once elegant building stood until 1961, when it was demolished to make way for the new office building of the federal government, which takes the place of the vast domed monument on the west side of Dearborn Street between Jackson and Adams. The site of the hotel was immediately adjacent to that once occupied by the Great Northern, a small part of the rear elevation of which appears in the illustration. The presence of the older hotel determined the fenestration and general exterior treatment of the Majestic. This is a good example of the strong sense of form correlation among the Chicago architects, which survived even after the old originality had disappeared, as the Michigan Avenue skyline impressively reveals.

The façade of the Majestic was an exact continuation of the street elevations of the Great Northern. The oriels, or projecting bays, and the size and spacing of openings in the newer structure were patterned directly after those of the older. The projecting belt courses were carried without interruption across both buildings. The one at the top of the thirteenth story, however, showed that the desire for continuity sometimes got the better of good sense. Since the Majestic had three full stories and a roof garden above the thirteenth, the interruption at this point was illogical. The horizontal course was repeated at the top of the fifteenth story, where it had some meaning. For the most part the Majestic Hotel was even more unified and homogeneous than the Great Northern, a consequence of a more strictly utilitarian approach to the design. Except at the sixteenth and seventeenth stories, the motive was uniform from end to end and top to bottom. The façade was perfectly neutral, a simple array of openings neither markedly horizontal nor vertical. Most of them were arranged in projecting bays for maximum light and air; all of them together directly expressed the pattern of the steel cage behind them.

With the completion of the Great Northern Theater Building (1895–96) at 20 West Jackson Boulevard, also designed by D. H. Burnham and Company, the Great Northern and Majestic hotels and the new theater and office block were merged into a connected and unified group arranged on an extensive U-shaped plan that covered more than half the block bounded by Jackson and Quincy east of Dearborn Street (for the theater, see Fig. 60, far right). The inclosure was described as the largest interior court in Chicago faced with glazed brick, or enameled brick, as it was then called. The court walls of both hotels and the theater were an inferior variation on those of The Rookery. Continuous bands of terra-cotta ornament extended around the three walls at the sill and lintel lines and thus enframed the high, narrow windows in a succession of horizontal strips. The windows were widely spaced in a pattern that in no way reflected the continuous cells of the steel frame. Again, as in the case of The Rookery, an iron stairway extended upward immediately outside the court-wall plane of the Great Northern Hotel and was housed in a clumsy glass and iron curtain well below the artistry that Root lavished on the similar inclosure of the earlier building (Fig. 26). Like the Majestic Hotel, the Great Northern Theater was demolished in 1961 for the federal office building.

The path that Burnham followed in the Majestic Hotel had been well explored and marked. But his next major commission, the Reliance Building, is astonishing in its daring pursuit of Chicago principles to their logical ultimate (Fig. 67). The designing architect was Charles B. Atwood, a member of Burnham's staff, whose reputation rested chiefly on two buildings done for the Columbian Exposition, the temporary Illinois Central Station and the Fine Arts Building.[1] One short step further in the design of the Reliance and he would have produced the transparent tower that Mies van der Rohe imagined in his Berlin project of 1919.

A commission for alterations to the previous building on the southwest corner of State and Washington streets was awarded to Burnham and Root in 1890, but sometime in the next four years the decision was made to demolish the earlier structure and erect the present fourteen-story Reliance Building, now known simply by its address, 32 North State Street. Atwood completed the plans in 1894, with Edward C. Shankland as structural engineer, and the building was opened for occupancy in the following year. The builders performed a remarkable feat of construction in erecting the steel frame of the top ten stories in fifteen days, from July 16 to August 1, 1895. The steel framing system included two unusual provisions for wind-bracing: 24-inch deep spandrel girders with either solid or trussed webs bolted to the columns through the web depth in rigid connections, and columns of two-story length disposed to provide staggered joints. The street elevations represent the goal that the whole functionalist wing of the Chicago movement was consciously or unconsciously striving to reach, for here the last vestige of a bearing element, or any indication of the hidden presence of one, has disappeared from the elevations.

The Reliance has no piers or columns in the exterior envelope, which is simply a vertical succession of broad glass bands divided into large panes by extremely tenuous mullions. The strong horizontality of the street elevations is a direct revelation of the internal floor system, a series of parallel, horizontal slabs carried to the columns by the girders and joists. Atwood succeeded in developing almost to its ultimate refinement the modern dematerialized curtain wall and thus made the building a direct forerunner of the work of Le Corbusier and Mies van der Rohe in the 1920's. The walls of the Reliance form a thin skin stretched over the skeleton of the building and exhibiting a neutral tension in all directions. The appearance of a dematerialized skin or envelope arises not only from the extraordinary proportion of glass but also from the fact that the glass is set nearly flush with the spandrels. The material of these narrow bands is glazed terra cotta, obviously without bearing capacity.

The windows of the Reliance form the most striking feature of the building. They represent the fullest development of the "Chicago window," in which a single large pane of glass fills the whole bay except for narrow movable sash at either end, immediately adjacent to the columns. The mov-

---

[1] The suburban station, with its three arched entrances, may well have suggested Reed and Stem's treatment of the main elevation of Grand Central Terminal in New York (1903–13). On the subsequent history of the Fine Arts Building, see p. 96.

97. STOCK EXCHANGE BUILDING, 1893–94   Adler and Sullivan

Main entrance. (From *Inland Architect and News Record*.)

98. STOCK EXCHANGE BUILDING, 1893–94   ADLER AND SULLIVAN

Detail of the main entrance. (*Institute of Design,
Illinois Institute of Technology.*)

99. STOCK EXCHANGE BUILDING, 1893–94   ADLER AND SULLIVAN
Grillwork of the elevator shafts at the top floor. (*Richard Nickel.*)

100. GUARANTY BUILDING, 1894–95 ADLER AND SULLIVAN

Now the Prudential Building, at the southwest corner
of Church and Pearl streets, Buffalo, New York.
(*Chicago Architectural Photographing Co.*)

101. GRAND CENTRAL STATION, 1889–90
SOLON S. BEMAN

Southwest corner of Harrison and Wells streets.
(*Chicago Architectural Photographing Co.*)

102. GRAND CENTRAL STATION, 1889–90   Solon S. Beman

Interior of the train shed. (*Allen Lein.*)

103. GRAND CENTRAL STATION, 1889–90   Solon S. Beman

Front curtain wall of the train shed. (*Allen Lein.*)

104. GRAND CENTRAL STATION, 1889–90 SOLON S. BEMAN

Glass roof of the mail and baggage platform. (*Allen Lein.*)

105. STUDEBAKER BUILDING, 1895   SOLON S. BEMAN

Now the Brunswick Building, at 629 South Wabash Avenue.
(*Commercial Photographic Co.*)

106. STUDEBAKER BUILDING, 1895   SOLON S. BEMAN

Main elevation. (*Commercial Photographic Co.*)

107. PHELPS, DODGE AND PALMER BUILDING, 1888
BURLING AND WHITEHOUSE

Now known by its address, 200 West Adams Street.
(*Kaufmann & Fabry Co.*)

108. YONDORF BUILDING, 1874, 1892

Now known by its address, 225 South Wacker Drive.
(*Chicago Architectural Photographing Co.*)

109. HYDE PARK HOTEL, 1887–88, 1891 THEODORE STARRETT

Formerly at the southwest corner of Hyde Park Boulevard
and Lake Park Avenue before its demolition in 1963.
(*Kaufmann & Fabry Co.*)

110. HYDE PARK HOTEL, 1887–88, 1891   THEODORE STARRETT

The elevation at the main entrance. (*Thomas Knudtson.*)

111. HYDE PARK HOTEL, 1887–88, 1891   THEODORE STARRETT
Detail of the main elevation. (*Thomas Knudtson.*)

112. VIRGINIA HOTEL, 1889–90 CLINTON J. WARREN

Formerly the Leander McCormick Apartments,
at the intersection of Ohio and Rush streets;
demolished in 1929. (*Commercial Photographic Co.*)

113. METROPOLE HOTEL, 1891   Clinton J. Warren

Northeast corner of Michigan Avenue
and Twenty-third Street. (*Commercial Photographic Co.*)

114. MICHIGAN HOTEL, 1891–92   CLINTON J. WARREN

Northeast corner of Michigan Avenue and Cermak Road.
(*Commercial Photographic Co.*)

115. PLAZA HOTEL, 1892   Clinton J. Warren

1553 North Clark Street. (*Commercial Photographic Co.*)

116. CONGRESS HOTEL, 1892–93, 1902, 1907
CLINTON J. WARREN, HOLABIRD AND ROCHE

504 South Michigan Avenue. (*Commercial Photographic Co.*)

117. CONGRESS HOTEL, 1892–93, 1902, 1907
Clinton J. Warren, Holabird and Roche

A later view showing the alterations to the ground floor.
(*Thomas Knudtson.*)

118. LAKOTA HOTEL, 1893

Formerly at the southeast corner of Michigan Avenue
and Thirtieth Street; demolished in 1959.
(*Commercial Photographic Co.*)

119. BREWSTER APARTMENTS, 1893   R. H. TURNOCK

Northwest corner of Diversey Boulevard
and Pine Grove Avenue. (*Kaufmann & Fabry Co.*)

120. BREWSTER APARTMENTS, 1893   R. H. Turnock

The interior light court above the fifth floor. (*Thomas Knudtson.*)

121. BREWSTER APARTMENTS, 1893   R. H. Turnock

Interior light court and skylight. (*Thomas Knudtson.*)

122. FRANCIS APARTMENTS, 1895   Frank Lloyd Wright

4304 South Forrestville Avenue.
(*Municipal Reference Library of Chicago.*)

123. CARSON PIRIE SCOTT STORE, 1899, 1903–4, 1906
Louis Sullivan, D. H. Burnham and Company

Southeast corner of State and Madison streets.
(*Chicago Architectural Photographing Co.*)

124. CARSON PIRIE SCOTT STORE, 1899, 1903–4, 1906
LOUIS SULLIVAN, D. H. BURNHAM AND COMPANY

The west elevation and the corner pavilion
showing the parapet that replaced the original cornice.
(*Ralph M. Line.*)

125. CARSON PIRIE SCOTT STORE, 1899, 1903–4, 1906
Louis Sullivan, D. H. Burnham and Company

Part of the corner pavilion and the west elevation.
(*Carl W. Condit.*)

126. CARSON PIRIE SCOTT STORE, 1899, 1903–4, 1906
Louis Sullivan, D. H. Burnham and Company

Detail of the west elevation. (*Carl W. Condit.*)

127. CARSON PIRIE SCOTT STORE, 1899, 1903–4, 1906
Louis Sullivan, D. H. Burnham and Company

Detail of the ornament at the first story
of the Madison Street elevation. (*Richard Nickel.*)

128. CARSON PIRIE SCOTT STORE, 1899, 1903–4, 1906
Louis Sullivan, D. H. Burnham and Company

Detail of the ornament over the entrance. (*Ralph M. Line.*)

able sash of the Reliance lies in the diagonal planes of the projecting windows and at the extreme edges of the openings lying in the main wall plane. "Ten years' experience," Giedion wrote, "lies behind the understanding treatment of the horizontally proportioned 'Chicago windows.' In earlier office buildings of the Chicago school the bow windows tend somewhat to be independent and isolated parts of the design. In the Reliance Building they project no more than they are required to in order to pick up light. They are wholly incorporated into the glass body of the building."[2]

The Reliance is not, like the Crystal Palace, a passing sensation produced for an exposition. It is a utilitarian structure commissioned as an office building, and it has been actively used as such since its completion. Yet if any work of structural art in the nineteenth century anticipated the future, it is this one. The building is the triumph of the structuralist and functionalist approach of the Chicago school. In its grace and airiness, in the purity and exactitude of its proportions and details, in the brilliant perfection of its transparent elevations, it stands today as an exciting exhibition of the potential kinesthetic expressiveness of the structural art. Although it is outrageously disfigured by signs and by a "modernized" base, the essential beauty of this slim glass tower still reveals that it "has its place . . . as a witness to the best of the spirit of the nineteenth century."[3]

Burnham and Company's designs after the Reliance show a progressive departure from its bold transparency. An increasing proportion of Daniel Burnham's enormous vitality was devoted to city planning and civic art, culminating in the celebrated Chicago Plan of 1909, which was prepared in collaboration with Edward H. Bennett. Although this grand scheme is excessively concerned with what Lewis Mumford has called Baroque monumentalism, it is the first comprehensive metropolitan plan prepared for an American city, organic and three-dimensional, and it reveals several important anticipations of contemporary town planning, especially its disposition

[2] Sigfried Giedion, *Space, Time and Architecture* (Cambridge, Mass.: Harvard University Press, 1941), p. 310.

[3] *Ibid.*, p. 310. At the time that the plans for the Reliance Building were being prepared, the architects Beers, Clay and Dutton designed what appears to have been the first steel-framed residence and thus applied the techniques of Chicago construction to the private dwelling. The house, built in 1894 for W. H. Reid, was planned as a completely fireproof structure. Built on a narrow city lot, the three-story house measured 25 by 89 feet in plan. All floor and roof loads, exterior walls, walls inclosing the central octagonal light court, and stairways were carried on a frame of steel columns, girders, and joists. The floors were constructed of concrete with expanded metal reinforcing laid over arched channels between the joists. The main girders spanned the full width of 25 feet. The Reid house thus constituted a miniature replica of the new office buildings that were multiplying in the commercial core of the city. Chief among the large commissions of Beers, Clay and Dutton were the Ward Building, 14 North Michigan Avenue (1885), and the Medinah Building, at the northeast corner of Jackson Boulevard and Wells Street (1892–93).

of major traffic arteries. The most important feature is its program for the exploitation of Chicago's natural setting along the shore line of Lake Michigan. Those portions of the plan embracing the lake-front development, the interior parks and parkways, and the through diagonal arteries were in large part realized. The magnificent achievement is Lake Shore Drive and its attendant system of parks, which rank with the greatest works of civic art in the past. The drive is the concrete embodiment of Burnham's brave dictum, "Make no little plans; they have no magic to stir men's minds."

Of the architectural features proposed or actually built as intentional elements in Burnham's plan, nearly all relied on the classical tradition for their formal character. Chief among the unbuilt proposals was the enormous civic center with its associated plaza, which Burnham planned to locate at the intersection of Halsted and Congress streets. His intention was to treat the approach drive as the westward continuation of the transverse axis of Grant Park, the east end of which is the site of the Buckingham Fountain. Fortunately for the city, this monstrous scheme was never realized. The proposed location is now wholly engulfed by the fantastic interchange system of John F. Kennedy (Northwest), Dwight D. Eisenhower (Congress), and Dan Ryan expressways—brilliantly engineered but equally space-consuming and with even less civic merit. A major loss for Chicago, however, was the failure to implement Burnham's perfectly sound proposal for a true union station to be located at Roosevelt Road and Canal Street. The desert of railroad trackage that extends south of the Loop between State Street and the Sanitary and Ship Canal represents a costly sacrifice of downtown land that the city can ill afford. The valuable lesson of Washington Union Station, which is one of Burnham's planning triumphs, was lost on his own city. This special genius for the design of railroad terminals was passed to his successors—Graham, Burnham and Company and Graham, Anderson, Probst and White—and the legacy survives in their design of the Chicago Union Station (1916–25), another masterpiece of railroad planning.

The history of Burnham as an architectural entrepreneur is an impressive example of correctly gauging the new public taste in building. He knew the path to success, and he was willing to sacrifice much that he had learned from Root and his Chicago experience in order to gain it. He willingly embraced the classicism that came from the East and controlled the program of design at the World's Fair. The First National Bank Building (1896) is a typical product of the transition from the commercial to the classical style. Except for the generous window area of its central portion and the structural and functional characteristics, this building makes us feel that the Chicago school existed in vain. Indeed, by the time the First National Bank was constructed many clients had come to believe that the school had been a passing phase, an old-fashioned thing with no place in the new gilded age. This belief persisted until well into the 1930's. If one took Sullivan's embittered view, his prophecy was fulfilled—"The damage wrought by the World's Fair will last for half a century from its date."[4]

Burnham's next important commission in Chicago, the Fisher Building, shows that in some respects he was still master of the structural art in the Chicago style. Still standing at 343 South Dearborn Street, the Fisher was erected between 1895 and 1896 (Fig. 68). Its structural system is another exhibition of E. C. Shankland's technical virtuosity. The eighteen-story, 230-foot steel frame embodies the same system of portal bracing that the engineer used in the Reliance Building. The spread footings rest on 25-foot piles introduced to consolidate the bearing soil and thus raise the allowable footing pressure to 6,000 pounds per square foot. The construction rate of the Fisher surpassed that of the Reliance: the steelwork of the top thirteen and one-half stories was erected in fourteen days.

The street elevations of the Fisher Building are those of the Reliance translated into terms of Gothic ornament and pseudostructural detail. But the essentials are there—the high glass walls stretched over the angled planes of the projecting bays, the thin bands of spandrel moldings and mullions, the open and airy grace. To appreciate the Fisher Building one has to see it in the late afternoon of a winter day. The fading daylight softens the redundant ornamental detail; the lighting within transforms the wall into a glittering and transparent sheath crossed by thin horizontal and vertical lines. The smoke-laden air of the city has covered the ornament of the Fisher with a black patina, so that the building has a gloomy appearance that it does not deserve. Cleaning would do much to restore its intrinsic beauty.

The Railway Exchange Building, erected from 1903 to 1904 at the northwest corner of Michigan Avenue and Jackson Boulevard, is one of the best designs that came from the office of Burnham and Company (Fig. 69). There is in it little dependence on historical forms and fairly consistent exploitation of Chicago construction. The extensive area of glass and the clean, sharp lines form a lively expression of steel framing. Above the course separating the thirteenth and fourteenth stories, the clarity is softened and obscured. The circular openings of the top story, like those of Sullivan's Wainwright Building, are an arbitrary decoration, but they soften the transition to the abrupt horizontal line of the cornice. The precision and openness of the Reliance Building were sacrificed for the gently undulating wall of terra

[4] Louis Sullivan, *The Autobiography of an Idea* (New York: Press of the American Institute of Architects, 1922), p. 325.

cotta and glass in which the extremely restrained and delicate ornamental bands subtly enhance the pleasing sense of movement.

The Railway Exchange was the subject of a confused and unconsciously ironic, though fundamentally perceptive, article on the skyscraper by H. W. Desmond, a critic on the staff of *Architectural Record*. Desmond, who saw most of the architecture of his time as a "mass of quotations" borrowed from unrelated sources and aiming at sensation, regarded Burnham's building as a sound starting point for a rational skyscraper design, but he seems to have been unprepared to accept the logical implications of the idea and hence the validity of this particular solution.

Looking at the Railway Exchange Building, the candid mind can hardly refrain from at least asking whether the theory and practice there exemplified are entirely without merit—whether, indeed, they are not after all very much closer to a thoroughly sound starting point for the design of a skyscraper than the more pretentious methods of our school-men.

But Desmond then went on to condemn what we would now applaud.

The Railway Exchange Building is monstrously ugly, a tremendous affair of window sashes, an aggregation of bird cages, lacking structural sufficiency as a matter of design in all its parts, but especially in the basement [that is, ground floor], in the piers, in the corner abutments, in all the horizontal lines, except possibly in the crowning story where . . . the architect . . . has departed from his practical theory and has inserted a row of round windows in a solid wall. . . . No! the design is not beautiful—it is merely interesting because it is rational.[5]

Burnham, of course, was not consistent in applying his own theory to the whole building. The lobby is a work of showy classicism in which the smooth white glaze of the terra-cotta sheathing has the effect of an expertly made but inedible frosting on a cake.

The Heyworth Building, constructed in 1905 at the southwest corner of Madison Street and Wabash Avenue, is somewhat like the Railway Exchange but is colder and more rigid in its flat, sharp-angled geometry. Unusual for Burnham's classical taste is the extremely subdued ornament, which reveals a geometrized foliate pattern suggestive of the designs of Sullivan and Elmslie. As a work of architecture in the Chicago style, the Heyworth was a farewell performance for D. H. Burnham and Company. The huge Marshall Field Store, completed in four stages, 1902, 1906, 1907, and 1914, is slightly in the Chicago tradition with its cellular walls, but the massive construction of the elevations is a throwback to classical masonry forms.

Although Daniel Burnham was almost exclusively preoccupied with city planning and civic projects in the last decade of his life, his office enjoyed

[5] H. W. D[esmond], "Rationalizing the Skyscraper," *Architectural Record*, XVII (May, 1905), 423.

an immense volume of major architectural commissions. After 1900 the administration of this designing corporation was in the hands of his chief partner, Ernest Robert Graham, who had joined the firm of Burnham and Root in 1888. When Daniel Burnham died in 1912, Graham, together with Burnham's sons, Hubert and Daniel, founded the organization of Graham, Burnham and Company. On the departure of Burnham's sons in 1917, the enterprising Graham established what was probably the most productive firm in the history of American architecture—Graham, Anderson, Probst and White, a corporation still in existence under the same title. The legacy of Daniel Burnham and his classical enthusiasm died with Ernest Graham in 1936.

CHAPTER VII

HOLABIRD AND ROCHE

In the long period of their practice, in the number and excellence of their buildings, in the consistency and uniformity of their designs, William Holabird and Martin Roche most completely represented the purpose and the achievement of the mainstream of the Chicago school. Individual buildings of Sullivan and Root are superior to anything they did; yet they discovered the simplest utilitarian and structural solutions to the problems of the big urban office block, and out of these solutions they developed a perfectly rational and standardized form adaptable with minor variations to the conditions imposed by the commercial structure in a crowded urban area. Early in their practice Holabird and Roche knew that they were on the right path, and they followed it with undeviating persistence. One of the consequences of this was that the original principles of the Chicago school survived longer in their work than in that of any other architect.

William Holabird was born in American Union, New York, in 1854. Two years at the United States Military Academy (1873–75) provided him with all the formal education that he received for his profession. He resigned from West Point over disciplinary action taken against him for aiding a sick friend—an act of charity that probably involved some minor infraction of the rules. He moved to Chicago in 1875 and decided, apparently with little previous thought, to become an architect. He acquired the best training he could have received by entering Jenney's office as a draftsman shortly after he arrived in the city. He formed a partnership with Ossian C. Simonds (1855–1931) in 1880 and expanded it to Holabird, Simonds and Roche in 1881. Two years later the firm became Holabird and Roche, which partnership survived until 1927. Forty-five years of unbroken success followed the establishment of the office.

Martin Roche, who was born in Cleveland in 1855, moved to Chicago with his family in 1857. He entered Jenney's office in 1872, shortly after completing his public-school education. There is little material on his early career, but he probably remained with Jenney's firm until joining the partnership of Simonds and Holabird in 1881. His role in the office was that of codesigner specializing in interior work. The whole program of design, however, was often divided equally between the two men until the number of commissions made necessary the organization of a large staff.

Holabird and Roche approached the problem of the commercial building in much the same objective, empirical, and businesslike way as Jenney did. Yet not only were they responsible for many structural and utilitarian innovations, but they also succeeded in developing the most effective architectonic expression of steel framing up to Sullivan's Carson Pirie Scott Store. The record of their commissions from 1883 to 1886 is meager, but their first great achievement, the Tacoma Building, undoubtedly marked a bold and unprecedented plunge into the new system of Chicago construction.

The characteristic originality and imagination of the Chicago school entered vigorously into the design of the Tacoma (Fig. 70). Holabird and Roche received the commission in 1886; the construction began two years later and was completed in 1889. The building stood on the northeast corner of La Salle and Madison streets until 1929, when it was demolished to make way for the present skyscraper known as Number One North La Salle. The Tacoma was the pride of the Chicago school in many ways, both structural and formal. Like the best work of Jenney, it represented the rational and realistic expression of a systematic scientific attack on the problems of construction and functional design.

The technical innovations were numerous. The foundations, both in type and construction, were at that time unique. Before excavation the builder made 50-foot test borings to determine the character of the subsoil. This preliminary investigation revealed the presence of several pockets filled with water and soft clay. These were excavated or pumped out and filled with concrete, which was forced in under pressure, or grouted in, as the process is commonly known. This method of soil stabilization is now used extensively not only to provide proper support for the foundations of buildings, bridges, and dams but also to fill soft spots in railway and highway embankments. The column footings of the Tacoma were floating rafts of concrete, 18 inches thick, reinforced with I-beams. The footings under the north wall of the building were used to support the party wall of the adjacent structure.[1]

The floor, roof, and wind loads of the Tacoma were divided between the frame, the brick walls of the inner elevations (opposite the streets), and two interior brick walls. The designing engineer of this mixture of old and new techniques was Carl Seiffert. The skeleton of the building included all the structural metals in use at the time—cast iron, wrought iron, and Bessemer steel. The spandrel beams and floor girders were wrought iron,

[1] The precautions taken with the Tacoma foundations were apparently insufficient to deal fully with the problem. When it was demolished in 1929, the wrecker discovered that the building leaned 11¾ inches out of plumb to the east.

the intermediate floor beams were steel, and all columns, mullions, and lintels were cast iron. The structural frame was the first to be erected by riveting and thus marked a great improvement in the speed and efficiency of construction. The disposition of framing members was unusual in one respect: the spandrel beams were anchored in the brick piers; the deep wrought-iron girders, on the other hand, spanned the bays from column to column, and the steel floor beams spanned between the girders in the usual way to carry the floor slab. Seiffert's intention apparently was to treat the framing system of each floor as an independent unit separate from the supporting beams of the curtain wall, probably to avoid internal buckling as a consequence of unequal settlement. Even more unusual was the presence of two transverse interior brick walls extending from foundation to roof and stiffened by diagonal reinforcing rods to carry part of the internal floor and roof loads and to provide rigidity against wind loads.

In its functional characteristics the Tacoma was one of the most advanced designs of its time. The L-shaped plan made possible an outer exposure for all offices. The floors rested on fireproof hollow-tile arches spanning between the steel joists, and all columns were completely incased in fireproof tile. For the first time in a large commercial building, all toilet and lavatory facilities were concentrated in a small area of two central floors, thus making it possible to minimize piping and to centralize it in a single service shaft. The projecting bays of the Tacoma were the product of careful study, through which the architects discovered the multiple value of such projections. The primary advantage was the admission of light from three directions. Second, they were useful in warm weather in catching the breeze blowing parallel to the building elevation. Third, they broke up the direct wind load and thus reduced lateral forces on the wall area. And finally, they had a distinct aesthetic value in their reflection of light in several directions and in increasing the sense of lightness and openness evoked by the great area of glass disposed in several planes. The well-integrated handling of the projecting bay, along with the extensive transparent area, gave the Tacoma its most striking architectonic quality. As we shall see, the architects employed this feature repeatedly in subsequent designs and always with great skill.

The basic form of the Tacoma was repeated by Holabird and Roche in three framed buildings—the Caxton, the Monadnock addition, and the Pontiac—erected shortly after the completion of their first major work. The first was the Caxton Building, 508 South Dearborn Street, which was constructed between 1889 and 1890 (Fig. 71). The bay-wide openings of the base, the projecting windows, the narrow openings grouped in the trapezoidal projections, and the brick and terra-cotta sheathing were used in this twelve-story structure approximately as they were in its more famous predecessor. The rich ornament of the Tacoma's top story, however, gave way in the newer building to a very simple treatment in which the windows lie in the primary wall plane. The Caxton was wrecked in 1947 as part of the extensive clearance necessary for the construction of Congress Parkway.

The commission for the south addition of the Monadnock (then Katahdin) Building was awarded to Holabird and Roche by Peter Brooks in February, 1892. The plans for the new block were completed in the summer of that year, after some hesitancy on the part of Brooks over steel construction (very likely the cost), and the building was extended south along Dearborn Street to Van Buren in 1893 (Fig. 72). The fact that the extension is a framed structure is apparent in the very wide openings of the base and in the relatively large area of glass compared with that of the original portion.[2] The structural system is a seventeen-story wind-braced steel skeleton with Z-bar columns resting on spread concrete footings reinforced with I-beams. The designing engineer was Corydon T. Purdy, who later achieved a national reputation as the structural engineer for a number of famous Chicago and New York skyscrapers. The entire east wall of the original Monadnock and the easternmost line of columns of the 1893 addition now rest on concrete caissons extending to hardpan, an alteration necessitated by the construction of the Dearborn Street subway in 1940. The walls were temporarily supported on hydraulic jacks during this operation.

In the elevations of the Monadnock addition we again see the narrow windows closely ranked in the projecting bays. Except for the heavy cornice, the arcade at the top story, and the sharp differentiation of the base from the main building mass, the extension is in general proportions and disposition of major elements like Burnham and Root's north half. Outer exposure for all offices in the Monadnock is made possible by the narrow slablike form of the entire block.

An unusual variation of the wall pattern first developed by Holabird and Roche appears in the Pontiac Building, erected in 1891 at 542 South Dearborn Street, where it still stands (Fig. 73). Instead of the usual projections whose individual width was limited to that of one bay, the architects here extended the wall outward in two wide projections, each spanning two bays. The projection at the center of each of the street elevations is conventional in form. No special functional requirement dictated this treatment, which gives the illusion of increasing the glass area of the wall. The Pontiac, like the Caxton and the Monadnock addition, shows a failure to exploit the steel frame to full utilitarian and formal advantage. The individual windows are small, and between the groups of openings, the envelope of the frame is solid brick throughout the height of the building. Shortly after the construction of

[2] For Burnham and Root's Monadnock, see pp. 65–69.

the Pontiac, however, Holabird and Roche took the decisive step in the architectonic revelation of steel framing in the design of the Marquette Building.

Later structures of the architects are clearer and more refined than the Marquette, but it is the point of departure for all of them. Peter Brooks was again the sponsor, and the letters that passed between him and Owen Aldis indicate that the plans were prepared in the spring and summer of 1893, when economic depression offered the possibility of reduced building costs, and that construction began in September of the same year. It was in connection with the preliminary planning of the Marquette that Aldis laid down the fundamental principles of the design and profitable management of a first-class office building, and they have been followed with variations to suit changing techniques and practices ever since.

First: The office building that gives up the most for light and air is the best investment.

Second: Second-class space costs as much to build and operate as first-class space. Therefore, build no second-class space.

Third: The parts every person entering sees must make the lasting impression. Entrance, first story lobby, elevator cabs, elevator service, public corridors, toilet rooms must be very good.

Fourth: Generally, office space should be about 24 feet from good light.

Fifth: Operating expenses must be constantly born in mind. Use proper materials and details to simplify the work.

Sixth: Carefully consider and provide for changes in location of corridor doors, partitions, light, plumbing and telephones.

Seventh: Arrange typical layout for intensive use. A large number of small tenants is more desirable than large space for large tenants because:

(a) A higher rate per square foot can be added for small tenants.

(b) They do not move in a body and leave the building with a large vacant space when hard times hit.

(c) They do not swamp your elevators by coming and going by the clock.

Eighth: Upkeep of an office building is most important. Janitor service must be of high quality, elevator operators of good personality, management progressive.[3]

The prescription was scrupulously followed in the case of the Marquette, which has been fully occupied and carefully maintained to this day.

The Marquette Building was completed in 1894 at 140 South Dearborn Street, where it stands in first-class condition, still one of the foremost office buildings of the Loop (Fig. 74). The steel frame of the sixteen-story structure, designed by the engineers Purdy and Henderson, includes Z-bar col-

[3] Quoted in Earle Shultz and Walter Simmons, *Offices in the Sky* (Indianapolis: Bobbs-Merrill Co., 1959 [copyright held by the National Association of Building Owners and Managers]), pp. 33–34.

umns of two-story length arranged so as to stagger the joints. The chief precedent for the exterior form of the Marquette is Jenney's Sears Roebuck Store. But Holabird and Roche turned away from the narrow openings and relatively heavy mullions of Jenney's buildings and their own earlier work to open the whole bay into a great horizontal sweep of glass. The so-called Chicago windows of the base and the narrow continuous piers standing out from the recessed spandrels became the distinguishing marks of nearly every office block designed by Holabird and Roche in the next fifteen years.

The plan of the Marquette is shaped approximately like a capital E (Fig. 75). The long elevation on Dearborn Street corresponds to the vertical line of the letter; the two wings extending respectively along Adams Street and the alley to the north are the upper and lower crossbars. A short, wide extension in the center between the two wings is the tongue of the E. The offices are disposed in a single row along Dearborn Street and in double rows along the two wings. Thus every office has a maximum exposure to natural light. The middle extension, relatively the darkest part of the building, is the elevator lobby around which the elevators are grouped in a spreading U. One valuable consequence of this careful planning is an extraordinary generosity of space in the elevator lobbies, in welcome contrast to the miserly planning of this area that has been the usual practice throughout the history of the elevator building. The first-floor lobby of the Marquette is surrounded by a mezzanine balcony the parapet of which is covered with brightly colored mosaics depicting scenes in the history of Chicago. The floor planning of the entire building is a model of functional design and has rarely been improved on in the subsequent history of commercial architecture.

The street elevations of the Marquette set it off from all its predecessors. The windows are long rectangular openings extending throughout the width of the bays. Most of them are divided into four openings separated by mullions so thin as to be almost unnoticeable. The sash in the two center divisions is fixed; that at the ends is movable. The true Chicago window appears in the base or first two stories. Here a very long, horizontally disposed, single pane of glass is flanked at either side by narrow sliding sash. This treatment of the windows not only allowed the maximum admission of light and the necessary quantity of outdoor air but also made possible the full and uninhibited expression of steel framing. The general impression of the street elevations of the Marquette is that of a pattern of large transparent areas set in narrow frames of piers and spandrels. The wall is a nearly uniform array of rectangular cells vigorously expressing the steel cage they cover. The deep reveals and the unusually fine proportions give the Marquette an incisive and dynamic quality that raises it to the level of superior architecture in any style.

There are architectonic defects in the building, lingering elements of misguided traditionalism that often appeared in the best Chicago work when the architects were striving for a monumental effect. The most obvious, perhaps, is the arbitrary horizontal division of the street elevations into the base-shaft-capital sequence: the two stories respectively at the base and the top are sharply set off from the twelve intermediate stories. The decorative treatment is redundant and hence obscures rather than enhances the structural and functional unity of the building. A further denial of the building's essential character exists in the enlarged width of the piers and the rustication of the brick envelope at the corner bays. The base and top, together with the corner bays, thus appear to inclose the entire façade in a heavy masonry frame devoid of any organic connection with the structural system of the building. The same treatment originally existed on the Adams Street elevation, but the later addition of the west bay (1905) upsets the symmetry and causes the decorative terra cotta and brickwork to appear even more inorganic.

But the virtues of the Marquette are so fine and many that we should hardly want to make an issue out of its superficial defects. The whole quality of the building is impressive: the wide, smooth expanse of glass transforms the big elevations into graceful patterns of light; the openings are perfectly scaled and proportioned; and the deep reveals give a powerful statement to the steel cage on which the walls are carried. The Marquette is a striking integration of technical necessities with their aesthetic statement.

The subsequent work of Holabird and Roche in the last decade of the nineteenth century reveals, with one exception, a systematic refinement and clarification of the fundamental form of the Marquette Building. The exception is interesting in several respects, however, and deserves separate mention before we proceed to more typical structures. The Old Colony Building is an unusual and arresting combination of elements developed by its own architects and engineers and by others who preceded them (Figs. 76, 77). The Old Colony was erected between 1893 and 1894 at 407 South Dearborn Street, one door removed from Jenney's Manhattan Building, which appears at the right edge of both illustrations.

The construction of the building was plagued by difficulties arising from inequalities of settlement and party wall problems. It was the original intention of the architects to use the north wall of the small building immediately to the south as a party wall with a joint footing (the neighbor is a narrow seven-story structure standing between the Old Colony and the Manhattan). Before the plans of the newer building were prepared, Adler and Sullivan signed a statement to the effect that the wall in question was strong enough for any building likely to be put up in the foreseeable future on that site. This rash assertion was apparently based on an inadequate investigation of the load concentrations of a high framed building, for it proved to be almost disastrously wrong. The footing of the party wall turned out to be wholly inadequate, and shortly after the beginning of construction of the Old Colony, the wall settled so far out of plumb that three stories above grade it leaned over the Old Colony lot line. The only feasible solution was the one that had been used four years earlier for the neighboring Manhattan: the south line of columns had to be carried on cantilevers anchored to the columns of the adjacent line. But the solution in this case brought more trouble: because of extremely high load concentrations on the second line of columns, the south end of the long, narrow building settled more than the north end. The designers called in as a consultant the bridge engineer William Sooy Smith, who solved the problem by jacking up the south end and introducing four hardpan caissons under the column footings at the anchor ends of the cantilevers, in this way equalizing the settlement at 4 $^3/_{16}$ inches all around.[4]

The framing system of the seventeen-story Old Colony is another exhibition of the engineering skill of Corydon T. Purdy. The skeleton is a curious mixture of the novel and the relatively old and well tried in iron-framed construction. The columns of the frame are wrought-iron Phoenix columns, which had been used for thirty years in American building.[5] The girders and floor beams, on the other hand, are steel members. The most impressive structural feature of the Old Colony is the system of windbracing, in this case a type of portal bracing in which the main girder is joined to the column by means of a deep fillet, thus giving the girder an archlike soffit (Figs. 78, 79). The resulting complex of the two columns and the horizontal member is in effect a rigid frame.[6] This elaborate system of bracing was dictated by the high,

[4] William Sooy Smith was one of the foremost bridge engineers of his day. He had a long series of major structures to his credit, but he was primarily known as the chief engineer of the first steel truss bridge in the United States, the Missouri River span of the Chicago and Alton Railroad at Glasgow, Missouri (1878–79). Smith had initially recommended caissons in building construction for Adler and Sullivan's Stock Exchange Building (see pp. 136–37. In 1947 hardpan caissons were introduced under the west column footings of the Old Colony in connection with the extension of the Dearborn Street subway south of Van Buren Street.

[5] The Phoenix column was invented in 1862 by Samuel Reeves of the Phoenix Iron Company, Phoenixville, Pennsylvania. It was a built-up member of four or eight flanged segments (like barrel staves) bolted together through the longitudinal flanges. Cross sections appear at the bottom of Fig. 79. Remarkable examples of the Phoenix column were used in the Garrick Theater Building (see pp. 128–29).

[6] I have not discovered any record of the previous use of portal arches of this kind in American building, but the portal frames of railway truss bridges may again have provided the precedent. The Old Colony may very well represent the initial application of the form to building frames. By far the most extensive example of arched portal bracing in the United States is the frame of the fifty-five-story Woolworth Building in New York (1911–13).

123

narrow, slablike form of the building, open on four sides, and by the absence of masonry bearing walls, which, as in the case of the Monadnock, provide some rigidity.

The standard paired openings and the continuous piers of the Old Colony are features common to many of the buildings of Burnham and Root and the earlier ones of Holabird and Roche. The cylindrical projections at the corners, forming the most striking characteristic of the building, are reminiscent of the pavilions that Root introduced at the corners of the Great Northern Hotel. The continuous piers of the long elevation produce an unobtrusive vertical accent. This is reversed in the narrow north elevation, where the continuous sills and lintels of the separate window groups provide a marked horizontality. One can see that the architects were attempting to contract the apparent width of the long elevations and to expand that of the narrow. The high slablike form again makes possible an outer exposure for all offices. The only disfiguring element of this otherwise dignified and well-proportioned building is the ridiculous colonnade at the fifteenth and sixteenth stories.

After the Pontiac and the Old Colony, Holabird and Roche rapidly developed a standardized form for the office building based on the design of the Marquette. From their drafting tables came one building after another, each almost identical with its predecessor. A single general description serves to cover the fundamental characteristics of all of them. The street elevations are cellular walls of large rectangular openings with the long dimension horizontal, each opening of glass filling the entire bay. The piers are almost invariably continuous, the spandrel panels generally recessed to the point of being nearly flush with the windows. Piers and spandrels are always much narrower than those of the Marquette. Chicago windows are common, but the narrow grouped openings separated by extremely tenuous mullions sometimes appear. Uniformity from end to end and from second story to top came to replace the decorative variations of the Marquette. This simplified treatment of the elevations, as we have seen in the case of the Marquette, answered the functional requirements of light and air and at the same time honestly and effectively expressed the structural system of steel framing.

The original Champlain Building, constructed in 1894 at the northwest corner of State and Madison streets, was typical of the large office blocks. Its fifteen stories were a succession of Chicago windows bounded by the terracotta sheathing of the slim piers and spandrels. The Champlain suffered the most outrageous premature demolition of all Chicago office buildings. It was razed in 1916—its twenty-second year—to make way for the extension of the Boston Store, a much larger building designed by the same architects.[7]

[7] For the Boston Store, see p. 175.

Especially refined examples of the later work of Holabird and Roche are the two little buildings at 24 and 30 South Michigan Avenue, which form, with Sullivan's façade immediately north of them, the three buildings of the Gage group (Figs. 80, 81). Construction of the first two was completed in 1898. The "modern" store fronts, appearing in the second illustration, are vulgarizations grossly inferior to the fine sweep of glass that originally characterized the base of these buildings. Their frank clarity and exactitude are the products of uniformity of treatment, the reduction of decorative detail to narrow moldings, and the presence of the big Chicago windows in the small façades.

A return to the paired standard openings recessed from the continuous piers marks the Williams Building (1898), at 205 West Monroe Street (Fig. 82). The sharp angle of the photograph obscures the unusually light and open quality of the façade. A building very much like the Williams was erected at 320 South Franklin Street in 1898, but it has been demolished. The former Cable Building (later the Hoops), at the southeast corner of Wabash Avenue and Jackson Boulevard, was completed in 1899 (Figs. 83, 84). Here the Chicago window was replaced by a group of four narrow openings of sliding sash separated by thin mullions. A suggestion of the Marquette was apparent in the way the heavy corner piers and the cornice enframed the otherwise light and graceful elevations. An unusual feature of the Cable were the continuous openings at the first and second stories.

The Cable Building was demolished in 1960 to 1961 to make way for the twenty-two-story addition to the Continental Companies Building, which fronts on Michigan Avenue. Since it was the first of four victims to the wave of destruction that hit Chicago architecture at the end of that year, the city and various professional societies acted quickly to save what they could of its appearance and structural character. In November, 1960, the city's Commission on Architectural Landmarks and the Chicago chapters of the American Institute of Architects and the Society of Architectural Historians cooperated to preserve portions of the Cable's rich spandrel ornament and the beaded work on the piers and sills at the second story (Fig. 84). The various societies involved in this enterprise believed that this was the first time an American city acted to preserve a physical fragment of its architectural heritage. At the same time Richard Nickel made his customary painstaking photographic record of the interior and exterior of the building, and the Landmarks Commission and the architects of the new Continental Building, C. F. Murphy Associates, assembled for preservation the original plans and the data on the genesis, construction, and subsequent history of the building. It is questionable whether the architecture of the Chicago school can survive an expanding economy, but it seems at least likely to become the best re-corded phase of our building history.[8]

The former McClurg (now Crown) Building, at 218 South Wabash Ave-nue, was erected between 1899 and 1900 (Fig. 85). This is an extraordinary example of how far Chicago architects could go in reducing the wide-bayed cellular wall to a pattern of mere lines. The presence of fluting on the knife-edged piers heightens the tenuousness of these members.

When we examine the work of Holabird and Roche in the twentieth cen-tury, we shall see a continuation of the same characteristics we have noted here.[9] The uniformity of their work is so striking that with little familiarity one can pick out their designs all over the Loop and adjacent blocks. Some critics have complained that, after the Marquette, their buildings reveal a monotonous repetition of a hackneyed formula. But those critics fail to appreciate the value of a true standard in architecture—that is, a basic norm or type exactly developed to fit a particular set of conditions and repeated wherever those conditions exist. Radical deviations from a formula that represents an adequate generalization would be mere caprice or illogicality. The work of Holabird and Roche is not sterile repetition; it represents de-tailed variations within the achievement of a stable form. It is to their credit that they rendered unnecessary a fresh act of imagination with every com-mission. Imagination and individual expression are vital to a living culture, but we should remember with Whitehead that "civilization [also] advances by extending the number of important operations which we can perform with-out thinking about them."[10]

[8] For a discussion of the general economic and historical problem of the preservation of American commercial architecture, see the discussion of the Garrick Theater Building, pp. 128–35.

[9] For the buildings of Holabird and Roche erected after 1900, see pp. 174–77.

[10] Alfred North Whitehead, *Introduction to Mathematics* (New York: Oxford University Press, 1948), p. 42.

CHAPTER VIII

ADLER AND SULLIVAN

Adler and Sullivan's first commission involving the use of complete iron and steel framing was the Wainwright Building in St. Louis, constructed in 1890 to 1891 (Fig. 86). This structure represents Sullivan's deliberate and most thorough attempt to create a special form appropriate to the multistory office block. We have already noted the long preparation for this celebrated design, beginning with the Rothschild Store among his own works and undoubtedly extending back to the mid-century in the vernacular buildings of Philadelphia that he very likely knew during his apprenticeship with Frank Furness.[1] The Wainwright represents the outcome of exactly the kind of sympathetic association between client and architect within which Sullivan's peculiar genius could flourish best. The building was commissioned by Ellis Wainwright, a wealthy St. Louis brewer who was a collector of painting and sculpture and something of an avant-gardist with a wide range of aesthetic tastes. It was an opportunity made for Sullivan's hand, and the resulting design left the earlier Chicago buildings and their possible Philadelphia ancestry far behind. As Hugh Morrison wrote:

It was the first true skyscaper built by Adler and Sullivan, and the surety, the justness, the completeness of this first attempt at solving a new architectural problem are astounding evidences of Sullivan's creative imagination and power of design. In the architectural world it was like an Athena sprung full-fledged from the brow of Zeus; the problem had been solved, a new need had called forth a new form.[2]

All the new technical elements that had become standard features of the Chicago office building are present in the ten-story Wainwright, for the first time in the Sullivan canon—the raft footings of reinforced concrete, the braced and riveted steel frame, the wall bays carried on spandrel shelf angles, the fireproof-tile covering of all structural members, movable interior partitions. Above the skylighted ground floor, the U-shaped plan provides an outer exposure for all offices. The formal and functional program derived

[1] For Sullivan's early work and the Philadelphia background, see pp. 37–42.

[2] Hugh Morrison, *Louis Sullivan: Prophet of Modern Architecture* (New York: W. W. Norton & Co., 1935), pp. 144–45.

from the structural basis and utilitarian demands had clearly been grasped by Sullivan in all its essentials.[3] The first requirement was to open the ground floor as fully as possible by using the entire area of the bay as a continuous window, while at the same time clearly stating the structural character of the building through the sharply defined envelopes of the columns and spandrel girders. This formal element, of course, was by 1890 part of a well-developed Chicago tradition. Above the base rises a succession of identical stories, terminating in an attic of mechanical utilities topped by the horizontal plane of the roof. For Sullivan, the potential aesthetic quality of the tall building lay in its unusual height, and it was this that he seized on to provide the expression of his intense personal feeling.

The particular device that he used to secure this expression was the system of closely ranked pierlike bands that give the street elevations their forceful vertical thrust. In order to emphasize the verticality to the maximum degree, he placed false piers between each pair of true piers, or envelopes of the wall columns. The result is a building with a strong, vigorously articulated base supporting a screen that constitutes a vivid image of powerful upward movement. The recessed spandrels, the intricate but flat and well-controlled ornament, and the warm red color of the brick give a rich texture to the plastic form. This personal treatment of the elevations in a sculptural way reveals Sullivan's feeling for the tall building to be strictly subjective and somewhat at odds with what one might call the more neutral and empirical character of the main body of Chicago work. His approach might be characterized as the higher functionalism of psychological as well as utilitarian statement. The major progress of the Chicago school lay in the direction of an articulated wall that expresses the structural facts of interior framing. The classic statement of this intention is Sullivan's Carson Pirie Scott Store, but a variety of experiments in form lay between the vertical movement of the Wainwright and the balanced structural articulation of the Carson building.[4]

The building in Chicago that stands closest in outward form to the Wainwright is the old Schiller Building, later the Garrick Theater, constructed between 1891 and 1892 at 64 West Randolph Street (Figs. 5, 87). Once again it is Adler's engineering skill that arrests our attention to almost the same extent as Sullivan's artistry. The familiar raft foundations of concrete were laid on huge grills of oak timbers supported in turn by eight hundred 50-foot timber piles driven to refusal in hardpan clay. The system was proposed by

[3] Sullivan later elaborated the principles of skyscraper design in a now classic source document in the history of the modern movement, "The Tall Office Building Artistically Considered," *Lippincott's Magazine*, LVII (March, 1896), 403–9.

[4] For a discussion of the subjective basis underlying Sullivan's treatment of the large urban building, see pp. 167–73. For a detailed analysis of the Wainwright, see Morrison, *op. cit.*, pp. 144–56.

William Sooy Smith, consultant in the design of the Garrick. The piling represents a forward step toward the true caisson foundation, which appeared for the first time in the Stock Exchange Building in 1893. Massive built-up girders on the footings of the Garrick Theater were cantilevered beyond the wall line to support the street columns of the building, and cantilevered footings at the sides carried party walls.

Above the foundations rose a complex braced frame of steel columns and beams to carry the office spaces and of iron ribs, hangers, and steel trusses of two-story depth to support the segmental vault over the theater and the office block above it. The most remarkable elements of the frame were the four Phoenix columns 93 feet high that carried the brick walls rising from the level of the rigging loft above the stage. The crown of the theater vault was level with the seventh floor, whereas the top of the rigging loft was at the eighth-floor plane (Fig. 88). Although the combination theater and office building followed the precedent of the Auditorium, the general form of the Garrick was unique among Sullivan's designs. The plan was shaped like the letter T with very short cross bars. The seventeen-story central tower was flanked by two nine-story wings. In back of the tower, corresponding to the stem of the T, was a fourteen-story wing. By means of this plan Sullivan was able to provide at least one outdoor exposure for every office and to admit some light into the offices along the long side elevations by setting these walls back a short distance from the walls of adjacent buildings. The disposition of the tower and flanking wings of the Garrick made it the first skyscraper to be designed on the setback principle, not only to admit light to its own interior enclosures, but also to prevent wall-to-wall building in solid blocks along a crowded urban street.

The entire ground floor of the building was taken up by the entrance lobby and the theater. The upper gallery extended to the fifth floor. The offices occupied the floors above the theater, the flanking wings on Randolph Street, and a narrow space above the lobby, between the theater and the street. The Garrick was originally built for a German theatrical society and once contained clubrooms and dining facilities. The theater proper, later devoted to movies and then to television broadcasts, was another good example of the workmanship and the fluent artistry that went into the Auditorium. The richly ornamented ceiling was again a series of expanding segmental vaults extending from the proscenium on the north to the forward edge of the balcony (Figs. 89, 90). Vision was unobstructed; acoustics were near perfect; scale and spatial relationships were exactly calculated to give a sense of intimacy while preserving the necessary spaciousness of a large theater. The Garrick was easily the best theater in Chicago after the Auditorium; indeed, as a movie house its only competitor was the Esquire Theatre on Oak Street.

129

The central and commanding feature of the Garrick Theater Building was the tower. This remarkable example of Sullivan's restless individualism stemmed in part from the Auditorium. The walls were a series of narrow piers extending to the sixteenth story, where they were joined by full-centered arches. Their slenderness and height, however, indicated that Sullivan's precedent was in greater part the Wainwright Building rather than the Auditorium, although without the Wainwright's false piers. Sullivan's intention in the Garrick Theater was to make of it "the proud and soaring thing" that he thought the tall building ought to be. He did everything to strengthen the upward sweep—it was "cast in one jet," as he described it. It was a superbly integrated and complex composition in both its exterior form and its rich interior ornament, the whole treated with a delicacy and a finish that seemed strangely out of place among the structures of Jenney and Holabird, and even Root at his most ornamental.

The details of the Garrick were perhaps questionable for a work of large-scale commercial architecture, although they were becoming to a theater. A highly ornamented arcade extended across the entire façade at the second story. A deep overhanging roof slab, or block-like cornice, incrusted with foliate ornament, sharply arrested the upward motion of the central shaft. This extraordinary cornice was replaced by an ugly parapet in 1948 (Fig. 87). The scale was exactly worked out for equal emphasis of the ornamentation at the base and the roof line. The total impression was one of elongated height circumscribed by an exuberant architectural lyricism. The Garrick Theater was an almost exotic exhibition of plastic and ornamental virtuosity, an arresting expression of its creator's inner feelings and his emotional response to the potentialities of urban building form.[5]

In May, 1960, the Balaban and Katz Corporation, owners of the Garrick Theater property at the time, decided to demolish the badly deteriorated and disfigured building and to replace it with a parking garage. The subsequent heroic but futile effort to save Sullivan's unique masterpiece brought to a focus for the first time all the factors involved in the formidable problem of preserving distinguished architectural works in the United States and at the same time provided lively evidence of the place of the Chicago achievement in the public consciousness. The city's Commission on Architectural Landmarks, implementing an ordinance of February 11, 1960, had awarded plaques to thirty-eight Chicago buildings, among them the Garrick. As a consequence of this award and the resulting public interest in the building, what would have been a routine request for a wrecking permit rapidly developed

---

[5] A vertical pattern with the piers joined at the top story by an arcade, like the main elevation of the Garrick Theater Building, appears in Sullivan's Bayard (later Condict) Building in New York (1897–98)—the Chicago school's only invasion of the eastern city.

into a political and legal issue with ever widening ramifications. On May 28, 1960, Alderman Leon M. Despres introduced a resolution into the City Council urging Mayor Richard J. Daley to defer issuance of a demolition permit to allow time to find means of saving the building. Mayor Daley, whose administrations were committed to one of the largest public building and redevelopment programs ever undertaken, quickly complied. The result was easily predictable: on June 1 the Balaban and Katz Corporation sued the city to compel it to issue the permit. The successive judicial decisions in this protracted case provide a concise summary of the issues involved, although they did not offer a solution to the fundamental problem.[6]

The suit between the corporation and the city reached the Superior Court on July 30. Arthur Goldberg, counsel for Balaban and Katz, argued that the city had no legal right to deny the wrecking permit. Judge Donald S. McKinlay was clearly sympathetic to the idea of preserving good building, and on August 23 he handed down a crucial decision that may constitute a landmark in legal issues of this kind. He ruled that the city could not be forced to issue the wrecking permit, that the city was not acting illegally or arbitrarily, and that aesthetic merit is a proper basis for protecting a building or any other landmark. He cited a unanimous decision of the United States Supreme Court, written by Justice William O. Douglas: "The conception of the public welfare is broad and inclusive. The values it represents are spiritual as well as physical, aesthetic as well as monetary. It is within the power of the legis-

---

[6] The municipal resolutions and the legal controversy were paralleled by an astonishing outburst of activity on the part of interested citizens. It began on May 28, 1960, when radio station WFMT broadcast a panel discussion in which the participants outlined the problem, urged preservation, and proposed various ways to make this possible. Early in the following month several enthusiasts led by the architectural photographer Richard Nickel formed the Chicago Heritage Committee to work out a program for the salvation of the Garrick and other threatened buildings. On June 8 the committee members and their associates picketed the building and secured thirty-three hundred signatures on a petition urging the municipal government to prevent the wrecking of the landmark. This action was a major factor in Mayor Daley's decision to hold public hearings on the question in the Council chambers on June 18, 1960. About a dozen people testified in favor of preservation and offered nearly as many ideas for its continued use (chief among them were dramatic productions, musical concerts and recitals, and adult-education programs). None of these proposals was the result of systematic planning, and none could be expected to raise the $1,500,000 that was then fixed as the minimum cost for rehabilitation of the building. Mayor Daley appointed a committee of fourteen to determine the feasibility of preservation, but in spite of the fact that the members included Augustine J. Bowe, Judge of the Municipal Court, and Ira J. Bach, Commissioner of City Planning, the committee had no success in finding a viable solution. A last-minute request for a grant from the Ford Foundation was denied. A second Council hearing, on August 17, 1960, produced a potentially more useful proposal, although again not one that could meet the immediate problem posed by the Garrick Theater. Alderman Despres pointed out that the threatened demolition of the building had become an international issue and urged that the federal government adopt a national policy, such as exists in France and Italy, for preserving fine works of architecture.

lature to determine that the community should be beautiful as well as healthy, spacious as well as clean, well balanced as well as carefully patrolled." Judge McKinlay added that the Garrick case was the first he knew in which "aesthetic and cultural values could be considered by a municipality under the police power." He pointed out that "under the Urban Redevelopment Act the city may consider whether 'faulty arrangement or design' is a detriment to the community." He concluded that "the [Supreme Court] might well decide that aesthetic, artistic and cultural values to the public could be considered not only in clearing a slum, but in preserving a landmark."[7] His final decision, of course, upheld the city, with the result that Balaban and Katz appealed to a higher court.

The case reached the Illinois Appellate Court in the fall, and on November 22, 1960, Justice James R. Bryant, taking a strictly legal and realistic view of the matter, ruled against the city and gave the Municipal Council fifty-five days in which to file an appeal with the State Supreme Court. The city realized that the case was hopeless and accepted the appellate decision as final. Justice Bryant's finding was based on the unassailable ground that the city had not worked out a definite plan for the preservation of the building and the adequate reimbursement of the building's owners. He recognized the injustice of the delay to the owners and realized that the situation had not in fact moved beyond the starting point of the problem. "In this case," he wrote, "there is no official action pending. There is but a bare expectation of a fortuitous development in the remote future. . . . It is laudable to attempt to preserve a landmark. However, it becomes unconscionable when an unwilling private party is required to bear the expense."[8] Time had run out on the Garrick close to its seventieth anniversary: on January 5, 1961, Mayor Daley announced that neither the city nor any private organization could raise the $5,000,000 then estimated as the cost of full restoration and ordered that the wrecking permit be issued. Demolition began on January 9 and was completed by the summer of 1961. The contract between Balaban and Katz and the Atlas Wrecking Company, however, contained a possibly unique provision. The wrecker was required to co-operate with a number of public and professional organizations to salvage representative samples of the building's interior and exterior ornament. In this way about three hundred pieces of plaster and terra-cotta work have been preserved, the consequence of a co-operative program established by the Balaban and Katz Corporation, a temporary Joint Preservation Committee, the Commission on Architectural

[7] All quotations from Ruth Moore, "Garrick Building Is Spared Again," *Chicago Sun-Times*, August 24, 1960, p. 3.

[8] Quoted in Ruth Moore, "Court Orders Garrick Razing Permit," *Chicago Sun-Times*, November 23, 1960, p. 3.

Landmarks, and the Chicago chapters of the American Institute of Architects and the Society of Architectural Historians.[9]

The practical exigencies involved in attempts to preserve a large building in a badly deteriorated condition and the legal issues arising from compensation to the owners brought the problem of the Garrick Theater to a perfect impasse. Judge McKinlay's ruling, derived from Justice Douglas' decision, expresses a moral principle that provides an adequate basis for state and federal legislation. The Landmarks Commission acted on the ruling when it prepared a bill for submission to the Illinois State Legislature giving the city power to purchase and preserve buildings of recognized architectural excellence. This bill was signed by Governor Otto Kerner in August, 1963. Justice Bryant's opinion, on the other hand, held that the owner of a private building cannot legally be compelled to preserve its aesthetic quality for public enjoyment if the cost exceeds that normally required to maintain the structure as a remunerative investment. Both opinions are equally valid, but they spring from the surface of the issue, so to speak. The heart of the problem is more profound, and it has to do with fundamental values in American culture.

There are many cases in which individual buildings and relatively extensive urban areas have been preserved for more than a century and will undoubtedly continue to be in the future. Among individual buildings the best known are the homes and estates of early presidents of the Republic, such as Washington's Mount Vernon and Jefferson's Monticello; the most conspicuous examples of restored or preserved areas are Williamsburg, Virginia, the Vieux Carré in New Orleans, and the Old City of Charleston, South Carolina. But the character of these examples serves nicely to define the nature of the problem. Where architectural landmarks are directly associated with important men or episodes in American national history, or where they

[9] The preservation of Sullivan's ornament constituted the most impressive effort in the whole struggle to save the Garrick Theater Building. The $27,000 cost of removal and salvaging was born by contributions from the municipal government, the Balaban and Katz Corporation, the World Book Encyclopedia, and various private individuals. The process of removal was supervised by Richard Nickel, who worked at the physical task himself. Several institutions acquired sections of ornamental panels and screens as parts of permanent collections, among them the Art Institute of Chicago, Illinois Institute of Technology, Southern Illinois University, and Beloit College. The architect of the parking garage, William M. Horowitz, used some of the ornament on the interior of the structure, and Seymour Goldstein, architect of the new Second City night club, incorporated part of the second-floor arcade of the Garrick into the façade of the building (1961). The city of Chicago was required to take out a special insurance policy to protect the Atlas Wrecking Company against damage claims arising from possible injury to the inexperienced men who worked on the removal of plaster panels during the demolition process. One result of salvaging the Garrick ornament was the discovery in one floor of hitherto unknown mosaic work long buried under asphalt-tile flooring.

have grown out of the early life of the Republic and its colonial past, especially if the architecture clearly suggests the Old World antecedents of that life, a vigorous effort to preserve such landmarks has generally been successful. The point is that the buildings are held in popular esteem because of strong emotional associations arising more from feelings of patriotism and pride in the local or national past than from admiration of their intrinsic architectural quality, although this too is felt and enjoyed in the popular consciousness. In Chicago, for example, only a fool would suggest the demolition of the Water Tower at Michigan and Chicago avenues. This charming relic of the Gothic Revival is as sacred as a religious symbol. On the basis of these popular feelings, many states and cities have established commissions to set aside areas for protection and to administer their preservation. Reservations of this kind are sometimes of great financial value: the Vieux Carré is again one of the most conspicuous examples.

On the other hand, buildings that are consciously designed and built strictly for a monetary return on the investment and that function throughout their lives as profitable commercial properties are regarded by the public as having no value beyond narrow economic satisfactions. When they cease to earn a return, or when a newer structure offers a greater return, the universal belief is that they are derelict and merely stand in the way of what is alleged to be progress. This attitude has been vigorously cultivated by building owners and managers, who regard architecture as a form of merchandising. The worst exhibition of this attitude in operation is the mid-town region of Manhattan. The relentless destruction of Park Avenue and the Grand Central area, the piecemeal erosion of the waiting rooms and concourse of Pennsylvania Station (to say nothing of its total obliteration), the grotesque proposal to instal bowling alleys in Grand Central Terminal, the strangulation of the city in this rage to rebuild—together they offer a picture of what can only be described as systematic vandalism. What one age builds is always threatened by the next; thus the good may as easily fall as the poor or indifferent. The basic truth is that there is a fundamental contradiction in the United States between the aims of commercial enterprise and the values of aesthetic achievement. At times they meet, but only temporarily and because of a fortuitous similarity of purposes. The overriding necessity, then, is to combine legislation for protecting architectural landmarks with education of the popular taste at least to the point where the commonplace emotions of local pride and attachment may be associated with buildings valuable chiefly because of their intrinsic aesthetic excellence. The most destructive consequence of a consumers' economy resting on a militaristic basis, other than war itself, is that works of art may be consumed like the most ephemeral of material goods. Indeed, we seem to have arrived at the stage where we consume buildings like clothing and household utensils. Only the most drastic effort to recover the sense of enduring value will prevent a regular repetition of the Garrick Theater disaster.

Sullivan's development from the Garrick and the Wainwright to the Gage Building and the Carson Pirie Scott Store was less irregular than his progress of the eighties. There was, first of all, a brief return to masonry construction and an attempt to refine it even beyond the severity of the Monadnock. This was the warehouse of the Chicago Cold Storage Exchange, completed in 1891 on West Lake Street at the Chicago River. The two blocks of the warehouse were nearly windowless above the second story, great solid masses covering an area of over 59,000 square feet. Sullivan deliberately and with considerable success set out to reduce architectural expression to the fundamental elements of volume and plane. It was a study in texture and geometric purism.[10] After an investment of $1,500,000 and a useful life of eleven years, the warehouses were demolished. The cost of progress has seldom been higher.

The little Victoria Hotel in Chicago Heights, built between 1892 and 1893, could hardly be classed with the commercial work of the Chicago school, but its originality of form bears the clear stamp of Sullivan and also indicates the presence of Frank Lloyd Wright, who had become Adler and Sullivan's chief designing assistant shortly before he left the firm in 1893. The over-all design of the Victoria is Sullivan's, but the surface ornament at the third story and the top of the tower is very likely Wright's (Fig. 91). The ornament is a regular geometric pattern that anticipates the tile ornament in the second-story elevations of the Coonley house in Riverside. The Victoria represents a romantic and even pastoral conception, perhaps befitting the near-rural nature of Chicago Heights before the metropolitan area engulfed it.

On March 10, 1961, the hotel was so nearly destroyed by fire that the remaining parts of the building had to be wholly demolished as soon as they cooled. The town had already granted a permit for demolition to make way for the inevitable suburban shopping center, but the new owners had intended to donate the clock in the tower to the municipality for use in the city hall and to preserve portions of the decorative tile and terra cotta for the Chicago Landmarks Commission. The fire prevented even this minimum effort to salvage a few remnants of the building.

The architecture of steel framing emerges with relative clarity in the Meyer Building, constructed in 1893 at the southwest corner of Franklin and Van Buren streets (Fig. 92). It still stands unchanged except for the replacement of the original cornice by the usual parapet. A wholesale store building, the Meyer is of brick facing devoid of ornament except for the

[10] For an illustration of the Cold Storage Exchange, see Morrison, *op. cit.*, Pl. 37.

narrow terra-cotta bands crossing the piers at the sill and lintel lines. Here Sullivan reversed for the first time the dominant verticalism of the Garrick Theater and the Wainwright and sharply emphasized the horizontality of the long, low block. It is a formal motive that was to become almost universal in the designs of the Chicago school after 1900. The uninterrupted continuity of the spandrels arises from their great width as well as from the bands of ornament across the piers. The exterior envelope of brick is heavy enough to suggest masonry construction, but the horizontality, the relatively narrow piers, and the large area of glass, especially at the base, belong to the architecture of steel framing.

Sullivan's excursion into the ephemeral architecture of fairs was his Transportation Building at the World's Columbian Exposition of 1893 (Fig. 93). For forty years the structure was the best known of Sullivan's designs and the one that was generally felt to be the most representative of his peculiar genius. It hardly stands on a level with many of his designs for permanent structures, but it was an honest, functional, and appropriately festive example of the architecture of temporary exhibition halls. The controlling classicism of the Exposition probably forced compromises that the architect would otherwise have been unwilling to make.

With the cornice height and the rhythm of the piers fixed by the Board of Architects of the fair, Sullivan was still able to turn out the only original and straightforward building on the site. He gave a frank statement of the temporary materials of which the structure was built: surfaces were perfectly flat, the profile sharp and rectangular, and the structural elements were reduced to a series of extremely shallow piers supporting an arcade without moldings or imitation stonework of any kind. The bright colors of red, orange, and yellow and the brilliant, if too obviously applied, decoration of the celebrated "Golden Door" (Fig. 94) gave the Transportation Building a liveliness and gaiety that the other structures lacked. The Golden Door was the most striking example of Sullivan's capacity for rich and intricate detail subordinated to great architectonic simplicity. It was for this element, more than anything else, that he received the medal of the Société des Arts Décoratifs. The architectural independence of the Transportation Building was consistent with Sullivan's estimate of the fair's achievement: "The damage wrought by the World's Fair will last for half a century from its date, if not longer."[11]

Of all the commissions of Adler and Sullivan or of Sullivan alone up to the Carson Pirie Scott Store, the one that enters most fully into the mainstream of the Chicago school is the original Stock Exchange Building, now

[11] Louis Sullivan, *The Autobiography of an Idea* (New York: Press of the American Institute of Architects, 1922), p. 325.

known by its address, 30 North La Salle Street (Fig. 95). The Stock Exchange was designed in 1893, while Wright was still with the firm, and constructed in 1894. It was the home of the Exchange until the present Board of Trade building was completed in 1930. Now given over entirely to offices, it has remained one of the most popular buildings in the Loop. Its rental record has been extremely good: even during the depression of the 1930's it was 95 per cent occupied. In both structure and form the Stock Exchange Building reflects the same fertility of imagination that Adler and Sullivan lavished on the Auditorium, after which the Stock Exchange was their largest commission.

The building is of standard fireproof, steel-framed construction. The most surprising feature of the framing system is the total absence of windbracing. This omission, which would seem fantastic today for a thirteen-story building, had previously been the conventional practice for buildings with relatively extensive horizontal dimensions, but it is unusual to find it at this late date. It was for the foundations that Adler and his engineering associate introduced another of the many technical innovations characterizing Adler's work. Over most of the building area the reinforced concrete footings rest on timber piles driven to hardpan about 55 feet below grade level. The footings of the west line of columns, however, rest on massive cylindrical concrete piers that also extend to hardpan clay. The concrete was poured in watertight drums that served as forms and as protection against seepage of the ground water under pressure. Thus, on the west wall, the Stock Exchange rests on the first caisson foundations for buildings. The idea came originally from William Sooy Smith, who acted as engineering consultant for the Stock Exchange, but it was Adler who worked up the details and hence translated it into practice. The decision to use the caisson foundation was made in order that the presses of the *Chicago Herald*, whose building was formerly adjacent on the west side, would not be damaged by the blows of the pile driver. Again a special problem gave rise to a great forward step in the progress of structural techniques. By means of the caisson foundation, Adler and Smith ended once and for all the hitherto discouraging problem of excessive or unequal settlement of the building.

The exterior form of the Stock Exchange is an organic outgrowth of steel framing without being a direct expression of it. Sullivan abandoned the plastic surface texture of the Wainwright and the Garrick Theater and treated the wall as a repetitive series of largely transparent planes. The general impression made by the street elevations is that of a great box composed largely of glass and poised lightly on the arcade of the third story. On the main portion of these elevations, between the three-story base and the top story, Sullivan scrupulously avoided the use of ornament and refrained from imposing either a horizontal or a vertical emphasis. Throughout its major area the wall becomes a thin curtain drawn in neutral tension over the projecting bow windows and the flat areas between them. The quality of a skin-like envelope is heightened by the shallow reveals and by the absence of continuous courses or bands, the narrow moldings around the windows forming closed rectangles.

But there is an ambiguity in the treatment of the Stock Exchange Building that seems more pronounced than in other commercial designs of Adler and Sullivan. It arises from the tension between the personal expression of the artist's individualistic temperament and the more impersonal statement of the structure and function of the building. The conflict appears primarily in the fenestration of the Stock Exchange. The narrow windows of the projecting bays stand independent of the large Chicago windows with their horizontal orientation. The two separate window sizes break up the elevations into numerous facets of glass that form a vivid play of light but are not unified into a coherent pattern. Again we find the familiar horizontal division, but here much exaggerated. The largely open base, extending to the top of the third story, is topped by semicircular arches and enframed in an ornamental band of terra cotta (Fig. 96). And the wall at the thirteenth story is recessed behind a low colonnade, a feature that recalls the Auditorium tower and that was to appear repeatedly in the designs of the second generation of the Chicago school. Sullivan's originality and proud individualism are emphatically displayed, not only in the somewhat restless treatment of the wall, but, as we might expect, in the ornamental detail. The entrance represents a peculiar combination of mass and depth with the screenlike pictorial quality of the ornamented surfaces (Figs. 97, 98). The only harshly discordant note is the heavy beadwork of the cornice. Among the interior details, the grills surrounding the elevator shaft were the best that Sullivan did—pure, delicate, perfectly controlled, and harmonious (Fig. 99). They were removed during the renovation of the interior, but one panel was preserved by the Art Institute of Chicago.

For an adequate understanding of the range and validity of Sullivan's large civic designs we must turn again to the buildings erected outside of Chicago. The Guaranty (now Prudential) Building in Buffalo (1894–95) represents the last commission of the firm of Adler and Sullivan (Fig. 100). In its functional characteristics and its formal quality, it is similar to the Wainwright in St. Louis, although a larger building by virtue of its thirteen-story height. The U-shaped plan, the braced steel frame, the open base, the circular windows in the attic story, the vertical pattern of the elevations—these and other technical details follow the precedent of the older building. But there are subtle differences that result in marked intensification of the whole effect: every formal detail of the Wainwright is enriched, heightened, stretched out, and slightly exaggerated in the Prudential. Paradoxically, Sullivan achieved a greater simplicity and harmony of over-all form with increased richness of ornamental detail. The cylindrical column envelopes of the first story and the bay-wide windows of the second open the base to such an extent as to suggest an anticipation of Le Corbusier's *pilotis*. The pierlike bands are more attenuated than those of the Wainwright, giving the newer building a greater lightness and openness and a more emphatic upward motion. The ornamental band at the attic story is effectively merged with the pier surfaces rather than separated by a slightly projecting course, as it is in the St. Louis building. The Prudential represents Sullivan at his best—an archetype of the skyscraper in the twentieth century, yet wholly unique and personal, impossible to duplicate. Indeed, it represents a union of creative gifts that only the Chicago movement could have called forth.

The Prudential commission brought to the fore the peculiar talents of George Grant Elmslie, who had joined the office of Adler and Sullivan in 1890.[12] Although the general scheme of the building's ornament was Sullivan's, its execution and detailed elaboration were Elmslie's work. In this first opportunity to try his hand on a major project, the younger man created the basis for the unique system of ornament that was to distinguish much of his subsequent work. As David Gebhard wrote:

Among the many imaginative patterns and forms which Elmslie developed for the Prudential Building were two basic patterns which he was constantly to use in the years that followed. The first of these was a richly developed three-dimensional plant-like pattern which was flowing in total character. The second was a very clear, direct, and precise two-dimensional linear pattern. In these designs Elmslie used a simple plane surface or low relief design as a foil for the three-dimensional foliate ornament. The movement of the three-dimensional patterns rose to skim the surface of the building; the effect was entirely opposite to the ornament of a Baroque or Gothic structure.[13]

In this way Elmslie's designs formed a perfect complement to Sullivan's general conception of the elevation, in which the essential idea is strong but controlled movement intensified by the intricate flow of the decorative patterns. On the completion of the Prudential, Elmslie became the major figure in the office next to Sullivan, and with Adler's departure in the following year his role quickly became indispensable.

The Prudential Building provoked a penetrating comment from Barr

---

[12] For the early life and subsequent career of Elmslie, see pp. 182–85.

[13] David S. Gebhard, "Louis Sullivan and George Grant Elmslie," *Journal of the Society of Architectural Historians*, XIX (May, 1960), 63.

Ferree, one of the more perceptive eastern critics, on the comparative virtues of the skyscrapers in Chicago and New York erected during the decade ending in 1895. The particular structure in New York against which he set off the work of the Chicago school was the dreadful American Tract Society Building, opened early in 1896.

Among many notable commercial buildings by [Adler and Sullivan] . . . is the Guaranty Building, at Buffalo. . . . The leading element of the superstructure is the vertical lines of the piers between the windows, which, at the 13th floor, are connected by small, round arches, and, in design, are joined with the circular windows of the frieze. The whole of the surface of this building is covered with ornament; not structural ornament, as columns and pediments and other artificial additions, but a finely designed, carefully modeled surface ornament, very rich in detail, yet kept well within the structural lines of the architecture. Though possibly the most richly decorated commercial building in America, the skill of the artist has produced a design of structural sobriety with great richness of effect. In both [the Schiller and Guaranty buildings] their success has depended, apart from the artistic feeling displayed in them, upon this unity. And this effect has been attained, not only by the correlation of the various parts of the façades to each other, but particularly by the long vertical lines of the superstructure, which naturally express the columns of the frame.[14]

Feree continues with a detailed condemnation of the American Tract Society Building, whose chief offense was the treatment of the street elevations as six-part horizontal compositions each part of which was confused, redundant, inappropriate, and in no way related to the others.

The error that led the designer of this building astray is very obvious; he did not understand the value of unity in a high building, and certainly did not know how to obtain it. Instead of unity, sobriety and strength, we have variety and change. . . . There is no structural significance in the design—simply a using-up of space, and a fear of long, uninterrupted lines.

It would be easy to multiply examples of badly conceived designs for office buildings, or to name buildings that violate the rules of art more flagrantly than the one we have just studied; but this must suffice. It is folly to deny that the average artistic standard of design in the modern office building is not good. The "skyscraper" has become a synonym for things of horror, and a blot upon the artistic aspect of our modern cities. That they are so is frequently true, but the error lies in the treatment, not in the dimensions of the buildings. Great office buildings like the Schiller Theater, the Stock Exchange, the Auditorium, the Old Colony, the Monadnock Block and others in Chicago; the Wainwright . . . in St. Louis; the Guaranty Building, in Buffalo; the Mills Building, in San Francisco [Burnham

[14] Barr Ferree, "The Modern Office Building" (lecture delivered at the Franklin Institute, Philadelphia, Pa., November 15, 1895), *Inland Architect and News Record*, XXVII (June, 1896), 45–46.

and Root] . . . and some few others in those and other cities, show that logically and artistically treated, the modern office buildings may be ornaments to our cities.[15]

The Stock Exchange Building proved to be Adler and Sullivan's last big commission in Chicago until 1899, six years after the Exchange left the drawing boards. The panic and the subsequent depression of 1893 stopped building once more and thus hit the architects hard. To Adler the situation looked dark enough to question the risk of hanging on. When Richard Crane in 1895 offered him the position of consulting architect and general sales manager of the Crane Elevator Company, he accepted. But the aggressive temperaments of the two men were antipathetic, and the contract was terminated six months after its acceptance. Adler wanted to reform the partnership, but Sullivan felt that he had deserted the firm in a trying period and refused. The two men founded separate practices in 1895, with Sullivan depending increasingly on Elmslie, and Adler on his sons Abraham and Sidney. Adler died in 1900, his name having already disappeared from the roll of the great Chicago architects. The refusal to reform the partnership may have been Sullivan's greatest mistake. Adler, the steady and practical man, was the necessary balance to Sullivan's reckless pride. The number of his commissions declined rapidly. He received only two more in Chicago before the dismal period from 1900 to his death in 1924, during which his business as an architect virtually disappeared. One was for the Gage Building, which involved only a façade; the other was for the Carson Pirie Scott Store, which had actually been offered to the firm before Adler departed. The latter was the pinnacle of Sullivan's achievement and the climax to the heroic age of the Chicago school.

We have already discussed the two earlier buildings of the Gage group in connection with Holabird and Roche.[16] They received the commission for all three, at 18, 24, and 30 South Michigan Avenue, in 1898. The treatment of the façade of Number 18 was later intrusted to Sullivan, and the entire structure was completed in 1899 (Figs. 80, 81). Originally, it was eight stories in height, but four more were added in 1902. Holabird and Roche drew the plans for the addition but followed Sullivan's design in all details. The actual execution of the façade design for Number 18 was the work of Elmslie, who again drew the ornamental detail.

The little Gage Building is important in two respects. It was the first structure from Sullivan's hand to take its form throughout the façade from the steel frame that supports it. In comparison with the frank clarity of Holabird and Roche's two buildings adjacent to it, Sullivan's personal idiom stands

[15] *Ibid.*

[16] For the Gage buildings, see p. 125.

out. Yet the expression is disciplined by the articulation derived from framed construction and by a sound functional approach to the special problem of lighting involved here. Across the top of each window group, which extends over the width of the entire bay, Sullivan placed a 4-foot-high band of translucent glass to reduce and diffuse the glare of direct sunlight. Since the building was originally designed for a millinery establishment, this diffusion of light was necessary for close needlework. Sullivan was criticized for his supposedly aesthetic innovation, but actually his solution is superior to the fully transparent openings of Holabird and Roche's buildings.

In the Gage Building extremely tenuous piers, narrow spandrels, flat glass base, and large openings set flush with the spandrel plane make the elevation a purer revelation of underlying structure than any of Sullivan's previous designs. The cage of the steel skeleton is plainly but delicately expressed in the light and graceful façade. The emphasis on thin horizontal and vertical elements and the resolution of these elements into a finely proportioned composition give the little structure a firm but subtle quality that is superior, as mature architectural artistry, to the vigor and directness of Holabird and Roche's buildings. But the lavish ornament created by Sullivan and Elmslie is somewhat redundant, especially in the foliation spreading out from the tops of the continuous piers and seeming so arbitrarily stuck on to the face of the parapet. The device was to appear in far more refined form in Elmslie's Edison Building.[17] The next step that Sullivan took, to the Carson Pirie Scott Store, has a perfectly logical starting point in the combination of Holabird and Roche's imposing simplicity and his own mature understanding of the complex quality of fine architecture.[18]

[17] For the Edison Building, see pp. 183–84.

[18] For the Carson Pirie Scott Store and a general evaluation of Sullivan's mature achievement, see pp. 161–73.

129. CARSON PIRIE SCOTT STORE, SOUTH ADDITION, 1960–61
    HOLABIRD AND ROOT

State Street midway between Madison and Monroe.
(*Carson Pirie Scott & Co.*)

130. KRAUSE MUSIC STORE, 1922   Louis Sullivan
AND William C. Presto

4611 North Lincoln Avenue. (*Richard Nickel.*)

131. CHAMPLAIN BUILDING, 1903   HOLABIRD AND ROCHE

Formerly the Powers Building, at the northeast corner of
Monroe Street and Wabash Avenue. (*Commercial Photographic Co.*)

132. BAILEY BUILDING, 1898, 1903
HOLABIRD AND ROCHE, NIMMONS AND FELLOWS

Formerly at 529 South Franklin Street; demolished in 1953.
(*Kaufmann & Fabry Co.*)

33. 325 WEST JACKSON BOULEVARD, 1904, 1911
   HOLABIRD AND ROCHE

Commercial Photographic Co.)

134. BORN BUILDING, 1908, 1927   HOLABIRD AND ROCHE, A. S. ALSCHULER

Formerly at 540 South Wells Street; demolished in 1953.
(*Chicago Architectural Photographing Co.*)

135. CHICAGO BUILDING, 1904   Holabird and Roche

Southwest corner of State and Madison streets.
(*Chicago Architectural Photographing Co.*)

136. REPUBLIC BUILDING, 1905, 1909   Holabird and Roche

Formerly at 209 South State Street; demolished in 1961.
(*Chicago Architectural Photographing Co.*)

137. REPUBLIC BUILDING, 1905, 1909   Holabird and Roche

Detail of the main elevation at the upper stories. (*Richard Nickel.*)

138. MANDEL BROTHERS ANNEX, 1900, 1905
HOLABIRD AND ROCHE

Northwest corner of Wabash Avenue and Madison Street.
(*Chicago Architectural Photographing Co.*)

139. BROOKS BUILDING, 1909–10   Holabird and Roche

223 West Jackson Boulevard.
(*Chicago Architectural Photographing Co.*)

140. HUNTER BUILDING, 1908 CHRISTIAN A. ECKSTROM

Now the Liberty Mutual Building, at the southeast
corner of Madison Street and Wacker Drive.
(*Chicago Architectural Photographing Co.*)

141. CHICAGO BUSINESS COLLEGE, 1910
D. H. BURNHAM AND COMPANY

Now the Adams and Wabash Building, at the
southeast corner of that intersection.
(*Commercial Photographic Co.*)

142. SOCIETY BRAND BUILDING, 1912–13
GRAHAM, BURNHAM AND COMPANY

Now known by its address, 416 South Franklin Street.
(*Commercial Photographic Co.*)

143. LEMOYNE BUILDING, 1914–15   MUNDIE, JENSEN AND McCLURG
180 North Wabash Avenue. (*Kaufmann & Fabry Co.*)

144. REID MURDOCH BUILDING, 1912–13 GEORGE C. NIMMONS

Now one of the municipal office buildings, at 325 North La Salle Street.
(*Chicago Architectural Photographing Co.*)

145. EDISON BUILDING, 1912   Purcell, Feick and Elmslie

Now known by its address, 229 South Wabash Avenue.
(*Purcell and Elmslie.*)

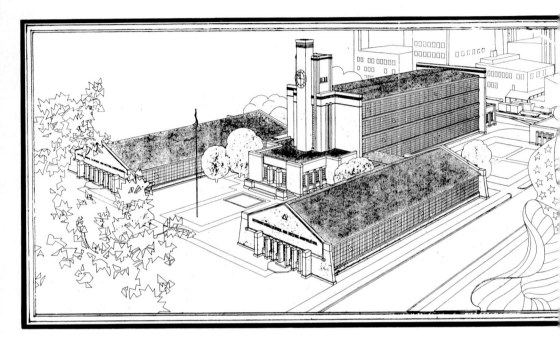

146. OFFICE BUILDING AND FACTORY, INTERNATIONAL LEATHER AND BELTING COMPANY, 1917–18
PURCELL AND ELMSLIE

Only the single-story unit to the right of the main block was built.
(From David Gebhard, "William Gray Purcell and George Grant
Elmslie and the Early Progressive Movement in American
Architecture from 1900 to 1920" [Ph.D. Dissertation, Art
Department, University of Minnesota, 1959].)

147. LORD'S DEPARTMENT STORE, 1905–6   W. M. Walter
625 Davis Street, Evanston, Illinois. (*Evanston Photographic Service.*)

148. CHAPIN AND GORE BUILDING, 1904   Richard E. Schmidt

Now the Union Life Building, at 63 East Adams Street.
(*Chicago Architectural Photographing Co.*)

149. POWERHOUSE, SCHOENHOFEN BREWING COMPANY, 1902
RICHARD E. SCHMIDT

Now the office and warehouse of the Morningstar-Paisley Company,
at Canalport Avenue and Eighteenth Street.
(*Municipal Reference Library of Chicago.*)

150. MICHAEL REESE HOSPITAL, 1905–6   Richard E. Schmidt
Ellis Avenue and Twenty-ninth Street. (*Michael Reese Hospital.*)

151. MONTGOMERY WARD WAREHOUSE, 1906–8
    SCHMIDT, GARDEN AND MARTIN

West Chicago Avenue at the North Branch of the Chicago River.
(*Montgomery Ward and Co.*)

152. MONTGOMERY WARD WAREHOUSE, 1906–8
SCHMIDT, GARDEN AND MARTIN

Part of the river elevation. (*Commercial Photographic Co.*)

153. PAVILION AND BOATHOUSE, HUMBOLDT PARK, 1907
SCHMIDT, GARDEN AND MARTIN

(*Leonard K. Eaton.*)

154. DWIGHT BUILDING, 1911   Schmidt, Garden and Martin

626 South Clark Street. (*Commercial Photographic Co.*)

155. OFFICE BUILDING AND FACTORY, BUNTE BROTHERS CANDY
COMPANY, 1920–21 Schmidt, Garden and Martin

3301 West Franklin Boulevard. (*Photocopy—Kaufmann & Fabry Co.;
John T. Hilborn.*)

156. KENILWORTH CLUB, 1904–6　George W. Maher

410 Kenilworth Avenue, Kenilworth, Illinois. (*Peter Weil.*)

157. UNIVERSITY BUILDING, 1905–6   George W. Maher

Northwest corner of Chicago Avenue and Davis Street,
Evanston, Illinois. (*Evanston Photographic Service.*)

158. PATTEN GYMNASIUM, NORTHWESTERN UNIVERSITY, 1908–9
George W. Maher

Demolished in 1940. (*Northwestern University*.)

159. PATTEN GYMNASIUM, NORTHWESTERN UNIVERSITY, 1908–9
George W. Maher

Interior view showing the three-hinged arched trusses supporting the
roof and skylights (*Northwestern University.*)

160. SWIFT HALL, NORTHWESTERN UNIVERSITY, 1908–9
George W. Maher

(*Evanston Photographic Service.*)

CHAPTER IX

IN THE WAKE OF
THE PIONEERS

Several architects whose work lacks the consistency and uniformly high level of that of the leaders nevertheless made important contributions to the total achievement of the Chicago school. Foremost among them, perhaps, was Solon S. Beman, a highly successful architect who received a considerable number of large commissions not only in Chicago but also in Milwaukee, Omaha, and Cincinnati. He was born in Brooklyn, New York, in 1853. After studying and practicing architecture in New York for eight years under Richard Upjohn, he came to Chicago in 1879. He enjoyed almost immediate prosperity: before the end of the eighties he had designed the Pullman Building at Michigan Avenue and Adams Street (now the site of the Borg-Warner Building), the original factories and company houses of the Pullman Company at Kensington on the far South Side of Chicago, and the first group of buildings of the Procter and Gamble Company at Ivorydale in Cincinnati. His office continued to flourish until his death in 1914. Grand Central Station is one of the most original of his designs and one of the least publicized of the important Chicago buildings.

The station was built between 1889 and 1890 at the southwest corner of Harrison and Wells streets for the now defunct Chicago and Northern Pacific Railway (Fig. 101). The company was originally planned by Henry Villard to extend his recently opened Northern Pacific Railway from St. Paul to Chicago, but the connection was never completed. The station property and the approach tracks were later acquired by the Baltimore and Ohio Chicago Terminal Railroad, which is now the proprietary company, the Chesapeake and Ohio being the only remaining tenant. By the standards of big metropolitan terminals, Grand Central is relatively small. It now handles only ten trains a day (1963), six of them operated by the Baltimore and Ohio, and includes only six tracks for passenger trains and three for mail and express. As in the case of all old terminals, platforms and canopies have been built far beyond the limits of the train shed to accommodate trains of fifteen or sixteen cars.

143

The station building is of secondary importance to the historian of the Chicago school. It has the common L-shaped plan of the grade-level terminal, with the shed embraced by the two wings of the L. The exterior walls are bearing-masonry construction resting on concrete footings supported in turn by 55-foot piles extending to hardpan clay underlying the layers of clay and sand that compose the overburden. The impressive clock tower at the corner, 222 feet high, was built first to avoid unequal settlement. The architectural treatment of the exterior represents a clean and handsome adaptation of Norman forms to the commercial style. The emphasis is on smooth planes and simple geometric masses, qualities enhanced by the superb brickwork of the walls. Until the completion of Cincinnati Union Terminal in 1933, the Grand Central building most closely approached the forms of modern commercial architecture among American railroad stations. The main floor, which contains the waiting room and ticket offices, is spacious and unusually warm and inviting. The interior cast-iron columns are covered with fireproof tile and imitation Mexican onyx, and the wall surfaces are finished in brown Tennessee marble. The functional and aesthetic superiority of the building is immediately apparent, especially if one compares it with some of its contemporaries, such as the Illinois Central Station or Dearborn Station prior to the modernization of the interior in 1946.

The feature that distinguishes Grand Central Station as a work of structural art is the glass and iron construction of the train shed, concourse, and taxi rotunda. The balloon shed has a clear span of 156 feet, a height of 78 feet, and an over-all length of 555 feet (Fig. 102). The vault itself is composed of overlapping panels of corrugated sheet iron supported on a series of parallel wrought-iron arched trusses of semicircular form. The spring line of the arches is nearly flush with the platform surface; thus the vault forms a half-cylinder of circular section. At the time of its construction, it was the largest train shed of its kind except for that of the original Grand Central Terminal in New York (1869–71). The New York structure was the native ancestor of all the American balloon sheds on iron arched trusses and the immediate prototype of its Chicago namesake. In construction and appearance, the two train sheds were at the end of the century the nearest American counterparts of the great sheds of Barlow and Brunel in London.[1]

The train shed is terminated at the front (toward the street) by a glass

[1] The shed of Grand Central Station is one of only two single-span balloon sheds surviving today, the other being that of the Reading Terminal in Philadelphia (1892–93). The largest continuous shed of all covers the tracks of St. Louis Union Station, but it is carried on intermediate rows of columns as well as those at the sides.

It is a curious and inexplicable irony that Chicago, where the modern commercial style was created and where the railroad reached an importance unparalleled in any other city of the world, failed to develop an architecture of railway terminals commensurate with that wall exactly conforming in shape to a right section of the vault (Fig. 103). The lightness and transparency of this wall is the consequence partly of the very thin sash inclosing the panes of glass and partly of the open trusswork brackets and columns supporting it. It is a superb example of functional glass and iron construction, another case of this favorite structural technique of the late nineteenth century. The warm light diffused throughout the station end of the train shed comes in good part through this glass curtain. Much of it, however, comes through the flat glass roof that spans the mail and baggage platform (Fig. 104). This roof is carried from the train-shed arches to the building wall by means of light horizontal trusses. The clean wall planes and fine brickwork, the weightless and translucent surfaces of glass, and the delicacy of the wrought-iron members combine to form the Chicago school's most beautiful and most nearly forgotten example of the advanced architecture of railway terminals at the end of the past century. Structures such as the balloon shed of Grand Central Station provided the precedent for the modern methods of spanning large areas by means of steel ribs or concrete shells with no intermediate supports.

The expert handling of large areas of glass appears again in Beman's Studebaker Building, now the Brunswick, constructed in 1895 at 629 South Wabash Avenue (Figs. 105, 106). In this building the exactitude of detail and the direct structuralism revealed in the Grand Central shed have been overlaid by a capricious and romantic Gothic ornament. For the most part, the ornament is well subordinated to the over-all form and the structural lines; at the top of the parapet, however, it became redundant and fantastic, as though it had completely escaped the architect's control. Aside from the former castellated parapet and the unnecessary contraction of the center bay, the façade is a great open area of glass crossed by the thin lines of the molded piers and the narrow bands of the spandrels. The spandrel panels are iron plates, representing the initial use of the structural material as a formal element throughout the façade of a fully framed building. The recent removal of the original parapet improved the profile of the whole façade, but the massiveness of the badly scaled brick substitute is radically out of keeping with the weightless transparency of the otherwise brilliant elevation. The Chicago windows and the delicately articulated wall provide the fullest exploitation of steel framing that the Chicago school could show at the time.

The former Phelps, Dodge and Palmer Building, at the northwest corner of Adams and Wells streets, now known simply as 200 West Adams Street, was erected in 1888 after the design of Burling and Whitehouse. Edward

---

of office and apartment buildings. Yet the architects had the opportunity to do so five times within the history of the Chicago school—Dearborn Station (1883–85), Grand Central (1889–90), Central (1892–93), La Salle (1901–3), and North Western (1906–11).

Burling, the senior partner, was the second architect to establish an office in Chicago. He was born in Newburgh, New York, in 1819. He started his career as a carpenter and at an early age became a housebuilder in his native town. He came to Chicago in 1843, worked with several builders for a few years, then founded an independent contractor's business. In the early 1850's, when John M. Van Osdel was the only architect in the city, he established an architectural practice with the engineer Frederick H. Baumann (1826–1921). Burling formed a second partnership with Dankmar Adler in 1871 but dissolved it to form another with Francis M. Whitehouse in 1879. The last firm continued until Burling's death in 1892.

Edward Burling had no technical training as an architect, his skill having sprung directly from the vernacular tradition of the carpenter-builder, who once dominated the structural arts in the colonies and the early Republic. In spite of this handicap, he was highly successful and designed a large number of buildings important in the history of Chicago if architecturally undistinguished. The building at 200 West Adams Street is apparently his one essay in the commercial style (Fig. 107). The east or side elevation of this structure, along Wells Street, is superior to the façade because, although it is no different in treatment, its greater length gives it greater unity. The building is chiefly interesting in that it represents an adaptation of the Richardsonian idiom to the architecture of interior framing. The influence of Richardson appears in the fenestration of the top story and of the end bays and in the emphasis on broad piers and extensive wall surfaces. It is original, however, in the absence of arches and in the rounding of the corners of the piers and the edges of the window reveals. As a consequence the street elevations suggest a refinement of masonry forms in the direction of the geometric exactitude appropriate to iron framing. The smooth planes and the general rectangularity of openings and over-all profile indicate that the architects were striving for a sense of volume rather than mass. The fine quality of the walls is another example of how the craftsmanship of the brick-mason can turn commonplace construction into a work of some aesthetic distinction. If Richardson had lived, his commercial architecture might very well have moved toward the expression of the 200 West Adams building. Indeed, the American Express Building of the previous decade suggests movement in that direction. A number of buildings in the Loop area, sometimes more refined in one detail and sometimes in another, are very much like Burling's design. A similar form, though on a larger scale and with more vigorously articulated walls, appears in the former Moses Building, constructed between 1911 and 1912 at the northwest corner of Jackson Boulevard and Wells Street.

One of the most remarkable structures in the strictly functionalist tradition of the Chicago school is the wholesale store and warehouse at 225 South Wacker Drive (formerly Market Street). Probably designed by Flanders and Zimmerman, it is an extension of an earlier building constructed in 1874 and known as the Yondorf. The extension was completed in 1893 (Fig. 108). This ten-story iron-framed warehouse represents the most nearly complete dematerialization of a wall with the traditional narrow windows rather than the Chicago type. Because of the narrow spandrels and the extremely thin mullions, it is virtually a prism of glass, all the more brilliant in its former setting among the begrimed buildings of the Market Street wholesale area. The base was originally a smooth plane of glass set flush with the outer surface of the slender columns, but this was cut off several feet above grade and treated to the usual modernization when Wacker Drive was extended south of Lake Street (the illustration shows the original appearance). Above the base rises a succession of horizontal glass bands stretched over alternate flat and projecting bays. Simple brick spandrels separate the standard windows, closely ranked with their thin mullions along the wall plane. The absence of any ornament except at the entranceway makes the building virtually a piece of pure structuralism, like a bridge, clearly anticipating the Reliance and strongly suggesting the early and highly mechanistic work of the so-called International school in Europe— the Bauhaus, the Van Nelle Tobacco Factory, the Maison Clarté.

It is in this vernacular essay that the geometric purism of much contemporary architecture appears in its embryonic form. A well-marked path points clearly from this functional and unpretentious warehouse to the symmetrically balanced prisms of glass and brick that distinguish Mies van der Rohe's buildings for the Illinois Institute of Technology (Figs. 189, 190). Thus the new architecture has come full circle, without quite realizing what it was doing, from Chicago through France and Germany and back to its native home.

CHAPTER X

HOTELS AND APARTMENTS

The Chicago school developed the modern office building, for which it now enjoys a world-wide reputation. Yet its equally influential though less spectacular work in the creation of the contemporary hotel and apartment building has gone largely unnoticed. The foremost architects of this type of structure—Theodore Starrett and Clinton J. Warren—were virtually unknown until Sigfried Giedion rediscovered them and published some of their work in *Space, Time and Architecture*. Chicago builders were the first to meet and deal directly with the problem of the multiple dwelling for a rapidly expanding urban population. The fire of 1871 and the headlong growth of the city made it necessary, and the elevator and the iron skeleton made it possible, just as these factors presented the challenge and offered the opportunity out of which came the modern office block.

The apartment house and hotel that evolved in Chicago were almost contemporary in their growth with the new office building. As we saw in the case of the Great Northern Hotel, the principles of construction and form developed by the Chicago architects were applied to the multiple dwelling with the same imagination and success. The architects made a direct functional attack on the apartment house, and the form that they developed was again an organic technical-aesthetic synthesis. The homogeneity and uniformity exhibited by the apartments and hotels is even more striking than in the case of the office building. It was once more a matter of developing the most rational standard, the generalization without exceptions, and using it wherever conditions indicated its propriety.

The technical innovations made or perfected by the Chicago architects are now so common that, like all the great basic inventions on which our lives depend, they have come to be regarded as natural things that have always existed. The important structural features were, of course, the iron and steel frame, hollow-tile fireproofing, and the curtain wall. Out of the old cruciform plan of the American house came planning variations that provided two- and three-way exposure of the main apartment rooms, making possible continuous cross-ventilation and at least two exposures to sunlight. In the matter of interior facilities, the Chicago architects developed one of the essential requisites of privacy, sound insulation. The innovations in plumbing were astonishing: hot and cold running water at all times, continuously circulating steam or hot-water heat, and the rational organization of plumbing facilities whereby the various supply and drain lines could be tapped into continuous centralized mains that formed separate circuits, one for each function. Electric lighting became standard early in the design of the Chicago hotel and flat, as did electric call bells and telephone communication. The first hotel to be equipped with electric lights, telephones, and elevators was the third Palmer House, by J. M. van Osdel, opened in 1875 at State and Monroe streets and replaced by the present building in 1925. Most important, perhaps, for the history of interior architecture were the development of the movable partition to vary the size and number of rooms in a suite and the creation of built-in service furniture such as chests, sideboards, and wardrobe lockers. And finally, in pursuit of their aim to free the resident of the last care of homeownership, the Chicago architects introduced the safe-deposit vault at the central desk.

It is impossible to track these many innovations to their points of origin in actual buildings. Many were patented inventions made by men who lived in other parts of the country and the world, but most of them received their first practical large-scale demonstrations in Chicago. Often they appeared simultaneously in several buildings. In some cases they were the work of anonymous contractors and engineering consultants. It is entirely possible that the Pullman Company's rapid development of the sleeping car offered as many suggestions to the architect of hotels as did the office building.[1] Precisely where the new architecture of hotels and apartments begins cannot be definitely established. The evolution away from traditionalism toward a new functionalism and a new organic expression occurred throughout the eighties. Some of the more significant of the early apartment buildings of masonry construction were the following: 3200 South Prairie Avenue, 1882, designed by Adler and Sullivan; the Geneva on Rush Street, 1884; the Lafayette on Dearborn Street, 1886–87; the Morton on Michigan Avenue

---

[1] It seems a plausible thesis that the exterior form and the interior arrangements of Pullman sleeping and lounge cars may have influenced architectural design, and it is even more likely that the converse is true. Soon after its introduction, the American Pullman car was elaborated into an astonishing range of accommodations and facilities, and the peculiar exigencies imposed by the size and shape of the car taxed the ingenuity of the designer, whose problem was essentially like that of the architect. The subject remains to be investigated. Except for H. H. Richardson, who proposed a design for a private car in 1884, the only American architect to design railway cars was Paul Cret of Philadelphia. As consultant to the Edward G. Budd Company, he was responsible for many of the early cars built for the "Zephyrs" of the Burlington Route, the "Rockets" of the Rock Island Railroad, and for the Santa Fe and the Seaboard Air Line. For further comment on the relation of building design to that of railway cars, see p. 190 n.

at Eighteenth Street, 1888–89; and the Parker on Cottage Grove Avenue at Thirty-first Street, 1889. *Industrial Chicago* singles out Clinton Warren's Virginia Hotel, 1889–90, as the first structure in which geometric simplicity and direct expression of function and structure became the basis of architectonic form. The Hyde Park Hotel, however, antedates it by two years, and it was probably the first building of its kind of fully framed construction.

Theodore Starrett designed the Hyde Park, which stood, somewhat worn but in full use, at the intersection of Hyde Park Boulevard and Lake Park Avenue until July, 1963 (Figs. 109, 110, 111). The main block of the building was constructed between 1887 and 1888 and the detached addition to the south in 1891. Starrett was not an architect by profession but a structural engineer; he had worked with Burnham and Root and was later associated with the George A. Fuller Company, builders of many of the structures we have mentioned here. It is very likely that the design of the hotel was the work of a staff assembled by Starrett and the Fuller Company to handle this particular commission, with Starrett as a designing supervisor. He took full advantage of the many structural and utilitarian innovations that were rapidly gaining acceptance in the large commercial buildings of the time. The Hyde Park contained so many of the features common to the new hotel and apartment house that a description of it fits nearly all of the same type of buildings that were growing up around it.

The main block of the Hyde Park was originally an open rectangle in plan, with the inner rooms receiving light from the interior court. The floors were later extended over the court, however, so that the building then had the conventional and uninteresting apartment plan of interior corridors without natural light. Both the original structure and the addition were of standard fireproof iron-framed construction. The exterior treatment plainly revealed the precedent for the Great Northern and many other hotels erected during the nineties and the early years of the twentieth century. Some of the details, such as the arched openings and the pattern of narrow embrasures in the parapet, suggested a simplified Romanesque character, but for the most part the architectonic effect of the two blocks was determined by the extensive area of glass, the grouped windows with their shallow reveals, and the smooth wall planes appropriate to the architecture of framed construction. The exterior finish was dark-red pressed brick with a brown sandstone trim. The rounded embayment, or pavilion, at each corner became the distinguishing mark of Chicago hotels in the decade following the completion of the Hyde Park. End and center pavilions of this kind were common features of the various neo-Baroque modes of Second Empire building in Paris from 1850 to 1870 and may have been the precedent for the Chicago practice. They were used in the Hyde Park to provide exceptionally spacious and well-lighted apartments at the corners. The repetition of the form on either side of the three center bays, however, was largely decorative, since the projection was too shallow to increase the admission of light. Originally a wrought-iron balcony on cantilevered brackets extended entirely around the main block of the Hyde Park, but it was later replaced by short lengths at the end elevations and across the façade at the center up to the sixth floor (Figs. 110, 111).

The main entrance of the hotel opened into a lobby 50 by 100 feet in plan, which originally included an interior court surmounted by a vaulted glass and iron skylight. The walls and columns of the main floor were richly finished in marble wainscoting. The rest of the lobby floor was originally given over to the usual assortment of lounges, reception rooms, public and special dining rooms, elevator bays, and other facilities, but these were removed over the years as the hotel was transformed into an apartment building for permanent residents. Of particular interest was the provision of a special inclosed area for small children and their attendants. This very useful feature is conspicuously absent from many large apartment and hotel buildings of the present time.

The three hundred rooms of the main block were arranged in suites of two- and five-room apartments. Utilitarian facilities such as electrically operated elevators, electric lighting, telephone service, electric call and return bells, and steam heat were standard from the beginning. Starrett carefully avoided the tunnel effect of corridors by making them unusually wide, airy, and well lighted. Wide windows opened to the cool breezes of Lake Michigan, which in 1891 was much closer to Lake Park Avenue than it is now.[2] The Hyde Park Hotel was a little shabby just before its demolition, but it was the ultimate in luxury, comfort, and refinement when it was constructed. Its bold and forceful architectural treatment would still place it above the extravagant hotel design that became the rule in the big cities around the time of the First World War.

The acknowledged leader among the architects of hotels and apartments was Clinton J. Warren. Born in 1860, he began his architectural career with Burnham and Root around 1880 and founded his own office in 1886. Before the end of the decade, he had established himself as a specialist in the work on which his reputation now rests. None of his early commissions as an independent designer shows the architectural vigor and originality of his hotels. His most important office building is the Unity, 127 North Dearborn Street, erected between 1891 and 1892. Its unusual technical feature is the

[2] The immense hydraulic fill underlying Burnham Park and South Lake Shore Drive from Grant Park to the Promontory moved the shore line to the east at varying distances from its original location.

presence of cast-iron columns in the frame of an eighteen-story building. The girders and floor beams are wrought iron, and the windbracing is a system of wrought-iron diagonal rods in the end bays (Fig. 55). The street elevation is a recognizable work of the commercial style, superior to Jenney's early work but hardly on the level of Root or Holabird. The familiar projecting bays are less exaggerated than those of the Manhattan and are thus better integrated with the over-all form of the façade.

Warren's first large commission for a multiple dwelling was the Virginia Hotel, originally known after its owner as the Leander McCormick Apartments. Erected between 1889 and 1890 at the intersection of Ohio and Rush streets (Fig. 112), it was demolished about 1929 for a parking lot. "All the modern improvements are found in this building," wrote the authors of *Industrial Chicago*.[3] And further, it revealed the most advanced architectural treatment of the time for its type of building. It was a ten-story and basement iron-framed structure sheathed in brown sandstone at the first story and dark-red pressed brick above. The hotel was divided into three parallel blocks separated by two 16-foot courts closed at the north end and open at the south. By means of this plan Warren was able, on a closely restricted lot, to provide the six apartments on each floor with east, south, and west exposures. The general exterior treatment depended for its architectonic effect on a composition of simple geometric elements—high, relatively narrow rectangular openings, uninterrupted wall planes, and slablike, sharp-edged volumes. Warren introduced the horizontal courses at the sill lines above the third story to offset the attenuated verticality arising from the vertically elongated windows and the high, narrow blocks into which the building was divided. A striking feature of this severe but effective design was the presence of the floor-to-ceiling windows separated on the vertical line by the narrow ribbons of the spandrels. All the external features of this design reappeared as a new fashion in many of the apartment and office buildings of the 1960's.

The individual apartment was divided into a living room, dining room, bedroom, library, kitchen, and bathroom. The major innovation in interior design was the introduction of movable (folding) partitions by means of which the living and dining areas could be opened with the library into a single continuous room. This open interior plan became an important feature of Wright's houses around 1900 and is now nearly universal in contemporary domestic architecture. Gas ranges were standard equipment in the kitchens of the Virginia. All kitchens connected directly with the service elevators. A reversal of the usual arrangement appeared in the location of the laundry rooms on the top floor and the main dining room in the basement.

---

[3] *Industrial Chicago* (Chicago: Goodspeed Publishing Co., 1891), I, 243.

Electric lighting and steam heat completed the catalogue of modern utilitarian facilities. The Virginia Hotel was justly described as one of the first and finest modern structures of its class.

The sharp-edged rectangularity of the Virginia gave way to cylindrical corners and projecting bow windows in Warren's next large commission. It was the Metropole Hotel, erected between 1890 and 1891 at Michigan Avenue and Twenty-third Street, where it still stands (Fig. 113). The Metropole, like the Virginia, is a series of separate blocks divided by deeply indented courts one bay wide that are open at the south end and closed at the north. Although it is three stories lower than the Virginia, its greater area of plan makes it about equal in size. Interior arrangements and facilities are essentially the same as those of the older building. Exterior treatment is considerably different and more nearly typical of the work of Warren and his contemporaries in the same field of design. Between the first story and the seventh Warren disposed all his windows in the circular and trapezoidal projections of the walls. The flat brick areas of the wall are relatively narrow; thus the total window area is about what one would find in many of the office blocks of the time. The projections not only provide for the admission of more light than would be possible with a flat wall but also give the impression that the glass area is greater than it is. The Metropole is throughout a distinguished design, more pleasing than the Virginia by virtue of its gently undulating wall and the softening effect secured through the rounded projections of the corner windows.

The present New Michigan Hotel was built between 1891 and 1892 and follows in general the exterior treatment of the Metropole (Fig. 114). Originally called the Lexington Hotel, the Michigan stands at the northeast corner of Michigan Avenue and Cermak Road, one block north of its forerunner. The strong feeling for form correlation and the development of a generalized form lie behind the similarity of the two structures. The projecting bays and pavilions of the Michigan are narrower and shallower than those of the Metropole and stop three stories short of the parapet. The whole formal design is consequently less unified and less well integrated than that of the older building. It is a much larger structure and is a true hotel rather than an apartment building.[4] It contains three hundred seventy rooms arranged around an open interior court. A steel frame carries the brick facing and the ornamental terra-cotta trim.

The Michigan and the Metropole stand in what was once the elegant residential area of the near southeast side, which later decayed into blighted

---

[4] The Chicago builders used the terms "hotel" and "apartment" interchangeably when they meant simply "apartment." Many of the so-called hotels, however, belonged to the intermediate category of the residential rather than transient hotel.

slum and industrial land. The entire area extending from Cermak Road to Fifty-fourth Street and from Burnham Park to the New York Central–Rock Island tracks is being redeveloped through an immense co-operative program carried out by the Chicago Housing Authority and Land Clearance Commission, Michael Reese Hospital, and the Illinois Institute of Technology. These well-built hotels could easily be renovated and brought to the condition of first-class residential buildings. There is every reason, practical and aesthetic, why they ought to be preserved in as near their original form as possible.[5]

The Plaza Hotel, erected in 1892 at 1553 North Clark Street, follows closely the plan, exterior form, and general functional arrangement of the two Michigan Avenue buildings (Fig. 115). The whole structure is divided into three equal blocks separated by narrow courts extending through the depth of the building. The cylindrical projections of the corners are repeated six times along the length of the façade, forming the dominant feature of the exterior design. The uniformity and regularity of the street elevations make this hotel one of Warren's best. The Plaza has deteriorated badly as a consequence of the urban blight that had spread throughout the central area of the near North Side with the haphazard location of industries and warehouses and the growth of slums. The Plaza Hotel now stands adjacent to the northeast corner of Sandburg Village (1961–64), the huge complex of apartment towers and row houses designed by Solomon and Cordwell and constituting the Clark–La Salle Redevelopment Project. The fate of the hotel is in the balance, although the owners announced their intention (1963) to renovate the structure.

Warren's largest and best-executed commission was that for the Congress Hotel, which stands in excellent state and full use today (Figs. 116, 117). It and the Sheraton are the only works of modern rather than eclectic design among the leading downtown hotels in Chicago or, for that matter, nearly any other city. The ten-story north block of the Congress, on the southwest corner of Michigan Avenue and Congress Parkway, was completed in 1893. The fourteen-story addition to the south was constructed in two parts: the first four bays in 1902, the remainder in 1907. Holabird and Roche received the commission for the annex but followed Warren's design exactly except for the treatment of the fenestration at the top four stories. Warren's handling of the original portion indicates a deliberate attempt to harmonize it with the Auditorium Building on the north side of Congress Parkway. Both the original block and the annex of the Congress are steel-framed structures with reinforced concrete floor slabs. The columns of the north block rest on the familiar raft or spread footings of concrete, whereas those of the south

[5] For Michael Reese Hospital and its urban renewal program, see p. 191.

annex are carried on smaller footings supported in turn by piles and caissons. The fireproof construction, the advanced design of mechanical and electrical utilities, and the generous opening of the east elevations to the view of Grant Park and the lake made the Congress the last word in hotel design at the turn of the century, and subsequent renovations have kept it to that standard throughout its history.

The greater uniformity of Holabird and Roche's exterior design is more appropriate to the steel frame and the functional character of the building than Warren's. The four upper stories of the north block suggest its architect's treatment of the Dexter Building as well as Sullivan's design of the Auditorium, but in the steel-framed Congress the arcaded windows are anachronistic. On the whole, however, the Congress is a highly expressive and well-integrated work of building art, with a vigorous rhythm imparted by the vertical window banks repeated uniformly down the long Michigan Avenue elevation. (This is especially noticeable in the second illustration, Fig. 117.) In spite of the relatively wide separation of the openings, the numerous projecting bays transform the wall into a lively play of surfaces and give it a light, glittering quality that well suggests the thin undulating curtain drawn over the members of the interior frame.

During recent years the Congress has been extensively remodeled, but fortunately this has brought little change to the general appearance of the building. The north bays of the original block, like the south bays of the Auditorium across the street, were placed under an arcade to allow the widening of Congress Street into the parkway that constitutes the easternmost mile of Congress Expressway. The rough limestone masonry of the piers was retained on the street side, but their lateral faces were covered with smooth envelopes of polished red granite. The present owner of the Congress, the Albert Pick Hotel Company, undertook from 1959 to 1962 a $4,000,000 renovation of the entire interior and part of the exterior of the building, which included the remodeling of all rooms, the relocation and expansion of ground-floor shops and restaurants, and the substitution of aluminum for the original wood of the sash and window frames. Although this program resulted in great and valuable improvement to the functional character of the hotel's interior, its success on the exterior is questionable. The original rough-faced limestone masonry of the base, designed to harmonize with the base of the Auditorium as well as the smooth limestone of the upper stories of the Congress, was replaced by an envelope of polished gray granite covering the piers and the first-story spandrel (Fig. 117). At the same time the windows were set flush with the outer pier faces. There are far worse examples of "modernization," but the new treatment of the ground floor can hardly be called an improvement over Warren's work. The addition of new restaurants, coffee shop, and meeting rooms left untouched the spatial and decorative character of the main lobby, on the express order of Albert Pick himself. Thus, on the whole, this program of renovation, along with the location and the original design, makes the Congress easily the best of the downtown hotels in Chicago. The improvements introduced into this fine building, which is unique in its class, form a welcome contrast to the deterioration and the thoughtless demolition that usually attend seventy-year-old structures. The treatment of the Congress offers an excellent example of how old commercial buildings of architectural distinction can be and ought to be preserved.[6]

Many Chicago architects whose names are not associated with the development of the office building contributed distinguished designs in the field of the multiple dwelling. One of the largest of the combined transient-residential hotels is the former Chicago Beach Hotel, at Hyde Park Boulevard and Cornell Avenue. It was first constructed about 1890, then rebuilt and enlarged in 1911. The appearance and functional arrangements were so much like those of the Hyde Park that it was probably the work of the same builders, Starrett and Fuller. The hotel is now the headquarters of the Fifth Army of the United States Armed Forces. Frederick Baumann and J. K. Cady designed a nicely detailed work at Roosevelt Road and Michigan Avenue—the Bordeaux Apartments, erected in 1891. The closely grouped windows in the projecting bays, characteristic of Warren's work, appear here in a precise geometric composition of horizontal and vertical lines. Flanders and Zimmerman directly applied the principles of office and warehouse design to the main elevations of the Park Gate Hotel (1891–92), on Fifty-ninth Street near Washington Park. They opened the wall into an unusually high proportion of glass extending over the flat surfaces and the projecting bays. The Park Gate was only six stories high but nearly a block long. Edmund R. Krause followed some of Warren's principles in his design of the Alexandria Hotel, built in 1891 at 542 North Rush Street, where it still stands under the original name. One of the handsomest products of the movement initiated by Starrett and Warren was the Mecca Apartments, erected between 1891 and 1892 at the northwest corner of State and Thirty-fourth streets after the plans of Edbrooke and Burnham. The structure was demolished for the southward expansion of the Illinois Institute of Technology's campus. The Mecca was particularly attractive because of its smooth plane surfaces and precise modeling, enhanced by the long Roman brick and the care with which it was

[6] The renovation and remodeling of the Congress Hotel were undertaken as a consequence of the completion in 1960 of McCormick Place, the city's lake-front fair and exposition building. The decision to remodel closely parallels the original motive for building the Congress, which was to secure a share of the enormous transient business brought by the Columbian Exposition of 1893.

laid. Each wing of the building embraced an interior light court roofed with glass and surrounded by continuous balconies on brackets, much like the court of the Chamber of Commerce Building.

The high standard of design established by Starrett and Warren persisted up to the depression of 1893. When construction was resumed again, the boldness of spirit and fertility of imagination exhibited by the hotel architects began to give way before the fashionable classicism of the Fair. But many fine buildings were completed before the failure of business and the shifting tides of taste undermined the spirit of the Chicago architects. The Omaha Apartments, designed by Irving K. and Allen B. Pond, were erected in 1893.[7] Although the window area was relatively small, covering less than half of the main elevation, the openings were distributed over the familiar projecting bays. The over-all treatment was crisp and precise, befitting the architecture of the new industrial and urban milieu. The ornament of the Omaha was reduced to an unobtrusive trim at the base and cornice, the main architectonic effect growing out of extensive planes and sharply incised openings. The Lakota Hotel (1893), at the southeast corner of Michigan Avenue and Thirtieth Street, was similar to the work of Clinton Warren—so nearly so, indeed, that it may very well have been a product of his hand (Fig. 118). The corner pavilions, the bay windows, the grouped openings, the deep, narrow court, the uniformity and regularity of the elevations—these together with its functional interior design made it one of the good late examples of its class. The Lakota was demolished in 1959 in connection with the Southeast Area Redevelopment Plan.

The Brewster Apartments, built in 1893 at the northwest corner of Diversey Boulevard and Pine Grove Avenue, are an unusual variation on the standard form (Fig. 119). The Brewster was designed by R. H. Turnock, an obscure product of Jenney's office whose name is not associated with any other noteworthy Chicago building. In the treatment of the openings and the projections in the wall it belongs to the mainstream of hotel architecture. What distinguishes it from the rest of its kind is the massive envelope of rough-faced granite blocks that extends around all four elevations. Turnock may have been influenced in this respect by Richardson, who was very fond of the romantic and sensuous effect produced by this rich and heavy texture.

No exterior detail of the Brewster matches the originality and daring that Turnock displayed in the interior construction. In order to admit the maximum amount of natural light to the lobby and to the corridors and apartments of the upper floors, he developed one of the most remarkable systems of interior planning in the building art of his time. The Brewster is a hollow rectangular block surrounding an inner court open from the second floor to

[7] For the later work of the Pond brothers, see pp. 205–7.

the roof and surmounted by a gabled glass and steel skylight (Figs. 120, 121). The opening originally extended from the lobby floor, but this part of the lobby was later covered by a ceiling. Access to the apartment entrances above the second floor is gained by a vertical series of glass-decked bridges extending across the long dimension of the court and branching into short laterals leading to the various entrance doors. Windows in the brick walls of the court provide daylight for the inner rooms of the apartments. Each bridge is supported by a pair of steel girders of I-section imbedded at their outer ends in the masonry of the brick walls and bolted together at the lateral connections. The bridge deck consists of 4-inch square glass blocks set in a grid of wrought-iron angles. The load of the deck is carried to the longitudinal girders by a series of shallow transverse members with a peculiar bowed shape that does not correspond to any standard rolled section. The bridge rails, which constitute the primary decorative feature, have the form of a simple latticework of wrought-iron strap. Against the middle bay of the west court wall the elevator shaft rises, inclosed in a delicate grill of iron strap similar to that of the rails. A cast-iron stairway extends in a floor-by-floor series, each composed of three flights wrapped in a square around the elevator shaft.

The entire complex forms a lively repetitive pattern of delicate iron screens and bands set off in black against the soft diffused light falling through the glass decks of the bridges. The whole impression is in extreme contrast to the heavy masonry of the external walls. On the lobby floor, all that is left of the original design are the curious columns, octagonal in section, unusually wide at the base, and marked by such an extreme entasis as to suggest the form of a squat wine bottle. The flaring capitals are covered with an ornamental pattern of intertwined tendrils and oak leaves. Certain formal elements of the Brewster appear to be of Second Empire French origin, and the iron grid of the court bridges was anticipated by Henri Labrouste in the cast-iron stack passages of the Bibliothèque Nationale in Paris (1858–68). Turnock's treatment of the court walkways, however, is derived chiefly from bridge design and is developed into a highly original tour de force that strikes us today virtually as a structural fantasy.

The original architecture of hotels and apartments survived throughout the nineties and in isolated buildings up to 1930. One of the more distinguished buildings of the last decade of the century is the Francis Apartments of Frank Lloyd Wright, erected in 1895 at 4304 South Forrestville Avenue (Fig. 122). Unlike most of the Chicago apartments, the Francis is marked by extensive areas of flat wall planes and sharp-edged windows rather than by the undulations of the repeated oriels or projecting bays. In Wright's building these are so reduced in number and height as to suggest a purely decorative rather than a functional purpose. The Langdon Apartments on Des Plaines Avenue is one of the late examples of the forms peculiar to the Chicago movement. The Langdon was designed by Dwight Perkins and constructed in 1903.[8] The projecting bays, the large openings, and the simple, straightforward treatment, with its usual emphasis on volume and plane, distinguish this structure from the borrowed forms then growing up around it.

Yet the sound principles of design developed in the late eighties never wholly disappeared. They survived, somewhat watered down, in scores of low-rise apartment buildings constructed as late as 1929, many of them architecturally anonymous, having been designed by unknown employees of the contractors who built them. They appear on the North Side and in Rogers Park and Hyde Park, among the Chicago neighborhoods, and in Evanston and some of the other outlying towns. Among the best of the isolated survivors is the apartment building at the southwest corner of Hinman Avenue and Lee Street in Evanston, designed by Lawrence G. Hallberg and erected between 1922 and 1923. In this building the nearly unbroken area of smooth wall planes has an unusually rich quality imparted by the warm tawny color of the carefully laid Roman brick. Only the undecorated and unmolded window openinges and the narrow panels of ornamental tile around the main entrance interrupt the flat surfaces of brick. One may distinguish all of these apartment buildings by their simplicity and honesty of appearance, their freedom from redundant and derivative ornament, their large grouped windows, and in many cases their deep glass-inclosed projections, usually square in plan, providing solariums or sitting rooms with a three-way exposure. They form part of the precarious but vital continuity that joins the Chicago school to the world-wide movement of the new architecture.

[8] For the later work of Dwight Perkins, see pp. 200–203.

CHAPTER XI

THE CHICAGO SCHOOL IN THE TWENTIETH CENTURY

1. THE MAIN TRADITION AFTER 1900

The year 1900 did not mark a turning point in the work of the Chicago school, although historians who follow Sigfried Giedion still contend that the death of Root in 1891 and the World's Fair of 1893 started the school on an irresistible decline. At the turn of the century it was clear that the heroic age was past: the ranks of the pioneers were rapidly thinning, and the original impetus that produced the great basic achievements was losing its drive. Root had been dead nearly a decade; Adler, parted from Sullivan, died in the century year; Sullivan's commissions were rapidly running out; Jenney was old and losing his powers; Burnham was turning increasingly to city planning and his Cleveland and Washington projects. These, with Holabird and Roche, were the men who had created the Chicago movement; most of them had done their great work, and only two were to survive in active practice beyond the first decade of the century.

But the passage of the pioneers meant not the ultimate conclusion but the end of one generation, the rise of another, and the establishment of new artistic directions. Many of the proudest achievements of the Chicago school came with the twentieth century, and many buildings constructed between 1900 and 1910 continued the tradition of commercial architecture established in 1880. The Carson Pirie Scott Store set a standard at the very beginning of the new century that others could only hope to emulate. The best work of Holabird and Roche outside of the Marquette Building was done in the twentieth century. Before 1910, however, a new generation of Chicago architects arose to challenge the creative powers of those who preceded them. Within a few years they were to multiply and enrich the new architectural forms beyond anything that the pioneers had imagined and to apply them to public and residential buildings in an extraordinary renewal of creative vigor.

If there was a turning point in the history of the Chicago movement, the most likely estimate of its date would be the period from 1905 to 1910, when the central concern of the Chicago architects shifted from commercial to public and residential building. The eclipse of this most prolific of all indigenous movements in American architecture came with the First World War. By 1920 it had very nearly spent itself, but it never entirely disappeared: it survived precariously in the Midwest through the work of Elmslie, Byrne, the Ponds, and a few less-well-known men until the first importations of the new European work began to come in around 1930. Until 1915, at any rate, the climate of the Chicago region was thoroughly congenial to the new architectural ideas advanced by Sullivan in his buildings and his writings. In our review of the Chicago achievement after 1900, the general historical pattern makes it logical to complete the chronicle of commercial architecture in the main tradition before turning to the public and residential work of the second generation. The obvious starting point is Sullivan's Carson store.[1]

Sullivan's career in the twentieth century was a record of neglect and poverty. A defiant and bitter rebel, he refused vehemently to compromise with the conspicuous extravagance that marked much of the new eclecticism. Emotionally erratic and given to strong drink in quantity, with an inflexible and arrogant personality, he made it difficult for even sympathetic clients to deal with him. He was a severe disciplinarian in his office, and he carried his extremely high standards into his business dealings. The result was that he was often admired and feared but rarely liked. He poured out his scorn for the World's Fair, the classicism of the East, Burnham the impressario, the Tribune Tower, and everything these phenomena represented in *The Autobiography of an Idea, Kindergarten Chats,* and numerous articles and letters. He became a crusader and a pamphleteer, turning the vision of a great creative artist into the only medium of expression left him. In his later life he was indeed a prophet without honor. He was often praised in Europe, where a number of architects and critics who regarded him and Wright as the foremost architects in the United States were astonished at his lack of commissions. How much of Sullivan's decline was a matter of national taste and how much the consequence of his own failings it is now impossible to say, but between the two they were enough to finish him.

[1] This second generation, as I have called it, is sometimes designated as the Prairie school, in part because of the dominance of horizontal motives in their designs. Equally striking features are the great variety and subjectivity of decorative forms in residential work, the breaking away from the comparatively rigid geometry of the commercial style, and the influence exercised on the members of the school by the arts and crafts movement in England. I shall not treat the residential architecture of this group beyond providing a few illustrations of the designs of the less-well-publicized figures who worked almost exclusively in this field. For a more extensive and detailed treatment of the domestic work, see the listings in the Bibliography under H. Allen Brooks, David S. Gebhard, and Mark Peisch.

It is fortunate for architecture everywhere that Sullivan enjoyed one more opportunity to design a large urban building. The commission for the Carson Pirie Scott Store was his last chance to express his powers on the scale and in the milieu to which the Chicago architects were accustomed. In the full vigor of his middle age, as yet free of the bitter contempt of his last years, he put into it everything that he had as a thinker, an artist, and a planner. The building is known and admired today wherever an interest in architecture flourishes.

Two firms of dry-goods and department-store merchants were successively involved in commissioning this celebrated building. The first was the Schlesinger and Mayer Company, owners of a dry-goods business that had been established during the Civil War. It was they who engaged Adler and Sullivan in 1891 to design an addition to their original building at the southeast corner of State and Madison streets and to bring the original and the addition together behind a uniform façade. The original structure had been designed by W. W. Boyington and erected in 1873.

The predecessor of Carson, Pirie, Scott and Company was the dry-goods business founded by Samuel Carson and John T. Pirie at La Salle, Illinois, in 1855. The two merchants opened their first Chicago store in 1864. The company has steadily expanded the sphere of its operations from retail to wholesale trade and from Chicago to the suburbs of the metropolitan area and eventually through a subsidiary to other cities of Illinois. The company's original wholesale store, which may have been designed by John M. Van Osdel, was built in 1875 at the northwest corner of Adams and Franklin streets. It was the first of the Carson establishments to achieve some distinction in the history of commercial architecture. The façade appears to have been cast iron or iron combined with narrow masonry piers and was a curiously proportioned composition of strict rectangularity. It exhibited a great horizontal elongation, with the wide openings between the piers filled by six windows separated by extremely thin mullions. The crude drawing of this elevation in the Rand McNally *Bird's-Eye Views of Chicago* (1898) suggests the appearance of the contemporary load-bearing screen wall. It is possible that the exaggerated horizontality of such vernacular essays as this may have influenced Sullivan's design of the big retail store.

The depression of 1893 discouraged the Schlesinger and Mayer Company from continuing with its project, which languished for six years. Meanwhile Adler and Sullivan had separated. In 1899 the company decided to build an entirely new building along Madison Street as a separate unit from the old building that stood at the corner of State and Madison and extended a short distance south along State. They selected Sullivan rather than Adler as the architect. The new 1899 structure was three bays wide and nine stories high and stood on Madison Street somewhat east of the intersection with State. It constituted the first portion of the present Carson Pirie Scott Store. In 1903 the old building at the corner and its neighbor immediately to the south were demolished, and in the same year Sullivan designed the extension of the original Madison Street building. This addition, twelve stories high and consisting of three bays along Madison and seven along State, was built between 1903 and 1904. In the latter year Carson, Pirie, Scott and Company bought the business from Schlesinger and Mayer. In 1906 D. H. Burnham and Company were commissioned to design the last addition of the original group, the five south bays on State Street, which were constructed in the same year. Burnham wisely elected to follow Sullivan's plans in every detail except in the treatment of the top story. Thus the completed building—six bays on Madison and twelve on State—emerged in steps (Fig. 123). It remained unchanged until 1948, when the original cornice or roof projection was replaced by a parapet (Figs. 124, 125).

The Carson Pirie Scott Store is for the most part a steel-framed structure the skeleton of which rests on caisson foundations extending to bedrock. The frame of the 1904 addition includes cast-iron columns, possibly representing the last use of this material in a major urban building. The outer columns and spandrel girders above the second story are sheathed in thin tiles of terra cotta. The first two stories, constituting the base, are clothed in cast iron covered with a remarkably profuse, delicate, and original foliate and floral ornament of low relief (Figs. 126, 127, 128). The elaborate pattern of intertwining plant forms on both the exterior and the interior was sketched in general form by Sullivan, worked out in detail by George Grant Elmslie, and executed in plaster molds by Kristian Schneider, a sculptor who had made Sullivan's ornament for twenty years. The cast iron of the base was originally painted a bronzed green by first covering the metal with a red coat and overlaying it with green in such a way as to allow the red color to show through in places. The intention was frankly to imitate the color of oxidized bronze. At the time of the Carson Company's centennial (1955), the ironwork was gilded and in the following year painted black. In 1962, after a good deal of experimentation with various colors, the ornament was painted a medium gray.

Elmslie explained that the main intention behind the lavish ornament at the base was to produce "a richly flowing picture frame . . . to surround the rich and ornate window displays."[2] Willard Connely, in his biography of Sullivan, expressed well the objective psychological import in the extreme

[2] David S. Gebhard, "Louis Sullivan and George Grant Elmslie," *Journal of the Society of Architectural Historians*, XIX (May, 1960), 64.

elaboration of the ornament and suggested something of the subjective meaning of its plantlike forms for Sullivan.

... The cunning in the design, and the bold originality of it, rested in the bottom two stories. The most delicate decoration adorned the level at which the passing crowd could see it. Whereas in the Guaranty Building Sullivan stressed masculinity—to bespeak drive, ambition, strength of purpose—in the present ornamentation his aim was to court unhurried femininity, to lure the susceptible women. He garnished the big display windows with lacy metal, flowers, vines, berries, geometrically arranged in cluster or scroll, and frieze or medallion, the whole instinct with vitality and rhythm, dancing by very grace of line. The effect was festive, a store permanently bedecked for a permanent commemoration; but the psychology of it was that an individual shopper should feel that her own visit was being celebrated. Even the great chains [now gone] which upheld the canopy over the broad side doors were not crude links, but iron garlands of flowers highly wrought. At the corner, the bulge offered a choice of five arched entrances, to invite approach from all directions, each door being topped with a great wreath of laurel, as if a customer who passed underneath invited a laurel crown for her discrimination. To cross such a threshold, the whole setting seemed to say, confirmed not one's interest in vulgar commerce, but one's devotion to art.[3]

Above the ornamental base of the Carson store rise the great cellular elevations, bold and exact, dynamically and perfectly proportioned articulations of the steel and iron frame. An overhanging roof slab or cornice originally topped the structure, a much more satisfactory element than the present parapet, which is badly out of scale with the spandrels (Figs. 124, 125). The transition between the two street elevations is harmoniously effected by means of a cylindrical pavilion at the corner, where the main entrance is located. The natural horizontality of the wide-bayed frame and the Chicago windows is deliberately emphasized by the ornamental bands extending continuously along the sill and lintel lines (Fig. 126). The elevations above the base have a cleanliness and precision so nearly absolute that the most minute change in proportions could be detected. There is no better revelation of the architecture of modern industry and commerce.

The flow of space in the interior of the Carson Pirie Scott Store has been dammed and parceled by the partitions introduced to form the many inclosures common to large department stores. The building is a closed rectangle of straight warehouse construction. The interior, consequently, appears as a series of broad avenues separated by the rows of slender, widely spaced columns. It rises with complete uniformity through one floor after another,

[3] Willard Connely, *Louis Sullivan as He Lived* (New York: Horizon Press, Inc., 1960), p. 235. For further discussion of the expressive and symbolic meaning of Sullivan's ornament, see pp. 167–73.

except for the ceiling height of the three top stories, which is lower than that of the first nine.

The department store of Carson, Pirie, Scott and Company is Sullivan's swan song as a civic architect and his unchallenged masterpiece. It is the ultimate achievement of the Chicago school and one of the great works of modern commercial architecture in the world. Probably the only commercial structure to rival it in sheer aesthetic daring was Wright's Larkin Company building in Buffalo (1904–5), destroyed in 1950 in what so far remains the most reckless act of architectural vandalism. In the Carson store both the system of construction and its formal expression evolved directly out of the work of Jenney and Holabird. What distinguishes it from the very best of their designs are the thoroughness of Sullivan's exploitation of the aesthetic possibilities of the big steel frame, his superior sense of scale, proportion, rhythm, and organization, and his unparalleled imagination as an ornamentalist. The street elevations present a dynamic revelation of the iron and steel cage that carries the building loads: thrust and counterthrust, tension and compression, give rise to powerful kinesthetic images in the observer. The long west façade is particularly impressive: it is a repetitive pattern of rectangular cells skilfully carried around the corner to the north wall by means of the pavilion, which repeats on smaller scale and in subtle variation the motive of the walls. The carefully calculated depth of the window reveals gives the cellular articulation clarity and incisiveness as well as force. The logic and precision of science and technology are here translated into an aesthetic discipline of grace and dignity born out of exact and controlled strength. Formal, structural, and utilitarian elements are fully integrated into a new synthesis the power and validity of which we have not yet been able to match.

An unusual tribute to the functional soundness of Sullivan's design as well as to his reputation was the decision of the executive officers of Carson, Pirie, Scott and Company to retain the original forms of the building in the latest southward extension along State Street. The eight-story addition, which extends the long west elevation by three bays, was designed by Holabird and Root and built between 1960 and 1961 (Fig. 129). The façade above the lintel line of the second floor exactly follows the proportions and ornamental patterns of the original; the different treatment of the base, however, is an unfortunate mockery of Sullivan and Elmslie's brilliant achievement to the north. In order to duplicate the original cast-iron ornament on the second-story spandrel, the numerous coats of paint were scraped off, a mold made from the exposed metal, and the new ornamental panel cast in aluminum.

The decision to build anew largely as the architect planned is an honor to Sullivan's memory, and it stands in happy contrast to the wanton destruction that ordinarily attends the expansion of commercial structures. Indeed, the company scarcely considered any alternative to retention of the original design. John T. Pirie, chairman of the Board of Directors, said, "We early decided to emulate Louis Sullivan's design and elaborate ornamentation even though we knew it was far from the cheapest way of doing the job." And C. Virgil Martin, the company's president, stated a simple fact when he added that "[it is] a remarkable tribute to the farsighted soundness of Louis Sullivan's genius that a completely modern new building can extend without change the classical lines and rich ornamentation of the older building."[4]

Along with the south addition, the Carson company undertook a renovation of the base of the original structure. The cast iron was cleaned and repainted and the projecting course at the top of the second story on the State Street elevation was replaced. This belt course, which constituted the cornice of the base, had fallen off. The ornamental detail of the new course was duplicated from the old by casting it in a mold obtained from a short length of the similar projection around the corner pavilion. The renovation work was carried out under the direction of Mason Walker, the staff architect of the company.

After the Carson store, Sullivan's commissions dwindled away into a handful of rural banks and suburban stores. There were three more in Chicago: the office building of the Crane Company, at Canal Street and West Twelfth Place, 1903–4; the Felsenthal Store, at 701 East Forty-seventh Street, 1905; and the last commission of his life, designed in collaboration with William C. Presto, the Krause Music Store, at 4611 North Lincoln Avenue, 1922 (Fig. 130). Of these the Felsenthal building is the most successful: the large areas of unbroken wall surface with its low ornament, the nicely proportioned window groups, and the simple cornice emphasize volume and basic geometric forms, qualities that were developed into extraordinarily effective compositions in the little banks. The Crane building followed a foundry and machine shop that Sullivan had designed for the same company and that had been built at Canal and Roosevelt Road between 1899 and 1900. The office building was a simple cube marked by extreme severity of form, but the windows were again grouped into horizontal bands by narrow projecting courses at the sill and lintel lines.[5] The Krause Music Store has many of the characteristic features of the Sullivan designs, but it is another case of

[4] Both quotations are from James Hoge, "Carson's Plans Major State St. Expansion," *Chicago Sun-Times*, July 15, 1960, p. 39.

[5] The Crane buildings were demolished in connection with the great expansion of rail facilities in the Canal-Roosevelt area that came with the construction of the Wisconsin Central (Soo Line) Freight Station (1912–14) and Union Station (1916–25). For illustrations of the Crane and Felsenthal buildings, see Hugh Morrison, *Louis Sullivan: Prophet of Modern Architecture* (New York: W. W. Norton & Co., 1935), Pls. 63, 64.

the ornament getting out of hand and dominating the basic forms of the building. Sullivan undoubtedly had little to do with this design. He had passed the time when he could create great architecture; such powers as he still possessed went into *The Autobiography of an Idea* and the comment on the *Chicago Tribune* competition.[6]

The centennial of Sullivan's birth brought forth a renewed stream of biographical and critical studies—lectures, articles, journalistic pieces, two books—yet none of it seems quite to have uncovered the essence of the man and his works. One major reason for this is that the theorists of the modern movement feel compelled to see him mainly as a prophet of the new style, with its structuralist and cubist manifestations. But Sullivan was the creator of an autonomous and permanently valid artistic world that arose from emotional and unconscious responses to his childhood experiences and to the age of his creative ascendancy. The key to his peculiar genius is in his writings as well as in his art, if the true meaning can be elucidated. It may be profitable for us to begin with the passages that lead us to the inner man rather than with the developed theory of *Kindergarten Chats*. Although this original work is a profound if inchoate ethicoaesthetic system, it is the product of conscious reflection aimed at developing a comprehensive social philosophy of art.

We have already noted that Sullivan was powerfully attracted to the building art as a child almost at the same time that he was drawn to books, music, and the world of natural phenomena, especially flowers. What seems to have excited him most intensely was the realization that men designed and built the structures that both terrified and delighted him. Years later the full meaning of this revelation began to emerge in the *Kindergarten Chats* description of Richardson's Marshall Field Wholesale Store (page 62 in this book). The significance of the description lies in its metaphors, the heart of all poetry. Sullivan was on one level celebrating the strong men who are creators and builders, like the workers at the Boston shipyard whom he saw as a child and described with typical passionate enthusiasm in his *Autobiography*.[7] On a deeper level, however, one is compelled to reflect on the fact that Sullivan identified the Field building with the man who created it, or transformed it into the man. The imagery is entirely associated with masculine energy and potency, sheer creative vitality in its basic physical sense. When one considers this along with the ascription of a Dionysiac quality to the tall building, the essential meaning becomes inescapable. For Sullivan the creation of a building is equivalent to the biological act of man recreating

[6] For the Tribune Building Competition and entries in the Chicago spirit, see pp. 209, 211, 217.

[7] *The Autobiography of an Idea* (New York: Press of the American Institute of Architects, 1922), pp. 85–86.

himself, as he does when he begets a child, the emphasis, however, being exclusively masculine.

But even a fine work of architecture like the Field store did not arouse in him the powerful emotions that were evoked by the achievements of the great bridge engineers of the nineteenth century. There are several illuminating passages in his *Autobiography*, among the most remarkable in the book, in which he tries to analyze his emotional and philosophic response to these monuments of pure structural form. The first records a childhood experience in which he saw a chain suspension bridge over the Merrimack River (possibly Finley's bridge of 1810, near Newburyport, Massachusetts). The description is loaded with the most extreme expressions of feeling.

Mechanically he ascended a hill . . . musing, as he went, upon the great river Merrimac. . . . Meanwhile something large, something dark was approaching unperceived; something ominous, something sinister that silently aroused him to a sense of its presence. . . . The dark thing came ever nearer, nearer in the stillness, became broader, looming, and then it changed itself into full view—an enormous terrifying mass that overhung the broad river from bank to bank.

He saw great iron chains hanging in the air. How could iron chains hang in the air? He thought of Julia's fairy tales and what giants did. . . . And then he saw a long flat thing under the chains; and this thing too seemed to float in the air; and then he saw two great stone towers taller than the trees. Could these be giants?

[A page follows in which Sullivan records how he ran frightened to his father to tell him that the giants might eat him.]

So [his father] explained that the roadway of the bridge was just like any other road, only it was held up over the river by the big iron chains; that the big iron chains did not float in the air but were held up by the stone towers over the top of which they passed and were anchored firmly into the ground at each end beyond the towers; that the road-bed was hung to the chains so it would not fall into the river. . . . On their way to rejoin Mama, the child turned backward to gaze in awe and love upon the great suspension bridge. There, again, it hung in the air— beautiful in power. The sweep of the chains so lovely, the roadway barely touching the banks. And to think it was made by men! How great must men be, how wonderful; how powerful, that they could make such a bridge; and again he worshipped the worker.[8]

It would be difficult to discover what complex emotions are imbedded in the first part of this passage, with its strange tone of the sinister and the threatening. But the predominant surface meaning is clear: the bridge, like Richardson's building, is transformed into a human figure, articulated, organically constructed, capable of sustaining itself erect over the waterway. Moreover, this feat is achieved by a kind of magic, such as one might expect from the

[8] *Ibid.*, pp. 82–85.

IN THE TWENTIETH CENTURY

dreamer who creates out of his own inner self. This sense of mysterious power born out of will is something that Sullivan retained all his life.

In later years, on his way to becoming an established architect in partnership with one of the leading building engineers of the time, Sullivan came to understand how these miracles were accomplished. Then he was prepared to pay his fullest tribute to the bridge engineers and to record it with his youthful enthusiasm in his *Autobiography*.

About this time two great engineering works were under way. One, the triple arch bridge to cross the Mississippi at St. Louis, Capt. Eades [*sic*], chief engineer; the other, the great cantilever bridge which was to cross the chasm of the Kentucky River, C. Shaler Smith, chief engineer, destined for the use of the Cincinnati Southern Railroad [*sic*]. In these two growing structures Louis's soul became immersed. In them he lived. Were they not his bridges? Surely they were his bridges. In the pages of the *Railway Gazette* he saw them born, he watched them grow. Week by week he grew with them. Here was romance, here again was man, the great adventurer, daring to think, daring to have faith, daring to do. Here again was to be set forth to view man in his power to create beneficently. Here were two ideas differing in kind. Each was emerging from a brain, each was to find realization. One bridge was to cross a great river, to form the portal of a great city, to be sensational and architectonic. The other was to take form in the wilderness, and abide there; a work of science without concession. Louis followed every detail of design, every measurement; every operation as the two works progressed from the sinking of the caissons in the bed of the Mississippi and the start in the wild of the initial cantilevers from the face of the cliff. He followed each, with the intensity of personal identification, to the finale of each. Every difficulty he encountered he felt to be his own; every expedient, every device, he shared in. The chief engineers became his heroes; they loomed above other men. The positive quality of their minds agreed with the aggressive quality of his own. In childhood his idols had been the big strong men who *did* things. Later on he had begun to feel the greater power of men who could *think* things; later the expansive power of men who could *imagine* things; and at last he began to recognize as dominant the will of the Creative Dreamer: he who possessed the power of vision needed to harness Imagination, to harness the intellect, to make science do his will, to make the emotions serve him—for without emotion—nothing.[9]

[9] *Ibid.*, pp. 246–48. Eads Bridge was built between 1868 and 1874 and the Dixville span from 1876 to 1877, so that Sullivan was twelve years old when the first was begun and at the threshold of his architectural career when they were completed. There are two particularly significant aspects of this testament: one is the fact that Sullivan identified himself with the bridges, possessed them, so to speak, and thus transformed them into a part of his own living spirit; the other is the hierarchy of doing, thinking, and imagining, with ultimate stress on vision and emotion.

The engineer in charge of the Dixville project was Louis F. G. Bouscaren, chief engineer of the Cincinnati Southern Railway. It was his decision to introduce hinges into the truss chords, which transformed the bridge into a cantilever structure. Charles Shaler Smith was the designing engineer. Bouscaren deserves as much credit for this work as Smith, but Sul-

There is a powerful strain of romanticism in this passionate devotion to the builder, even a Nietzschean quality in the worship of creative power. And it is here that the secret of Sullivan's achievement lies, as we shall see when we re-examine the major buildings. For Sullivan came to see in science and technology the triumphant assertion of man's will expressing itself in a new way. As he himself put it:

Louis saw power everywhere; and as he grew on through his boyhood, and through the passage to manhood, and to manhood itself, he began to see the powers of nature and the powers of man coalesce in his vision into an IDEA *of power*. Then and only then he became aware that this idea was a *new idea,*—a complete reversal and inversion of the commonly accepted intellectual and theological concept of the nature of man.[10]

Sullivan's intuitive grasp of the meaning of the Eads and Dixville bridges was perfectly sound. The union of science and technology that made them possible was the creation of men who possessed a rare combination of faculties: they were men who could imagine and think things and who, when they translated the products of imagination into physical fact, did so on a heroic scale. It was difficult not to be impressed, however little one understood the methods of their achievement. Sullivan was profoundly moved, and he knew that he would have to create a building art that could give voice to these powerful feelings and thus evoke them in others. Sullivan's personal as well as his professional relationship with Adler represented something of the same union. According to Frank Lloyd Wright, the architect regarded the engineer with profound admiration. Indeed, the strength of this emotion may well have accounted for Sullivan's bitterness over Adler's dissolution of the partnership. He felt that he not only had to build *on* the empirical forms of Adler's engineering but had to transform them into architecture that would express publicly the personal feelings they aroused.

We have already considered the nature of these feelings, which focus on masculine energy and potency and on will as the energizing force that transforms dreams into concrete realities. Sullivan's big urban buildings—Auditorium, Schiller, Wainwright, Guaranty, Carson Pirie Scott—are direct outgrowths of this process of Nietzschean sublimation. The Auditorium, relying on the masonry pier for its exterior wall supports, is a transition to the fully developed expression of the three tower-like skyscrapers. After meeting the empirical requirements of structure and utility, Sullivan turned in these buildings to the plastic implementation of what appealed to him in the skyscraper structure. In the terms of his own celebrated description—"The lofty

---

livan and the rest of posterity have always honored the latter and forgotten the other half of the team.

[10] *Ibid.,* p. 248.

steel frame makes a powerful appeal to the architectural imagination where there is any. . . . The appeal and the inspiration lie, of course, in the element of loftiness, in the suggestion of slenderness and aspiration, the soaring quality of a thing rising from the earth as a unitary utterance, Dionysian in beauty."[11]

In the light screens of terra cotta that constitute the street elevations of the skyscrapers, the basic theme is precisely this soaring movement, the dynamic transcendence of space and gravitational thrust, qualities Sullivan long before felt in the "floating" chains and roadway of the Merrimack suspension bridge. In a broader sense, the theme suggests the underlying energy of a world of process, of evolution and growth in living things, or the dynamics of the electric field in physics. The bridge, like the building, is not seen by Sullivan as a static thing but as something that leaps over its natural obstacle and thus becomes a living assertion of man's skill operating through his simultaneous dependence upon and command over nature. Again Sullivan's intuition led him into the right path, for this is exactly how the bridge behaves. We can sense this directly in the suspension bridge with its wire cables and suspenders: it seems alive, constantly quivering under its changing load. Although we can never see it and seldom feel it, the same thing occurs in the dense and massive members of the big railroad truss as the internal stress continuously adjusts itself to the moving weight that it sustains. It took a century and a half of painstaking scientific inquiry to discover this hidden and vital activity. This is the scientific and technical material that fed Sullivan's feelings and imagination, producing the complex and powerful psychological responses recorded in his *Autobiography*. The mode of expression came wholly from within the architect: the exuberant upward thrust is the natural symbol for a driving self-assertion and an untrammeled will energized by masculine potency.

The Carson Pirie Scott Store offers a somewhat different problem. Here he turned to a new kind of expression for him, one derived from the dominant tradition of the Chicago school. Whereas in the older buildings he used the close vertical pattern, in the department store he opened the main elevations into great cellular screens expressive of the steel cage behind them. The form was dictated initially by the requirement for maximum light in the store, but again in many subtle ways, he translated the practical functionalism into art. If the theme of the Wainwright and the Guaranty can be said to be primarily movement, that of the Carson store is articulated power. Here the elaborate interplay of tension and compression in the bridge truss is given an intensified statement by means so delicate as almost to escape notice—the carefully calculated depth of the window reveals and the breadth of the terra-cotta

[11] *Ibid.*, pp. 313–14.

envelope on the columns and spandrel girders, the narrow band of ornament that enframes each window, the even narrower band that extends along the sill and lintel line to give the façade a tense, subdued horizontality.

The ornamental detail of all the buildings—in good part the joint achievement of Sullivan and Elmslie—is much more difficult to interpret in symbolic terms. It is radically subjective, and it evokes from the observer so many different responses and associations that it is scarcely possible to find objective experiences that might have led to the feelings out of which it grew. In its naturalistic character—its iconographic content, so to speak—it clearly represents the organic world of growth and fertility. It is sensuous and erotic, feminine, as Willard Connely suggests; and in its continuous rhythmic movement, it is strongly expressive of the basic rhythms of life comprehended in the cycle of birth, death, and rebirth. Indeed, the idea of the Dionysian seems as appropriate to the ornament as it does to the upward sweep of the skyscraper walls. The careful formal control of the intricate details symbolizes the inexhaustible diversity that covers the unified organic world. On the Carson store the lavish ornament of the screenlike base combined with the powerful cellular wall above it leads to a curious tension in which we sense a deliberate masculine-feminine ambiguity. They are both necessary for the fulfilment of Sullivan's architectural myth.

On one level his civic architecture is a celebration of technique, as is most of the contemporary work of which he was the foremost pioneer. He was not himself an engineer, but he grasped with a sure intuition the inner character of the great structural achievements. He controlled with perfect skill the intricate utilitarian details of the big office and store buildings, and he planned them with an exact sense of functional propriety. He was imbued with the scientific spirit of his age and he felt compelled to find a means of expressing it in his art. In all these ways he belonged to one of the mainstreams of his time; he sought and found a union of the technical with the emotional and the poetic. This aspect of his life and work was summed up well by Albert Bush-Brown.

For Sullivan taught that the language of modern society is both science and romance, both fact and belief, and that the two must be wedded in one statement. He broadened the technology of his own day by making it poetic, and he brought it as a symbol to serve the institutions of industrial society; his art arose from his organization of the scientific ideas, technical means, utilitarian demands, and romantic beliefs of his age.[12]

His revolt against the complacencies of his time was broad enough to embrace both feeling and reason, and it had affinities with the new pragmatism and the more seminal radical empiricism.

[12] Albert Bush-Brown, *Louis Sullivan* (New York: George Braziller, Inc., 1960), p. 32.

But the pragmatism was mature, for it never insisted, as many who came late to the industrial machine . . . naïvely insisted, that utilitarian expedience and economy should be declared in bald and mechanistic displays of raw technology.[13]

On the deepest level, however, Sullivan was a poet profoundly imbued with the romantic spirit that survived intact from the great age of Words-worth and Goethe. His last commissions, the rural banks of the Midwest, bear unqualified witness to this fact. In his writings he frequently referred to him-self as a poet, sometimes in conjunction with the experience of structural or mechanical objects such as buildings, bridges, and trains. Another passage of his *Autobiography* highly charged with emotional imagery provides a typical illustration: "The train now well under way for Newburyport, our poet, he of the dream-life, crawled forth from his cave of gloom and began to take notice."[14] A fuller revelation of the poetic character of Sullivan's artistic spirit is embodied in the letter he wrote to Walt Whitman in 1887, when he sent the poet a copy of his essay "Decadence" after reading *Leaves of Grass*.

To a man who can resolve himself into subtle unison with Nature and Humanity as you have done, who can blend the soul harmoniously with materials, who sees good in all and o'erflows in sympathy toward things, enfolding them with his spirit:—to such a man I joyfully give the name of Poet:—the most precious of all names.[15]

This feeling of sympathy uniting the young architect and the poet in an inner bond indicates that Sullivan's own creative urge was like that of Whitman's. And a further identity exists in the architect's looking upon democracy as the only social milieu that could liberate the artist's creative power through the free expression of his love for nature and his fellow man. "Blending the soul harmoniously with materials" is exactly what Sullivan did, in an almost lit-eral sense. Like the poet in the great age of romanticism, he transformed his sensuous and intellectual experiences into emotional states, then expressed these in forms derived from a union of the feeling and the kind of experience that evoked it. When we see a building of Sullivan's, we see not only struc-ture and material form but also the creator's own inner world of emotions and dreams. We are compelled to share them.[16]

[13] *Ibid.*

[14] *The Autobiography of an Idea* (New York: Press of the American Institute of Architects, 1922), p. 72. The imagery in this passage has an almost mythopoeic quality.

[15] Letter dated February 3, 1887, from the collection of Charles Feinberg of Detroit. I am indebted to Ernest Samuels for showing me this letter. Mr. Feinberg kindly allowed me to quote from it.

[16] The romantic strain in Sullivan was not an isolated phenomenon, as is attested by a curious historical coincidence. He died in 1924, the year that also saw the deaths of Joseph Conrad and Giacomo Puccini. The artistic achievements of the three men are utterly dispa-rate; yet all three shared a common quality: they were the last great romantic creators,

After the Carson Pirie Scott Store the commercial work of the Chicago school seems anticlimactic; nevertheless, some of it produced in the new century stands comparison with the best of the old. The basic type of office block that Holabird and Roche perfected continued to appear in a number of good designs up to 1910. The cellular elevations, the continuous piers, the wide Chicago windows, or grouped windows of standard size, reveal themselves in the same clean-cut lines and careful proportions. They have been described at length before and need no extended comment here. The important commissions of Holabird and Roche that show little variation on the fundamental theme are the following: the original Powers Building, now known as the Champlain, northeast corner of Monroe Street and Wabash Avenue, 1903 (Fig. 131); the two north bays of the Bailey Building, 529 South Franklin Street, 1898, of which the two south bays, erected in 1903, were designed by Nimmons and Fellows (Fig. 132); the 325 West Jackson Building, 1904, 1911, particularly good in its regularity and harmony (Fig. 133); the Boston Store, extending along the north side of Madison from State to Dearborn Street, 1904–5, 1917; the Bauer and Black Building, 2500 South Dearborn Street, 1907–8; and the Born Building, 540 South Wells Street, 1908 (Fig. 134). An addition to the Born, identical in treatment with the original, was designed by A. S. Alschuler and constructed in 1927.

All but three of these buildings survive in active use at the present time, and all but two are or were steel-framed structures. In the case of the Champlain, several bays of the first two stories at the corner were remodeled in 1946 for the ticket office of the Trans World Airlines, designed by Skidmore, Owings and Merrill. This handsome work of contemporary design involved the replacement of the original subdivided glass curtain at the base with a continuous area of transparent glass. The result is that the alterations to the interior and the modernization of the exterior envelope are entirely in keeping with the over-all form of the building. The best as well as the simplest and least expensive way to modernize the structures of the Chicago school is to do as its own architects did, that is, to clothe the base in glass. The common use of various kinds of shiny synthetic materials as an envelope for many contemporary store fronts and entrance bays has ruined the ground floors of a number of fine Chicago buildings (see, for example, the damage done to the Gage group, Figs. 80, 81).

The Bailey and the Born were among four blocks of buildings demolished in 1952 and 1953 to make way for the Congress (now Eisenhower) Express-

---

but they were simultaneously men of our own century. Unique in their respective ways, they left little continuing influence; they brought a great cultural movement to its end point and at the same time helped to reformulate its various modes of expression into the artistic idiom of our time.

161. SHERIDAN HOUSE, 1910–11   GEORGE W. MAHER
310 Church Street, Evanston, Illinois. (*Peter Weil.*)

162. JOSEPH SEARS ELEMENTARY SCHOOL, 1912   GEORGE W. MAHER

542 Abbotsford Road, Kenilworth, Illinois. (*Wayne Andrews.*)

163. GROVER CLEVELAND ELEMENTARY SCHOOL, 1911
  DWIGHT H. PERKINS

3850 North Albany Avenue. (*Chicago Board of Education.*)

164. LYMAN TRUMBULL ELEMENTARY SCHOOL, 1909–10
Dwight H. Perkins

Northwest corner of Ashland Boulevard and Foster Avenue.
(*Chicago Board of Education.*)

165. CARL SCHURZ HIGH SCHOOL, 1908–10
   Dwight H. Perkins

Northeast corner of Milwaukee Avenue and Addison Street.
(*Chicago Board of Education.*)

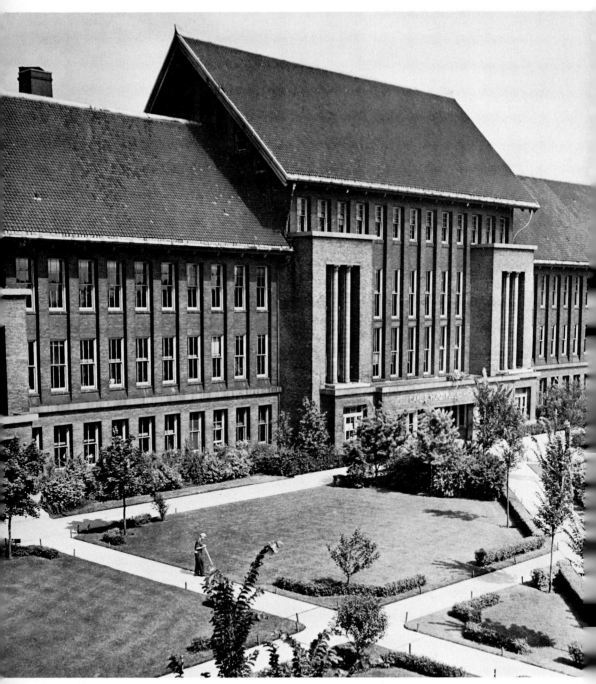

166. CARL SCHURZ HIGH SCHOOL, 1908–10 Dwight H. Perkins

Main elevation at the entrance. (*Chicago Board of Education.*)

167. IMMACULATA HIGH SCHOOL, 1921–22 Barry Byrne
640 West Irving Park Road. (*Photo—Henry Fuerman; Barry Byrne.*)

168. IMMACULATA HIGH SCHOOL, 1921–22 BARRY BYRNE

View from the southwest showing the main entrance and the sculpture by Alfonso Iannelli. (*Photo—Henry Fuerman; Barry Byrne.*)

169. TOLL BUILDING, ILLINOIS BELL TELEPHONE COMPANY, 1908
    IRVING AND ALLEN POND

111 North Franklin Street. (*Illinois Bell Telephone Co.*)

170. PART OF THE HULL HOUSE GROUP, 1890–1908
Irving and Allen Pond

The group surrounds the original Hull mansion, at 800 South Halsted Street.
(*Photo—Allen, Gordon, Schroeppel and Redlich, Inc.; Hull House.*)

171. LINTHICUM HOUSE, 1907–8   TALLMADGE AND WATSON

1315 Forest Avenue, Evanston, Illinois.
(*Evanston Photographic Service.*)

172. 608 DAVIS STREET, EVANSTON, ILLINOIS, 1910
TALLMADGE AND WATSON

(*Evanston Photographic Service.*)

173. FIRST CONGREGATIONAL CHURCH OF AUSTIN, 1908
WILLIAM E. DRUMMOND

Now the West Central Church, at Waller Avenue and Midway Park.
(*J. Carson Webster.*)

174. LORIMER BAPTIST CHURCH, 1914 Guenzel and Drummond

St. Lawrence Avenue and Seventy-third Street. (*J. Carson Webster.*)

175. UNITARIAN CHURCH OF EVANSTON, 1903–4
MARIAN MAHONEY

Formerly on Chicago Avenue near Dempster Street, Evanston, Illinois; demolished in 1961. (*Peter Weil.*)

176. CARTER HOUSE, 1910   WALTER BURLEY GRIFFIN
1024 Judson Street, Evanston, Illinois. (*Peter Weil.*)

177. FIRST COMSTOCK HOUSE, 1911–12   WALTER BURLEY GRIFFIN
1416 Church Street, Evanston, Illinois. (*Peter Weil.*)

178. SECOND COMSTOCK HOUSE, 1912 Walter Burley Griffin
1631 Ashland Avenue, Evanston, Illinois. (*Peter Weil.*)

179. PROJECT, TRIBUNE BUILDING COMPETITION
1922 Walter Burley Griffin

(From Chicago Tribune, *The International Competition
for a New Administration Building for the Chicago Tribune,
MCMXXII* [Chicago: The Tribune Co., 1923].)

180. BERSBACH HOUSE, 1914   John S. Van Bergen

1120 Michigan Avenue, Wilmette, Illinois. (*Peter Weil.*)

181. 5730 SHERIDAN ROAD, 1914–15   JOHN S. VAN BERGEN
Demolished in 1960. (*Peter Weil.*)

182. PROJECT, PAVILION AND BOATHOUSE, COLUMBUS PARK, 1920
JOHN S. VAN BERGEN

(*Chicago Park District.*)

**183. DEMPSTER STREET STATION, CHICAGO, NORTH SHORE
AND MILWAUKEE RAILWAY, 1924–25 A. U. GERBER**

5001 Dempster Street, Skokie, Illinois.
(*Chicago, North Shore and Milwaukee Railway.*)

184. CARSON PIRIE SCOTT MEN'S STORE, 1926–27
HUBERT AND DANIEL (JR.) BURNHAM

Northwest corner of Wabash Avenue and Monroe Street.
(*Williams and Meyer.*)

185. CARSON PIRIE SCOTT MEN'S STORE, WEST
ADDITIONS, 1940, 1949–50 LOUIS KROMAN

North side of Monroe Street midway between
Wabash Avenue and State Street. (*Allen Lein.*)

186. PAVILION, ROOKERY, LINCOLN PARK ZOOLOGICAL GARDEN
1936   Landscape Architect's Staff, Chicago Park District

(*Robert Fine.*)

187. PAVILION, ROOKERY, LINCOLN PARK ZOOLOGICAL GARDEN
1936 LANDSCAPE ARCHITECT'S STAFF, CHICAGO PARK DISTRICT

Detail of the timber and masonry work. (*Robert Fine.*)

188. PROJECT, TRIBUNE BUILDING COMPETITION
1922 WALTER GROPIUS AND ADOLF MEYER

(From Chicago Tribune, *The International Competition
for a New Administration Building for the Chicago Tribune,
MCMXXII* [Chicago: The Tribune Co., 1923].)

189. ALUMNI MEMORIAL HALL, ILLINOIS INSTITUTE OF
TECHNOLOGY, 1945–46   Ludwig Mies van der Rohe,
Holabird and Root

(*Hedrich-Blessing Studio.*)

190. CROWN HALL, ILLINOIS INSTITUTE OF TECHNOLOGY, 1955–56
LUDWIG MIES VAN DER ROHE, PACE ASSOCIATES

(*Photo—Hube Henry, Hedrich-Blessing Studio; Illinois Institute of Technology.*)

191. PROMONTORY APARTMENTS, 1948–49   Ludwig Mies van der Rohe,
Pace Associates, and Holsman, Klekamp and Taylor

South Lake Shore Drive near Fifty-sixth Street.
(*Bill Hedrich, Hedrich-Blessing Studio.*)

192. INLAND STEEL BUILDING, 1955–57
SKIDMORE, OWINGS AND MERRILL

Northeast corner of Monroe and Dearborn streets.
(*Photo—Kaufmann & Fabry Co.; Inland Steel Co.*)

179. PROJECT, TRIBUNE BUILDING COMPETITION
1922 WALTER BURLEY GRIFFIN

(From Chicago Tribune, *The International Competition
for a New Administration Building for the Chicago Tribune,
MCMXXII* [Chicago: The Tribune Co., 1923].)

180. BERSBACH HOUSE, 1914   John S. Van Bergen

1120 Michigan Avenue, Wilmette, Illinois. (*Peter Weil.*)

193. HARTFORD FIRE INSURANCE BUILDING, 1960–61
SKIDMORE, OWINGS AND MERRILL

Southwest corner of Wacker Drive and Monroe Street.
(*Ezra Stoller Associates.*)

194. CONTINENTAL CENTER, 1961–62   C. F. MURPHY ASSOCIATES

Southeast corner of Jackson Boulevard and Wabash Avenue.
(*Richard Nickel.*)

195. CHICAGO CIVIC CENTER, 1963–65 C. F. Murphy Associates,
Skidmore, Owings and Merrill, Loebl, Schlossman and Bennett

North half of block bounded by Clark, Randolph, Dearborn,
and Washington streets. (*Photo—Bill Hedrich, Hedrich-Blessing;*
Skidmore, Owings and Merrill.)

196. STANLEY R. PIERCE HALL, UNIVERSITY OF CHICAGO, 1959–60
HARRY WEESE AND ASSOCIATES

Southwest corner of Fifty-fifth Street and University Avenue.
(*Photo—Hedrich-Blessing Studio; University of Chicago.*)

way–Wacker Drive interchange. The extensive demolition made possible a welcome area of landscaped open space and provided an adequate foreground for Grand Central Station. Unfortunately, the Baltimore and Ohio Railroad took advantage of the opportunity to reach a new audience and installed an enormous billboard across the top of its handsome station. The Born Building, a twelve-story structure on wood piling, was the first building in Chicago with a reinforced concrete frame of flat slabs and mushroom columns, a system patented in 1908 by the Minneapolis engineer Claude A. P. Turner. The Bauer and Black Building was also supported on a reinforced concrete frame, but in that case the structure was the more traditional column-and-beam system of the type developed by Julius Kahn of Detroit. The Bauer and Black Company's office was demolished in 1962 for the construction of Dan Ryan Expressway. The former Boston Store is a typical steel-framed building on concrete caissons. A huge seventeen-story block, its incisive cellular screens are marred only by the absurd colonnade at the top two stories. In 1948 the Boston Company withdrew from the department store business and sold the building, which was converted to office use and renamed the State-Madison Building.

Holabird and Roche returned to the projecting bay windows of the Tacoma in the Chicago Building, erected in 1904 at the southwest corner of State and Madison streets (Fig. 135). In this structure, however, a modification of the Chicago window takes the place of the narrow sash in the older building. The wide windows of the Chicago almost fill the alternate flat and projecting bays along the Madison Street elevation, with the result that the now blackened piers and spandrels enframe a lively pattern of light reflected from several angles. The unification of this diversity of elements is well handled from the standpoint of proportion, but an ambiguity appears in the contrast of the sharp verticalism of the projecting bays and the horizontality of the rest of the wall plane. The enlargement and rustication of the corners recall the Marquette Building.

Further variations on the flat cellular wall appear in three later structures. The nineteen-story Republic Building, with a steel frame on concrete caissons, was one of the cleanest and lightest of all Holabird and Roche designs, a consequence in part of its height and its very tenuous piers (Figs. 136, 137). The Republic stood at 209 South State Street, at the intersection with Adams. When the building was opened in 1905, it was twelve stories high; seven more stories were added in 1909. After a half-century of dominating the State Street scene, it was acquired by the Home Federal Savings and Loan Association and demolished in 1961 to make way for the company's new office building, designed by Skidmore, Owings and Merrill.

The decision to replace the fifty-five-year-old structure seemed plausible enough to those concerned with the ownership and management of commercial buildings, but a minimal concern with the total function of good architecture can only lead to the conclusion that the Republic's destruction was a major civic loss. Throughout most of its history the Republic was a popular, high-rent office building with its own merchants' association, organized in 1915 and still flourishing in 1955. By the latter date, however, the quality of management had begun to decline and with it the management's interest in adequate maintenance. For many years there had been no improvements in the mechanical and electrical equipment, and the tenants had been given a free hand to alter interior space to suit themselves. It was a typical pattern of what is known in the business as dissipated management, which is inevitably accompanied by falling rents. At the same time the powerful State Street Council, determined to make the great shopping artery as modern and fashionable as the current taste dictates, vigorously encouraged the idea of new up-to-the-minute construction. In terms of the narrow economic satisfactions of the money and real estate interests, it was easy to make the usual financial survey and come to the expected conclusion to tear down and build anew. Whether this decision led to an improvement on the work of Holabird and Roche is a debatable question. The simple truth is that the Republic could have been thoroughly renovated at a small proportion of the cost of the new building and its honesty and vigorous articulation thus preserved for the benefit of the whole urban core. Instead, the owners chose to replace it with the already omnipresent curtain wall of glass. The whole episode must be set down as another triumph of the architecture of public relations. Again, as in the case of other demolished buildings, a physical description and a graphic record of the Republic were preserved for the Commission on Architectural Landmarks. Skidmore, Owings and Merrill prepared a history of the design, construction, and subsequent use of the building, and Richard Nickel made another of his photographic surveys.

One of the most impressive designs to come from the office of Holabird and Roche is the annex of the Mandel Brothers Store, built in two sections in 1900 and 1905 at the northwest corner of Wabash Avenue and Madison Street (Fig. 138). The street elevations are particularly striking because of the great horizontal elongation arising from the unusually wide bays, the narrow spandrels, and the sharp-edged projecting courses of ornamental detail. Equally arresting is the continuous opening of the second story, which is a true ribbon window divided into extraordinarily large panes of glass. A small portion of this window appears in the lower right-hand corner of the illustration.

The Brooks Building, erected between 1909 and 1910 at 223 West Jackson Boulevard, provides still another variation on the basic pattern (Fig.

139). It is one of the most open and vigorously articulated of the Holabird and Roche designs by virtue of the round moldings on the piers, which elongate and narrow their appearance and enliven the whole elevation. The essential form of the original work of these prolific architects persists in three commissions that came near the end of the Chicago movement. The Great Lakes Building, on the southwest corner of Wacker Drive and Lake Street (1912), and the Crane Building (1912–13), 836 South Michigan Avenue, reveal the familiar cellular pattern of the articulated wall. The Century Building, on the other hand, stands in marked contrast to the usual designs of Holabird and Roche. Erected between 1914 and 1915 at the southwest corner of State and Adams streets, the sixteen-story Century is distinguished by street elevations that present an extremely attenuated vertical pattern, produced by continuous, closely ranked mullions sheathed in terra cotta.

William Holabird died in 1923 at the age of 69, but the partnership was continued by his son John until the death of Martin Roche in 1927. In the following year John A. Holabird and John Wellborn Root, Jr., established the highly successful firm of Holabird and Root, inheritors of the commissions for or authors in their own right of some of Chicago's best-known skyscrapers, most notably the original Daily News, the Palmolive, and the Board of Trade buildings. The older partnership was extraordinarily productive: in its forty-five-year history the firm designed seventy-two major buildings within the central commercial area of Chicago. Holabird and Roche were fortunate in the preservation of their buildings: many of their good designs after the Tacoma stand today, but the unplanned construction of expressways and new office buildings constantly threatens them, as it has swept away those that have fallen.

That other architects sought the formula that brought Holabird and Roche prosperity is revealed in a number of good commercial buildings. Some of these architects were less-well-known men whose designs were mostly of transitory interest; others were famous and well-established figures who contributed valuable work to the Chicago movement. The original Hunter Building, designed by Christian A. Eckstrom, is the best of these isolated achievements (Fig. 140). Now the office building of the Liberty Mutual Insurance Company, it was constructed in 1908 at the southeast corner of Madison Street and Market (now Wacker Drive). The base of the twelve-story block was greatly improved in 1947 to 1948 when the old ground-floor stores were removed and the windows widened out to the full area of the bays, as they are at the second floor. This change provided a handsome open base for the glass and brick cellular wall above it, but unfortunately the improvement was short-lived. The extension of Wacker Drive south of Madison Street three years later made it necessary to raise the street grade six feet to provide adequate clearance for the lower level of the double-deck drive. This necessitated reducing the first-story height above grade by about half the original figure, which spoiled the fine proportions of the big ground-floor windows.

The old Chicago Business College, now the Adams and Wabash Building, is very much in the spirit of Holabird and Roche (Fig. 141). The narrowness of the piers in relation to the width of the spandrels, together with the unusually wide Chicago windows, produces the exaggerated horizontality. The building was erected in 1910, after the plans of D. H. Burnham and Company, on the southeast corner of the intersection from which it takes its present name. It is the only example of the Chicago window other than the Reliance Building to come from Burnham's office.

The adaptation of the Chicago office building to industrial purposes was a logical consequence of opening the wall to the maximum extent allowable with wide-bayed steel framing. Many factories exhibiting the same basic form were built in the manufacturing districts on the periphery of the Loop area from 1900 to the time of the First World War. One of the most imposing is the high slablike building at 416 South Franklin Street, immediately behind Sullivan's Meyer Building. Originally the Alfred Decker and Cohn and later the Society Brand Building, it was designed by Graham, Burnham and Company and erected between 1912 and 1913 (Fig. 142). This combination office block and factory belongs to the strictly empirical tradition and thus stands in marked contrast to other buildings by Burnham and his successors that represent a mixture of the realistic and the monumental. Of these the largest examples are the Marshall Field Store (1902, 1906, 1907, 1914), on State Street between Washington and Randolph, and the huge Butler Brothers warehouses (1913, 1922), stretching for nearly two blocks along Canal Street opposite the train shed of the North Western Station.

One of the last structures in the Loop to be built in the old commercial style is the Lemoyne Building, originally a combination of hotel, offices, and stores but now simply an office block (Fig. 143). It was erected between 1914 and 1915 at 180 North Wabash Avenue after the plans of Mundie, Jensen and McClurg, the inheritors of Jenney's business. Completed just thirty years after the opening of the Home Insurance, it represents the concluding episode in the Jenney phase of the Chicago movement.

The work of George C. Nimmons (1865–1947) and William K. Fellows (1870–1948) is to a certain extent derived from that of both Jenney and Holabird, although the younger architects generally introduced a greater variety of elements and a livelier and more original ornament into their elevations. The partnership of Nimmons and Fellows was established in 1898 and flourished until 1910, when the latter left and founded a new business with Dwight H. Perkins and John L. Hamilton in the following year.[17] Except for the Bailey Building, this firm did little to attract the historian's attention for the first half of its existence, but its place in the hierarchy was suddenly and dramatically changed early in the new century.

In 1904 Nimmons and Fellows were awarded what was very likely the largest single commission in the history of Chicago building up to that date. Sears, Roebuck and Company selected the relatively young firm as the designers of their warehouse, distribution, and administrative center on West Arthington Avenue at Homan. Nothing better demonstrated the power and efficiency of the building industry of Chicago than the construction of this immense complex. The five main structures of the group are the merchandise, administration, and machinery buildings, the printing plant, and the power and steam generating plant. It was said to be the largest mercantile establishment in the world at the time, and subsequent expansions have probably maintained this record. The Merchandise Building, nine and one-half stories high with a five-story tower over the main entrance, covers 160,000 square feet in area of plan and embraces 14,000,000 cubic feet of space within the main block. In addition to this immense enclosure, there is a long unloading and freight-handling wing extending along the railroad sidings at the rear of the building. For all their unprecedented size, the five major structures and their subsidiary facilities were built in exactly twelve months, from January 24, 1905, to January 22, 1906. Only the exigencies of war have brought comparable feats of construction.[18]

The Merchandise Building alone reveals an architectural character expressive of this technical prowess. Except for the Doric columns and entablature at the main entrance and the Roman arcades on all four elevations at the top of the tower, the walls are the typical cellular screens of window groups enframed in spandrels and continuous piers of brick. The regular pattern of openings is interrupted only at the corners, where the windows are reduced to a single opening in each bay, and at several places along the front and side elevations, where the window area is again sharply contracted in the bays housing utilities, stairways, and elevators. The tower stands out as a distinct entity because of the skyscraper verticalism that bears some resemblance to the façade of Sullivan's Garrick Theater Building. For the most part the Sears Roebuck Merchandise Building is a straightforward utilitarian

[17] For the work of Dwight Perkins during this period, see pp. 200–203.

[18] A few of the more spectacular statistics may give some idea of the size of the Sears Roebuck complex: the five buildings rest on a total of 1,563 rock caissons sunk to a maximum depth of 90 feet below grade; the total quantity of lumber for framing, flooring, formwork, and miscellaneous uses measured 20,505,000 board feet; a maximum volume of 60 carloads of supplies and equipment were unloaded in a single day. The Thompson-Starrett Company were the contractors for this staggering achievement.

work with undeniable power in its combination of great size and simple rectangular geometry. The warm color of the brickwork and the heavy rhythm of the unbroken piers adds a measure of richness and dignity to a severely functional design. The whole group was once isolated from surrounding buildings and could be seen with generous foreground. The Sears executives clearly wanted everyone to know that they conducted business on a grand scale. The company's facilities at this location have been progressively enlarged over the years to accommodate a store and mail-order business with annual revenues now above $5,000,000,000. The major step in this expansion, accomplished from 1917 to 1918, again found Nimmons in charge of the design.

Among the less prominent works of Nimmons and Fellows, the Arthur Dixon Building represents a transition from the orignal forms of the Chicago school to the new essays that came after 1900. Erected in 1908 at 411 South Wells Street, the Dixon is a small seven-story building with a simple, articulated façade whose somewhat enlarged piers and spandrels of brick suggest the work of the second generation of the school.

Nimmons' familiarity with warehouse design and construction brought him the commission for the big office and storage building of Reid, Murdoch and Company, built between 1912 and 1913 and extending for 320 feet along the north bank of the Chicago River between Clark and La Salle (Fig. 144). The steel- and concrete-framed building stands eight stories above water level, with a three-story clock tower rising above the center bay. Piers and spandrels are brick, and the floors and footings are reinforced concrete. The footings are supported by wood piles driven to hardpan. The severity of the cellular elevations is relieved by a variety of details that form a well-integrated composition. Chief among these are the raked horizontal joints that intensify the natural horizontality of the long building, the separation of the two end bays, the enlargement of the piers at the ends and at the center, the low arcade of the top story, and the heavy projecting course that separates the parapet from the main wall. The formal elements of the tower—the shallow balconies, the close vertical pattern arising from the grouped windows and the strongly emphasized mullions, the wide overhang of the roof that terminates the upward movement with a broad horizontal sweep—all of these are prominent features in the work of Sullivan, Wright, and the twentieth-century generation of the Chicago movement. The low-pitched gables over the paired end bays were probably introduced to relieve the 320-foot long line of the parapet. They were later felt to be anachronistic and were replaced by a continuation of the flat coping. The Reid Murdoch Building was subsequently acquired by the Monarch Foods Company, which in turn leased it to the city as a municipal office building. Somewhat heavy and static in its dead-center symmetry, although warm in color, it remains one of the impressive façades among the fantastic assortment of river-front buildings that face the spectator on Wacker Drive.

2. THE SECOND GENERATION, OR THE PRAIRIE SCHOOL

The work of Nimmons and Fellows belongs mainly to the original and for long the dominant tradition of the Chicago school, which was highly empirical in its concern with utilitarian and structural ends. The new generation of architects that began to flourish after 1900 were imbued with a different spirit. Their aesthetic mentor was Sullivan, and like him they were more concerned with ornamental variety and originality and with the plastic possibilities of building design than with functionalist theories. This later development of the Chicago movement was astonishingly vigorous, especially in the field of residential architecture, and the rapid growth of the architects' powers exactly paralleled the decline of the older forms of structural expression. The fertility of the movement and the volume of its work were great enough to command the attention of the authoritative critics of *Architectural Record* at the very beginning of the century. Arthur C. David wrote one of the most perceptive essays on the characteristics of the new residential work, but its general evaluation is applicable to commercial and public building as well.

It is beginning to be more and more apparent that a number of the better architects of the West have a tendency consciously to break away from the time-honored European tradition to which their eastern brethren devotedly cleave. . . . The number of the protestants is not as yet very great; several of the architects whose work shows the influence of the different ideal are by no means consistent in their devotion thereto; and the different members of the group differ considerably in the extent to which they push their search for an original vehicle of expression. In the case of some of them the desire to free themselves from tradition does not go much further than a search for irregularity in exterior design and for certain novel details in the interior. Others have become absolutely revolutionary in their ideals and in their technical means. They are seeking to make one big jump from a condition of stylistic servitude to that of irreverent and self-assured independence. They do not seek originality, however, as the "great American architect" once did by combining a number of traditional types into one incongruous hodge-podge. The radicals among the group are seeking for a rational and consistent basis for American design and ornament. The more conservative are merely seeking to reduce their debt to the European tradition to a few fundamental forms and to work out on the basis of those forms some new types of design. . . . The forms which they devise occasionally suggest the influence of the "New Style," which is so popular abroad; but when this is the case the suggestion points rather to the German than the French variety of movement. For the most part, however, it borrows little either from "L'Art Nouveau" or the "Jugend Style." It really derives its momentum and inspiration from the work of Mr. Louis Sullivan, and from a very able architect, who issued from Mr. Sullivan's office, Mr. Frank Wright. But it is still too young to have a history, and probably ten years must pass before any very intelligent estimate can be placed upon its value.[19]

The final sentence of this quotation is peculiarly ironic: in ten years the Chicago movement was moribund, and by the end of the First World War it was dead as a coherent school. Even worse, there was no one left who was interested in making an appraisal of its achievement, as Frank Lloyd Wright was to learn in the decade of the 1920's. Indeed, the sudden death and virtual oblivion of the midwestern architectural movement, which was so prolific up to 1915, continues to be one of the unexplained phenomena of American cultural history. The Chicago literary renaissance of the same period moved to New York and on to greater heights, but there was no place in the United States that was hospitable to original architecture. The fact that the second-generation Chicagoans—the Prairie school, as they are sometimes known—turned almost exclusively to residential building around 1910 indicates that the big commercial clients had already begun to lose that flair for the bold and the emancipated that they had once regarded as the proper hallmark of their power.

Of all the Chicago architects whose independent work lies in the twentieth century, George Grant Elmslie was the most skilful and imaginative, although very few of his commissions came from the city itself. This was partly a consequence—ironically enough—of his long association with Sullivan. He was born in Huntly, Scotland, in 1871, emigrated to Chicago in the early 1880's, and entered the office of Joseph Lyman Silsbee as errand boy and then apprentice in 1885. Wright and George Maher had already joined Silsbee's staff by that date.[20] Elmslie must have been strongly influenced by Wright's example, for he followed the pattern of Wright's moves almost exactly. In 1890 he joined the firm of Adler and Sullivan, by the end of the decade rose to the position of a designer second only to Sullivan himself, and in 1909 left to help found the partnership of Purcell, Feick and Elmslie, with offices in Chicago and Minneapolis. This became the firm of Purcell and Elmslie in 1913, to be dissolved in turn in 1921.[21] Elmslie continued to

[19] Arthur C. David, "The Architecture of Ideas," *Architectural Record*, XV (April, 1904), 361–64. Among the foreign influences on the residential work of the Chicago group was the English Arts and Crafts movement.

[20] For the work of George Maher, see pp. 195–200.

[21] William Gray Purcell was born in Chicago in 1880. He enrolled as an architectural student at Cornell University in 1899 and graduated in 1903. He founded a partnership

maintain an office in Chicago until his retirement in 1935; he died in 1953. Much of the work of Elmslie and his partners was residential, the major part of it in Minneapolis and the smaller towns of Minnesota and Wisconsin. There were several eastern commissions, most notable among them the Bradley house at Woods Hole, Massachusetts (1911), and a particularly brilliant triumph in the Midwest, the Woodbury County Court House at Sioux City, Iowa (1915–17).

By 1895 Elmslie had become the leading figure in Sullivan's office, both in designing and in dealing with clients. When Sullivan started on his decline after the Carson Pirie Scott Store, it was Elmslie who maintained the flow of commissions by meeting clients and acting as a buffer between them and the unpredictable Sullivan. The older man came to rely on Elmslie to an increasing extent, eventually to such a degree that it is now difficult to decide when the designer's pencil, so to speak, passed from the former to the latter. David Gebhard, the leading authority on Elmslie, believes that Sullivan's legacy had already passed to his Scottish assistant at the time when he left the firm.

The continuity of design of the Sullivan office, then, lies in the work of Purcell and Elmslie after 1909, rather than in the few banks which Sullivan designed after this date. . . . The creative and original design solutions which were expressed in the later buildings of the Sullivan office before 1909 were not then an indication of a resurgence of Sullivan's creativity, but rather they demark the architectural development of George Grant Elmslie as a designer in his own right. With this in mind the work of Sullivan's later years becomes comprehensible, and the later designs of the firm of Purcell and Elmslie assume a new and increased importance in the history of American architecture.[22]

The first commercial work of Purcell, Feick and Elmslie in Chicago is the former Edison Building, constructed in 1912 and still standing at 229 South Wabash Avenue (Fig. 145). Originally a store and sales office of the Chicago Edison Phonograph Company, it was commissioned by Henry Babson of Riverside, who held title to the property. Sullivan had designed Babson's house in Riverside (1907), although Elmslie was chiefly responsible for the details of ornament and planning. Because of this association, Babson first intended to offer the Edison commission to Sullivan, but when he learned

---

with George Feick in Minneapolis in 1906. Elmslie joined them, as we have noted, in 1909. Feick left the firm in 1913, and Purcell moved to Portland, Oregon, in 1920 to establish an independent practice. He eventually retired to Pasadena, California, where he still lives (1963).

[22] David S. Gebhard, "Louis Sullivan and George Grant Elmslie," *Journal of the Society of Architectural Historians,* XIX (May, 1960), 68.

that Elmslie had left Sullivan's office, he thought that the older man could not handle the work and thus offered the commission to the new firm.

The adjacent Wabash Avenue elevated line and the later disfigurement of the ground floor for a restaurant make it nearly impossible for the spectator to see that the Edison store is one of the most imaginative small buildings of the Chicago school. Only one bay wide and four stories high, the façade is the nearest thing to the dominant structuralism of the Chicago tradition that Elmslie did. Within this simple concept and the confines of a narrow lot, the architects transformed a strictly functional idea into a minor masterpiece. Two narrow brick piers, which are actually the widened ends of the side walls, extend continuously upward from grade level to a high spandrel band formed partly by the front of the parapet and capped by an ornamental coping. Each of the bays in vertical succession is thus a Chicago window in which the mullions are extremely tenuous brick piers again extending continuously up the height of the façade. The wonder is that so much brickwork in so narrow an area could be composed into the delicacy and strength and sharp-edged clarity of this elevation. The light buff brick contrasts strongly with the dark areas of the windows shadowed by their deep reveals. The base of the glass curtain is set far back from the pier faces to make a sheltered entranceway that once must have been irrestibly inviting amid the noise and frantic traffic of Wabash Avenue. The elegant Roman brick; the varying depths of recession of the spandrel faces, windows, and base; the rich and original ornament concentrated at the capitals of the piers, in the center of the top spandrel, and along the coping—these and the expert proportions make the Edison store a little triumph of plastic design. It and the courthouse at Sioux City, completed five years later, are enough to establish Elmslie as a creative architect of the first rank.

After the Edison store the work of Purcell and Elmslie was increasingly confined to the Twin Cities region. There were few commissions in the Chicago area. Henry Babson employed their talents once more when they designed the service buildings for his farm in Riverside (1915).[23] Their last work in the city of Chicago and their only industrial commission is the factory built for the International Leather and Belting Company (1917–18), whose headquarters and main plant were in New Haven, Connecticut (Fig. 146). The company's original program embraced a fairly extensive group of factory and office buildings, but the bankruptcy of the firm about 1919

[23] The suburban town of Riverside still remains an architectural and planning showplace, especially the part south of the Burlington Railroad line. Lying on a narrow tongue of land in a tight S-curve of the Des Plaines River, the winding and heavily shaded streets were originally laid out by Frederick Law Olmsted in 1869. Foremost of its architectural works is the celebrated Coonley house (1908), a work of controlled extravagance that established once and for all Wright's supreme virtuosity in residential design.

prevented the realization of all but a small part of the plan. Purcell and Elmslie's complete project included an office building and three manufacturing units, two of which were to be single-story structures flanking the main four-story factory. A single-story office block was planned to stand in front of the higher manufacturing unit and to be marked by a slender tower rising to a height of about six stories above grade. The office wing and tower formed a complex of narrow rectangular prisms with a pronounced vertical accent. The entire group suggests an anticipation of the work of Willem Dudok and the cubistic skyscrapers of the *Esprit Nouveau* period in the mid-twenties.

Of the four structures composing the belting company's project, only one small factory building was constructed.[24] Its side walls of glass make it one of the early industrial buildings with walls of continuous glazing, a technique which dates from about 1910. A one-story factory with a gabled roof on trusses, its façade is distinguished by a common characteristic of the late Chicago school—the vertical pattern made by a series of closely ranked piers extending as mullions across the horizontally disposed window group. The massive brick piers at the corners and the heavy stone caps that top them are also familiar features of the time, especially in Wright's work, although the battered outer edges of the piers in the International Leather factory seem to be unique to Purcell and Elmslie's design. The simple building is an excellent example of how creative architects can transform a straightforward industrial structure into a warm and lively design.

After the dissolution of the partnership with Purcell in 1921, Elmslie continued the business alone. His final commissions in the Chicago metropolitan area came from Aurora. The first was for the American National Bank Building, completed in 1922, and the second for the Healy Chapel, 1926. The earlier building followed a number of banks designed by Purcell and Elmslie that had given the firm a position of some eminence in this specialty. The chapel is unusual among Elmslie's designs because of its severe economy of detail. The building is approximately T-shaped in plan, the long wing one and one-half stories in height under a gabled roof and the short wing three stories under a hipped roof. The walls are simply unbroken planes of brick opened into horizontal groups of Chicago windows.

The ornamental style established by Sullivan and Elmslie enjoyed a considerable vogue in the early years of the century and produced several imitators among less-well-known architects. A number of store, office, warehouse, and apartment buildings in the Chicago area reveal decorative details that

[24] I have not been able to discover the address of the International Leather factory. The bankruptcy of the firm occurred during a six-year hiatus in the publication of the *Chicago Directory* (1917–23), and the name of the corporation was changed before the next volume of the directory was issued.

seem clearly to have been derived from the work of one or the other of the two architects. One of the best of these is the façade of that portion of Lord's Department Store that fronts at 625 Davis Street in Evanston (Fig. 147). The entire store consists of three separate iron-framed buildings constructed between 1905 and 1906, which together form an L-shaped plan with one unit fronting on Orrington Avenue and two on Davis Street. The unit at 625 Davis, designed by W. M. Walter, is distinguished chiefly by continuous openings at the first and second floors that are surrounded by bands of terra-cotta tiles with an ornamental pattern that could only have been derived from the floral designs of Sullivan and Elmslie. The other Davis Street unit, at 621–23, originally known as the Witkower Building and designed by George H. Edbrooke, offers a typical example of the store front in the functional Chicago tradition. Separate windows nearly equal to the bay span in width are set in deep, sharp-edged reveals cut directly into the brick wall plane. Similar in general form is the two-story building at 1014 Davis Street, Evanston, designed by E. O. Blake and built in 1905.

In the number and size of their commercial and public buildings, Richard E. Schmidt and his associates were the most prolific of the Chicago architects whose major achievements came after the turn of the century. Schmidt could design with equal facility in the classical and the Chicago modes, and his important work is good in proportion to the consistency with which he pursued the aims of the Chicago school. The basic form of his strictly utilitarian buildings was usually derived from the underlying structural frame and thus belonged more to the tradition of Holabird and Roche than to that of Sullivan and Elmslie. But Schmidt was equally interested in the plastic modeling of wall surfaces, which he treated in such a way as to give either a vertical or a horizontal emphasis. In this respect he was working in the new forms that Sullivan, Elmslie, and Wright were developing around the turn of the century. His attitude toward design thus embraced both the expression of a personal idiom and the impersonal revelation of the structure and function of the particular building.

Richard Schmidt was born at Ebern, Bavaria, in 1865 and was brought to the United States by his family in the following year. He enrolled in the architectural school of the Massachusetts Institute of Technology in 1883 but left two years later, having decided to begin his career as an architect before completing the curriculum. He started to practice in Chicago in 1887 and soon established an independent firm with a solid reputation. A capable and energetic young man, he was awarded a major skyscraper commission within a decade and was thus quickly launched on a fifty-year career of unbroken success that included the design of some of the most prominent buildings in Chicago. His first big commission was the Montgomery Ward Building at the northwest corner of Michigan Avenue and Madison Street (1897–99)—the beginning of a profitable association with this rapidly expanding mail-order business. Now known as the Tower Building, the Ward was originally built as a narrow twelve-story, steel-framed tower, but subsequent additions raised its height to twenty stories. The pyramidal roof that was once its most conspicuous feature was removed at the time the new stories were added. But Schmidt was unsure of himself in the high building: the main elevations represent a confused attempt to create an appropriate expression for the skyscraper out of classical details, horizontally disposed openings, and the new verticalism that had been developed by Root and Sullivan.

It was the utilitarian and unpretentious warehouse that seems to have freed Schmidt's hand and to have given him the kind of opportunity he needed to show his real ability. The first of these structures is the former warehouse of the Grommes and Ullrich Company, erected in 1901 at 108 West Illinois Street and now owned by the W. H. Long Company. Associated with Schmidt in this design was a talented young newcomer from Toronto, Hugh M. G. Garden (1873–1961), who was ultimately to be responsible for most of the actual designing work in Schmidt's office. The Grommes and Ullrich warehouse is a four-story timber-framed building with a typical cellular wall of bay-wide Chicago windows. The openings are enframed in patterned brickwork marked by horizontal bands of projecting courses on the pier faces and the top spandrel or parapet face. The base of the building is opened to a generous area of glass that fills the bays defined by the narrow piers and spandrel panels. The greater height of the first story, however, makes the individual bays square in elevation and thus out of proportion to the horizontally elongated windows of the upper three stories. The Grommes and Ullrich warehouse attracted the attention of the architectural critics and theorists Russell Sturgis and Peter B. Wight. The latter, who enjoyed great success as a Gothic revivalist, was beginning to lose something of his medieval enthusiasm in the first decade of the century and to see the possibilities of a new realistic and organic architecture in modest buildings like the Grommes warehouse.

The ambiguity that may result when a functional and organic form is inadequately harmonized with personal expression appears in Schmidt's Chapin and Gore Building, erected in 1904 at 63 East Adams Street, where it still stands with little change from the original design (Fig. 148). This eight-story office block, later known as the Nepeenauk, is now the Union Life Building. The façade is the product of a free plastic handling of the major elements. Above the third story the wall appears to start from the formal expression of the iron and timber frame behind it; yet the unusually deep reveals, the wide piers with their heavily ornamented capitals, and the deep spandrel at the top suggest masonry construction that has been molded to produce the sharp edges and plane surfaces of an architecture appropriate to mechanized industry.[25] The seemingly capricious change in the treatment of the wall at the second and third stories may have been the outgrowth of structural exigencies, but the details arise from pure personal feeling and are not well harmonized with the base and the upper stories. The original glass areas at the end bays of the first story and between the entrances remain but have been cluttered up by the window paraphernalia of a store and two restaurants. Alteration has not improved the appearance of the building, although it is less offensive than the usual variety of modernization.

The same interest in modeling surfaces in a subjective and plastic rather than an organic way lies behind the outer form of the powerhouse of the Schoenhofen Brewery, erected in 1902 at Eighteenth Street and Canalport Avenue (Fig. 149). The main street elevation is a clean-cut rectangular plane that in profile and texture clearly expresses the nature of the brick curtain wall. But the openings are grouped in arbitrary vertical bands separated by false piers with recessed spandrels between them—a small-scale variation on the skyscraper accent of the Wainwright and Guaranty buildings. The vertical lines are grouped in turn into five panels extending from end to end of the elevation. The wall is thus treated like an abstract pictorial composition of vertical window groups enframed by an all-embracing rectangle of narrow brick moldings. The disposition of elements bears no relation to the structural frame of the building. The Schoenhofen Brewing Company (now Schoenhofen-Edelweiss) has moved to other quarters, and the dirty and disfigured building at present serves as a distribution center of the Morningstar-Paisley Company, a manufacturer of glues.

The powerhouse impressed Russell Sturgis so much that he devoted a special article to it in *Architectural Record*. To him it was a work of realistic and functional design, something that could never be taught in the schools of the time.

No school of architecture can teach a man how to design such buildings as this brewery. At least, if there be any school of architecture of that stamp, it should really proclaim itself—its power of inspiring liberal and practical ideas in the

[25] The frame of the Chapin and Gore Building is virtually two separate structural systems with a great difference in the bearing capacities of the individual members. Up to the fourth floor the frame is a massive construction of cast-iron columns and timber beams designed for a floor load of 250 pounds per square foot; for the upper five stories it was designed for a 100-pound load. This difference may have suggested, or even dictated, the special treatment of the second and third stories. The pier width is greatly increased, and the recessed edges in the broken rectangular moldings may represent Schmidt's attempt to harmonize the changed proportions with those above and below the two stories.

youthful mind should be widely advertised. As things are, we dread the going of a student to an architectural school, and we dread accepting him as an assistant when he leaves that school; and this because of the perfunctory nature of what he learns there. No blame to anyone! He would be a bold professor of architecture who would try and lead his boys to the designing of things according to the requirements of the situation.[26]

An unusual example of the new idiom of warehouse design that Schmidt was developing is the structure originally built for Kelley, Maus and Company in 1903 and now occupied chiefly by the Graham Paper Company. Designed by Jarvis Hunt, the building is trapezoidal in plan because it stands on a narrow irregular lot bounded at the ends by Lake and Randolph streets and at the sides by the Chicago River and the tracks of the Milwaukee Railroad.[27] The warehouse is constructed with solid bearing walls of brick on the exterior and an unusually massive and elaborate system of timber framing on the interior. The plank floors are carried directly on joists supported in turn by immense timber girders of square section. Since the joists rest on top of the girders, the total depth of the floor framing system, which is wholly exposed, appears to be at least 36 inches. The columns are wood incased in fireproof tile and cast-iron sheathing. This primitive but perfectly sound system of construction is in its external appearance a solid brick prism punctuated by small, widely spaced windows of square outline. By using brick of three different colors, Hunt transformed the otherwise unrelieved walls into a mosaic-like design in which the windows form an integral part of the over-all pattern. The brick of darkest color is disposed in groups of four narrow ribbons, two at the sill and lintel lines of each window row and two equally spaced between them, all of the ribbons extending entirely around the four elevations. In this way the walls are divided into a series of horizontal bands forming a repetitive pattern of three different widths. The exterior brickwork of the building is now so discolored by soot and smoke that the once colorful mosaic pattern is almost invisible.

What is important in this decorative motive is the applied horizontality that is secured wholly through surface color. This horizontal accent made its first appearance in the Montauk Building and reached its culmination in Chicago with Wright's Robie house and Schmidt's Montgomery Ward warehouse. And many more architects were to use it before the Chicago movement spent itself. With the exception of Wright's work in the 1920's, however, it dis-

[26] Russell Sturgis, "The Schoenhofen Brewery," *Architectural Record*, XVII (March, 1905), 201.

[27] Jarvis Hunt (1863?–1941) was a highly successful Chicago eclecticist whose largest commission was Kansas City Union Station (1910–13). His best-known works in Chicago are the American Trust and Savings Bank (1906), the Lake Shore Club (1924), and the 900 North Michigan Avenue Building (1927).

appeared from American architecture until it was reintroduced by way of the European International Style around 1930. Raymond Hood's McGraw-Hill Building in New York, completed in that year, is probably the first of the new skyscrapers with a horizontal accent.[28]

Russell Sturgis felt that the Kelley Maus warehouse offered another salutary lesson to the architects of the time.

There is something to be said for the theory broached now and then by persons not enamored of our present architecture of mere pretence, that the designers should be restrained to square masses and sharp corners and plain windows for twenty years to come—with sculpture denied them and all the bad achitectural forms *tabu*. Then, it is thought by some, a chance for design rightly so-called, might be found in the very inability to misuse the old forms. At all events there is great delight in watching the attempts of those who willingly take up that course of thought and push it in a sensible way and with energy.[29]

Jarvis Hunt's subsequent career, however, was hardly one to fit this description. He seldom found any of the traditional forms taboo, and the black-

[28] Horizontal patterns had been common features of the American scene for a long time before the Chicago architects employed them as formal elements in building. Clapboard siding of houses and barns, long rows of closely ranked windows in mills and warehouses, the roof, sill, and upper and lower window lines of railroad passenger cars, and the deck lines of river steamboats are the most obvious examples. As a matter of fact, the wood-sheathed passenger car and the steamboat reveal the peculiar combination of long horizontal lines holding between them a densely grouped array of short vertical lines that appears again and again in the Chicago work. The view that this horizontality was inspired by the level sweep of the prairie and Lake Michigan is a romantic and oversimplified explanation. All-embracing physiographic features of this kind do not lead to such carefully shaped ornament.

In addition to the horizontal motives in some of Root's designs and in Sullivan's Meyer Building and Carson store, there were other architectural antecedents in the work of the English Arts and Crafts group. Conspicuous examples appear in certain of the residential designs of C. F. A. Voysey in the late 1890's.

The renewed popularity of the horizontal motive in building during the 1930's led to its being arbitrarily applied to the decorative scheme of the first so-called streamlined Pullman cars, which date from 1938. Horizontal stripes exactly like those of the Kelley warehouse in Chicago were added to the car wall along the upper and lower window lines and between the windows to exaggerate the already pronounced horizontality of the roof, car sill, and top and bottom window edges. The industrial designer Henry Dreyfuss appears to have been the first to design railroad passenger cars in this way.

The Chicago pattern (long horizontal lines bounding a close vertical array) is again becoming common through the use of concrete sun screens and load-bearing screen walls. An example of the first is the Water Tower Inn, Michigan and Chicago avenues, designed by Hausner and Macsai, and an example of the second, the University Apartments, Harper Avenue and Fifty-fifth Street, by I. M. Pei and Loewenberg and Loewenberg. Both were completed in 1961. But these features arise, of course, from structural and functional elements.

[29] Russell Sturgis, "The Warehouse and Factory in Architecture," *Architectural Record*, XV (February, 1904), 133.

ened warehouse on the Chicago River is an isolated phenomenon among his works.

Before Richard Schmidt returned to the design of warehouses, he was awarded a series of commissions for hospitals, a building type in which his successive firms were to continue to specialize throughout their history. The first of these, St. Anne's Hospital at 4950 West Thomas Avenue (1902–3), shows no distinction in its conventional classicism. The next, however, not only marked a radical break with architectural tradition but was ultimately destined to grow into one of the great hospital and medical research centers in the world. Michael Reese Hospital was planned in 1905 and completed the following year along Ellis Avenue at the east end of Twenty-ninth Street (Fig. 150). The plan of the central building in the original group has the shape of a widespread blunted V in which two long wings extend at 45 degrees from a central pavilion. The projecting piers at the inner corners of the main elevation and above the entrance, along with the high, narrow, widely spaced windows, give the walls a vertical movement, but this is decisively overlaid by a strong horizontal pattern secured by means of continuous projecting courses at the sill and lintel lines and the overhanging roof. The narrow windows and the large unrelieved areas of brick, now badly discolored, give the whole building a rather forbidding institutional character, but this was very likely less pronounced before the original light-colored brick acquired its patina of soot.

At the end of the Second World War Michael Reese Hospital began a program of expansion that eventually extended its elaborate facilties for research, treatment, and staff housing southward to Thirty-second Street. The curtain walls of buff brick match the original color of the older buildings, although this is difficult to believe now. At the same time the hospital undertook the construction of the huge urban renewal project known as Prairie Shores, of which the five apartment buildings completed by 1963 represent about half the total plan.

Henrotin Hospital, built in 1906 at the southeast corner of La Salle and Oak streets, is the least interesting of Schmidt's designs. The six-story building, L-shaped in plan, is supported on a reinforced concrete frame of the conventional column and beam system.[30] All elevations of the hospital are

[30] Schmidt was one of the pioneers in the use of concrete construction in Chicago. The first essay in reinforced concrete framing appears to have been the Winton Building (1904), at the northeast corner of Michigan Avenue and Thirteenth Street. The architect was James Gamble Rogers, and the engineer E. Lee Heidenreich. The Winton is a small three-story building constructed with exterior bearing walls and an interior frame of columns and beams reinforced with bars according to the system patented by the French inventor Joseph Monier. The year 1904 was a rather late date for the original work of concrete framing in Chicago, but the form of the reinforcing suggests that it may well have been the pioneer.

extremely severe and wholly devoid of ornamental detail. The horizontal pattern common in Schmidt's work is here transformed into nearly unbroken verticality. Only the horizontal courses at the second-floor line and at the top of the parapet interrupt the vertical lines of the continuous piers and the window rows with their recessed spandrels. The pattern is exactly like that of the advanced skyscraper design of the late 1920's and by virtue of its color bears a striking resemblance to Raymond Hood's Daily News Building in New York. The white glazed brick of Schmidt's building may suggest the necessary sterile quality of a hospital interior, but it also serves to increase the coldness of the exterior design. A new wing was added to Henrotin Hospital in 1935. Although the addition was designed by Holabird and Root, the architects made no change in Schmidt's treatment of the exterior walls.

In 1906 Richard Schmidt formed a partnership with Hugh Garden and Edgar Martin (1871–1951) that was to flourish for the next twenty years. Martin left the firm in 1925 and was replaced in the following year by Carl A. Erikson, who is now the senior member of the business. The expanded office, embracing engineering as well as architectural design, immediately had its hands full with a commission probably second only to the Sears Roebuck merchandise plant in total size. The mail-order business founded in 1872 by A. Montgomery Ward had expanded with such rapidity that within little more than a generation it required virtually unparalleled facilities for administration and distribution. Ward decided at one stroke to build an entirely new plant to house the various operations of his company. On an open site along the North Branch of the Chicago River at Chicago Avenue construction began on the whole complex in 1906. The office building on the south side of the street was completed in 1907, and the tremendous warehouse and distribution center on the north side in 1908. Both buildings are supported by a reinforced concrete frame on wood piling, but the architectural treatment of the two is radically different. The office block, with a corner tower and smaller dimensions in plan, is treated in the vertical manner through continuous piers and mullions, whereas the great elongation of the warehouse is intensified by a horizontal emphasis. This building stands by itself as one of the most powerful works of utilitarian architecture that our building art has produced (Figs. 151, 152).

In the warehouse the plastic handling of form characteristic of Sullivan and Wright is subordinated to and informed by the structural and functional nature of the building. The whole block is a bent trapezoid in plan, nine

---

Frank Lloyd Wright's factory for the E-Z Polish Company, built in 1905 at 3005 West Carroll Avenue, is an early work in bar-reinforced concrete framing. Schmidt adopted concrete construction in 1905 and was soon using it for very large buildings. For the initial use in Chicago of Turner's flat-slab system, see p. 175.

stories high along the river, 800 feet long, with an average width of nearly 200 feet, and 158,000 square feet in area of plan. This immense volume was treated with a boldness, assurance, and directness worthy of the best architects of the Chicago school. The elevations take their basic form from the system of construction, but they are at the same time revelations of a purely personal idea that was an outgrowth of the new aims of the Chicago movement. In this respect the building is comparable to the Carson Pirie Scott Store: both represent a complete integration of the two fundamental themes of the school.

The Montgomery Ward warehouse is the largest building of the Chicago school to be supported on a reinforced concrete frame. The massive columns and girders of the skeleton are directly reflected in the pattern of horizontal and vertical bands that forms the dominant accent of the elevations. In fact, with the exception of the brick facing on the spandrels, the elevations are composed of the peripheral members of the frame itself. On this direct revelation of structure, the architect imposed a strong horizontality achieved by means of narrow projecting bands at the top and bottom of each spandrel (Fig. 152). It is the horizontality that we have noted with growing frequency following Sullivan's Meyer Building, but here it is a more logical product of the form dictated by the material of the structural frame in addition to being an intensified expression of the natural horizontality of the multistory building. The sweeping horizontal planes and long bands of Wright's Robie house, also completed in 1908, represent the same aesthetic interest, but in that case they were employed for strictly formal purposes.

At the other end of the building spectrum from the Montgomery Ward warehouse are the recreational and ornamental buildings of Humboldt Park, the design of which was intrusted exclusively to Hugh Garden. They were completed in 1907, while Jens Jensen's masterpiece of landscape art was being laid out by the gardeners of the West Park District.[31] The park structures included the main pavilion and boathouse, the pergola, and the music pavilion. Of these only the boathouse is a true building (Fig. 153). It is a remarkably open and delicate structure, perfectly appropriate to its landscaped setting and its recreational function. The long elevations are divided

[31] Jensen was at the time chief landscape architect of the West Park District and the designer of Garfield and Columbus parks as well as Humboldt. He was another gifted Chicagoan who received international attention while remaining virtually unknown outside the Lake Michigan region. His plan for Humboldt Park was published in Hugo Koch's *Gartenkunst im Städtebau* (Berlin: E. Wasmuth, 1914), a volume devoted to the work of Jensen and other leading landscape designers of the time. He belongs squarely in the Chicago tradition, and the spirit behind his art reveals the same attitude that one finds in Wright's approach to architecture. Jensen was deeply impressed by the subtle beauties of the prairie landscape and sought to re-create them in artistic form in his landscape work.

primarily into three arched openings flanked by a simple vertical pattern of narrow columns; the entire structure is covered by a broad, low-pitched roof that sweeps well beyond the wall planes and imparts a dominant horizontal movement to the whole composition.

The three-story factory of the Garden City Plating and Manufacturing Company, at Tallmadge and Ogden avenues, lies closest to the mainstream of the commercial work of the eighties and nineties. Erected in 1910, the factory has the articulated cellular wall of the Holabird and Roche designs, but the excessively wide piers and spandrels suggest masonry construction and detract from its potential clarity and force. The Garden City factory is a simplified, purely functional verson of the incisive, open, and finely proportioned façade of the Dwight Building, a warehouse with a reinforced concrete frame constructed at 626 South Clark Street in 1911 (Fig. 154). The treatment of the main elevation recalls the Grommes and Ullrich warehouse, but the narrower piers and spandrels, the more organic horizontality of the wide windows with their continuous sills, the shallow reveals, and the uniformity of the whole composition make it much superior to its forerunner. The Dwight Building is certainly equal to the best work of Holabird and Roche—superior, perhaps, in the absence of the heavy cornice and stout corner piers common to their work.

The subsequent commissions of Schmidt, Garden and Martin are mostly anticlimactic. The famous Ambassador Hotel (now the Ambassador West), built between 1918 and 1919 at the northwest corner of State and Goethe streets, brought the firm further prominence but hardly added to its architectural stature. The office and factory building for the Bunte Brothers Candy Company (now Bunte Brothers–Chase) is a late work in the early creative spirit. Built between 1920 and 1921 at 3301 West Franklin Boulevard, it is the last design of the Schmidt firm that belongs to the great tradition of the Montgomery Ward warehouse (Fig. 155). The Bunte building is unlike any other of Schmidt's designs or, for that matter, any other work of the Chicago school. The entire structure, which covers 400,000 square feet of floor area, is disposed in a T-shaped plan of which the stem is the office block and the long wings the manufacturing areas. The office portion is an extraordinary complex of huge rectangular prisms—a central five-story block, two blunt four-story wings set back slightly from the entrance façade, a massive flat-topped tower, and two great pylons flanking the entrance—the forms of which are emphasized or repeated with variations in horizontal courses of stone, tower balconies, deep piers, and high ornamental caps on the pylons. The whole composition suggests the cubistic experiments that followed the *Esprit Nouveau* exhibit in Paris in 1925 and that strongly influenced the architects of the New York skyscrapers in the late twenties. The Bunte plant

194

is now largely empty and was put up for sale in the summer of 1961. The Gothic entry submitted by Schmidt, Garden and Martin for the Tribune Building Competition of 1922 marked the end of original work by this once imaginative firm of architects.

One of the most prolific and original of the Prairie school of residential architects was George W. Maher, who designed several public and commercial buildings that represent unusual variations on the basic Chicago principles. None of these commissions, however, came from the city itself. Maher was born in Mill Creek, West Virginia, in 1864 and began his architectural career in 1878 as a draftsman in the office of Augustus Bauer, with whom Adler had been briefly associated around the time of the Civil War. Maher went on to join Wright and Elmslie in the office of J. L. Silsbee, where he remained until 1888 and where he seems to have developed much of his highly independent talent. Like the two younger men under Silsbee's tutelage, he was soon imbued with the new spirit; deeply impressed by the work of Richardson and Sullivan and by the latter's ideas, he set himself the goal of creating a native architectural style that he hoped would express American democracy. He was strongly influenced by the Arts and Crafts movement in England and was one of the founding members of the Chicago Arts and Crafts Society, established in 1895.[32] The others in the charter group were Frank Lloyd Wright, Dwight Perkins, Robert C. Spencer, Jr., and Myron Hunt. The fundamental principles of their credo were simplicity of forms, the elimination of excessive detail, and respect for materials. To these they soon added the open interior plan.

Having established himself as an independent architect, Maher began to exhibit his prolific imagination in a series of markedly original residential designs, the first dating from 1894. Before the end of the decade, he became a leading figure in the Chicago Architectural Club, which was the representative organization of the Prairie movement and which made its work known to the public through a succession of exhibits beginning in 1898.

The most important of Maher's early non-residential commissions is the community clubhouse and recreational center of Kenilworth, Illinois, designed in 1904 and completed in 1906 (Fig. 156). A long single-story building that hugs the ground, it stands under a deep hipped roof that overdominates the low elevations. The main formal element of the exterior walls is a succession of vertical bands defined by the widely spaced floor-to-ceiling windows, plaster wall panels, and groups of closely ranked exposed posts.

[32] The leading figure in the Arts and Crafts group was William Morris. For the relation of this movement to the history of modern architecture, see Nikolaus Pevsner, *Pioneers of the Modern Movement from William Morris to Walter Gropius* (New York: Museum of Modern Art, 1949), chap. ii.

The whole treatment constitutes a unique variation on the familiar theme of Sullivan, Wright, and the other Prairie architects—the repetitive pattern of vertical elements bounded by strong horizontal lines. But in the case of the Kenilworth Club the irregular rhythm and the breadth of the wall panels tend to separate rather than unify the horizontal and vertical lines of the composition. On the whole the clubhouse is a pleasing little building in its heavily shaded suburban setting, but at the same time it is unsatisfactory in the excessive dimensions of the roof and the shifting proportions of the wall elements. The tree that grows through the roof over the entrance lobby is a piece of romantic naturalism popular with Wright and other Chicago architects. William Drummond, for example, deliberately designed his house so that trees grew through the floor and roof of the front porch.[33]

In the University Building, erected between 1905 and 1906 at the northwest corner of Davis Street and Chicago Avenue in Evanston, Maher developed several variations on characteristic features of the commercial work of the Chicago school (Fig. 157). The narrow south elevation of the building is entirely open to glass at the base and is divided at the second floor into a succession of Chicago windows that are separated by engaged octagonal columns with curious capitals. A rich foliate ornament starts on the upper shaft and spreads up and over a flat capital in the form of a rectangular plate extending well out from the outer column surface. This detail was repeated in a number of Maher's residential designs. In the long (east) elevation of the University Building, the Chicago windows are separated by relatively broad bands of the smooth limestone envelope of the wall. The building contains a store on the first floor and twelve offices disposed around a central skylighted court on the second.

In 1907 George Maher began a brief but fruitful architectural association with Northwestern University. He received the commission for two large buildings and prepared a comprehensive campus plan, thus becoming the first architect to design in a native and modern style for an American university. The plan remained an unexecuted project, but Patten Gymnasium and Swift Hall of Engineering were built simultaneously from 1908 to 1909. Maher had drawn the plans for James A. Patten's house in Evanston (1902), and it was probably this association that led to his choice as architect of the gymnasium that Patten endowed (Fig. 158). The central and dominant part of the building was the great single-span vault that covered the gymnasium floor and was supported by a series of steel three-hinged arches (Fig. 159). As a structural form the vault was derived from the armories and balloon train sheds, which by 1890 were nearly always built with hinged-arch framing. The façade was Maher's boldest non-residential design: the striking

[33] For Drummond's work, see pp. 208–9.

feature was the curved upper profile, which was exactly determined by the transverse section of the vault and which enframed the dominant formal pattern of the wide wall panels and vertically accented openings. Although this composition recalled the Kenilworth Club, the powerful curve incisively cutting off the whole upward movement was unique in the work of the Chicago school. The verticality of window groups, mullions, and solid wall panels was intensified by the thin shafts in the wall niches and by the light standards with lanterns in the form of narrow rectangular prisms. The front elevations of the low flanking wings, blank stone panels of square outline, were not well integrated with the main composition, but on the whole the façade possessed a true monumental force that stood in refreshing contrast to the heavy-handed eclecticism of most twentieth-century campuses. As Northwestern University expanded, Patten Gymnasium eventually became inadequate to serve the needs of the institution. Its demolition in 1940 and its replacement by the present featureless building, however much dictated by practical necessity, proved to be the first of a series of architectural disasters for the university. The brave program inaugurated by George Maher succumbed to newer and shallower fashions.[34]

Swift Hall was the original home of Northwestern's engineering school and although its function has changed, it is fortunately still standing (Fig. 160). For the more sober character of technological education, Maher turned to the functionalism of the commercial style as his guide. The long (east and west) elevations of the building are treated as cellular walls of Chicago windows very much in the tradition established by Holabird and Roche. The chief difference is that, whereas the latter always set the windows in deep reveals and frequently used continuous piers for vertical emphasis, Maher kept the whole wall screen nearly in a single plane, to a great extent like the contemporary curtain wall. A prominent motive in the composition of the façade is the system of tripartite divisions: there are three full stories above the grade level; the entrance is divided into three openings; the bays are grouped by threes within frames of narrow inflectional lines; and there are three such groups in the full elevation. As in the Patten Gymnasium, Maher again introduced thin shafts set in niches on either side of the entranceway. In Swift Hall, however, these shafts terminate in a curious ornament that seems to have been derived from a seed and thistle form. Maher's ornamental details were never fixed and suggest a restless search for some

[34] No American university was to be wholly freed from historical eclecticism until 1938, when Maher's fellow Chicagoan Frank Lloyd Wright began the campus plan of Florida Southern College in Lakeland, Florida. Two years later Mies van der Rohe created the original campus plan for the Illinois Institute of Technology, the architectural character of which lies much closer to the mainstream of the Chicago movement. For buildings on this campus, see p. 218.

kind of expression that he never quite reached. The ornamental motive of Swift Hall is repeated in abstract geometrized form in the outside doors, the windows of the entranceway, and the light fixtures of the entrance portico and lobby. Although the narrow two-level lobby is badly planned in a spatial sense, the primary elements of light standards, limestone-sheathed columns, and brick wall panels are composed into a harmonious decorative scheme.

Maher was consciously trying to create a native collegiate architecture in Swift Hall, and he defended his aims in a statement specially prepared for submission to the trustees of the university.

The design of the Swift Engineering Hall . . . marks a new era in College Architecture. The purpose of the design is not only to emphasize present day themes in the realms of art, but also the practicality of the design for the purposes intended.

Light and ventilation are of the first import in an educational building and in this design the façade lends itself to ample window treatment.

These windows are relieved of any monotony by means of a strong band motif which forms a parallelogram around the façade.

This band course arises from the base of the building, at the ends, forming strong courses and returning over the tops of the windows, combines the frieze and cornice treatment in one.

In the center of the main façade are two huge wall supports, moulded and ornamented, dividing the elevation into three equal sections. These supports rise organically from either side of the main entrance obtaining stability to the elevation and support for the frieze and cornice treatment. . . .

The horizontal effects predominate and all projections are subdued, the value of simplicity being thus enhanced. The main entrance loggia is directly in the center of the façade and the wide approach of steps extended to abutments on either side support large bronze lamps.[35]

The university's engineering school was moved from Swift Hall in 1941, when the present Technological Institute was completed. The older building was twice expanded in recent years: a new wing was added at the north end to house the gunnery room of the Department of Naval Science, and another wing, much longer, was built at the south end for the Cresap Laboratory of the Department of Biology. The north wing includes large areas of glass to provide a maximum amount of daylight for the study of naval gunnery, but the general treatment is in keeping with Maher's design. The long elevations of the Cresap wing closely follow the rhythms and the window treatment of the original building.

In the spring of 1908 Maher submitted a general campus plan to the university trustees. This valuable idea for the design of an entire campus was never realized, although it generated considerable enthusiasm among some

[35] Undated typescript over Maher's signature, University Archives, Deering Library, Northwestern University.

of the university's administrative officers at the time, particularly President Abram W. Harris, who recommended it to the trustees.

Mr. Maher would exploit to the fullest the natural advantages of the campus, which borders Lake Michigan for 4,000 feet. . . . [The plan involves] the adoption of a distinctly American type of architecture. . . . The arrangement of the landscape [is] to harmonize with the building scheme. It is his purpose to make a harmonious creation, to make it monumentally one of the great educational centers of the Middle West, and to express Americanism in architecture and landscape.[36]

As near as one can tell from the obscure surviving drawings, the plan was more classical than American in its monumental axiality. Yet it is a serious loss to university building and planning that something like this example of civic art in the Chicago style was never attempted. Maher and the university administration were probably influenced in this plan by the projected lakefront program of the city of Chicago. As in the case of the city itself, the site was ideal for the type of plan that included a harmonious association of building, landscape, and shore line together with adequate shore protection. The water of the lake and the planted grounds of the campus are separated by so narrow a strip of beach that the entire landscaped bank along the shore was totally destroyed by waves in the 1950's. The university has now started (1963) to expand its campus by building on fill raised behind cofferdams in the lake, in emulation of Chicago's immense waterfront development.

The commercial style from which Maher derived the elevations of Swift Hall reappears with variations in the house originally built for A. D. Sheridan between 1910 and 1911 at 310 Church Street in Evanston (Fig. 161). Although the treatment of the façade is perfectly appropriate to a detached residence, it contains many of the familiar elements of the Chicago office building: the wide Chicago windows, the regularity of the pattern formed by the openings and the brick wall areas, the emphasis on unbroken planes and severe geometric outline. Only the arched opening of the entrance interrupts the exact rectangularity, but single arches and arcades were fairly common features in the work of the Prairie school. The simple and handsome residence is still standing, well maintained and pleasingly situated along one of Evanston's little lake-front parks.[37]

[36] Annual Report of the President to the Board of Trustees of Northwestern University, June 2, 1908, pp. 592–93.

[37] Many of Maher's houses have a smaller window area than the Church Street house. He preferred large areas of smooth unbroken brickwork and was particularly adept at integrating it with his heavily molded windows and entrances. Two good examples of the more common design still stand on the portion of Sheridan Road between Hollywood Avenue and the right-angled turn in the line of Devon. They will not long survive, however, for this one-mile length of Sheridan is rapidly being transformed into a canyon of high-rise apartment buildings.

One of the last of Maher's non-residential commissions is the Joseph Sears Elementary School in Kenilworth, completed in 1912 (Fig. 162). This building differs radically from any of his previous work by virtue of the absence of windows in the front elevation and the extremely spare ornament. The simple rectangular planes of the walls and the flat overhanging roof represent a geometric purity that is rare in the late Chicago work. The shafts terminating in square tablets are a repetition of a similar theme in the Patten Gymnasium, and the engaged octagonal columns had previously appeared in the University Building, although their capitals are unique. Eight of these columns are symmetrically arranged in pairs on either side of the main entrance on the south elevation. The checkerboard pattern of the brick panels and the window groups of the long side elevations are familiar elements in the Prairie work. Geometric patterns in brickwork were distinguishing features in houses designed by Philip Webb and Norman Shaw in England. Since Maher was strongly influenced by these architects and their associates in the Arts and Crafts movement, he may have derived this decorative element from their work. There is enough of a resemblance between the Sears School and Wright's Unity Church in Oak Park (1906) to suggest another possible influence. After the Sears School, Maher's work was progressively eclipsed by the eclectic fashions that returned at the time of the First World War, with the result that he receded steadily into obscurity as the years passed until his death in 1926.

The architect who set the standard for scholastic building in Chicago was Dwight H. Perkins. Born in Memphis, Tennessee, in 1867, with two years at the Massachusetts Institute of Technology behind him (1885–87), he came to Chicago and entered the office of Burnham and Root in 1888. He must have exhibited unusual maturity and ability almost immediately, for they placed him in charge of the office during their activities with the World's Columbian Exposition in 1891 to 1893. Perkins established his own office in the year of the World's Fair and within two years received a fairly large commission for the design of Steinway Hall, built between 1895 and 1896 at 64 East Van Buren Street. The building housed Frank Lloyd Wright's office for a few years around the turn of the century and the Chicago Musical College until it was merged with Roosevelt University. The Steinway is a typical though undistinguished example of the tall, narrow office block in the manner of Holabird and Roche, with projecting bays and Chicago windows.

In 1901 Wright was commissioned by his uncle Jenkin Lloyd Jones, a Unitarian minister, to design the Abraham Lincoln Center, a settlement house founded by Jones and affiliated with his church. The minister apparently disliked the exterior design and turned the job over to Perkins, who was asked to redesign the elevations and possibly part of the interior. Perkins was thus largely responsible for the present appearance of the building, which was constructed between 1902 and 1903 at 700 East Oakwood Boulevard. The main elevation is another rectangular composition in which the vertical pattern secured through continuous piers is bound within strong horizontal bands at the base and the parapet. The whole block is a simple rectangular prism of excessive severity, a rather heavy design although arresting in its smooth planes of warm red brick.

Neither the Steinway nor the Abraham Lincoln building gave an indication of the imaginative designs that Dwight Perkins was to develop for public schools. The Chicago Board of Education appointed him as its chief architect in 1905 and thus pioneered in the adoption of a modern American architecture for school buildings.[38] It was thirty years before the practice began to spread, largely through the efforts of Richard Neutra in California and Perkins' son Lawrence in the Chicago area. Dwight Perkins was associated with the Board for only five years, but in that time he designed about forty new schools and additions to existing schools. The three most striking and original among them were completed in the years 1908 to 1911. Grover Cleveland Elementary School, the smallest of the three, is located at 3850 North Albany Avenue (Fig. 163). The plan of the building has the shape of a short-stemmed T with the three wings nearly identical in appearance and dimensions. In this way Perkins was able to secure the maximum amount of light and ventilation for all classrooms and offices. The predominant accent in all elevations between the base and the fourth floor is a verticalism arising from the deep continuous piers, but this is strongly bound by the heavy slab-like course of smooth stone at the sill line of the second floor and by the high parapet of brick surmounted by a stone coping. The walls are further enriched by a repetition of inverted U-shaped motives formed in a variety of ways—by the piers and lintels of the base, the patterned bands of brick enframing the individual bays of the fourth story, and the similar bands inclosing the entire window area of each elevation.

Variations on similar themes produce a markedly different effect in the Lyman Trumbull Elementary School, at the northwest corner of Ashland Boulevard and Foster Avenue (Fig. 164). The dense array of continuous brick mullions on the long elevations and the tower-like projections provide a strong vertical pattern, which, however, is sharply contrasted with the horizontality of the entablature over the main entrance and the alternate bands

[38] The private school appeared in modern form at about the time that Perkins' schools were completed: the initial work was the kindergarten and nursery school that Frank Lloyd Wright designed for Avery Coonley in Riverside (1910–11).

of light- and dark-colored brick. The opposing movements are partially unified through the use of two ornamental devices: one is the complete enframing of the window groups between the broad piers, and the other is the extension of the light and dark bands continuously over mullions, piers, and
projecting masses. The monumental treatment of the façade is distinctly
inferior to the lively rhythms of the long elevations. There are too many
diverse elements, and they are too heavy for the scale of the building and
for the light and open character of the grouped windows. When the entranceway is seen head-on, however, this elevation is less awkward than it appears
from the sharp angle of the photograph. The brickwork of the Trumbull
School is now badly discolored, which has the effect of making the building
seem heavier and hence more institutional than it really is.

Perkins' masterpiece is the big Carl Schurz High School, at Milwaukee
Avenue and Addison Street (Figs. 165, 166). The school is an impressive
example of the late Chicago style on a large scale. In plan it consists of a
central east-west portion from which two long wings spread out on diagonal
lines, the whole structure being about half a block in over-all length. The
building is dominated by a huge, steeply pitched roof of red tile and green
copper trim, almost overpowering in its immediate effect. Its is a thoroughly
functional design except for the dark interior corridors, which receive little
natural light. The spreading plan and the placing of the building well back
from the streets on spacious lawns represent a happy solution to the problem
of orientation for light and air and reasonable freedom from the noise of
traffic.

The exterior treatment of Carl Schurz is a more sober case than the elementary schools described above of molding the exterior form of a building
in a plastic way. Pure forms exactly repeated, sharp-edged intersections, uninterrupted planes, the close vertical pattern under a dominating horizontal
line—all are characteristic features of the time, but they appear in the school
in a unique and personal way. The major emphasis of the wall treatment is
the verticalism secured by Sullivan's technique of introducing false piers
between the true piers, which are impossible to discover except at the entrances. Elsewhere this accent is uniform throughout the length of all the
elevations. The vertical movement is abruptly terminated one story below
the roof line by the stone course at the top of the heavy pylon-like projections
at the corners, along the wings, and flanking the entranceways. It is a formal
element characteristic of several of Wright's designs at the time, especially
the Larkin Company building in Buffalo. Part of the effectiveness of Carl
Schurz High School lies in its color: the brick envelope of the wall is burnt
red, the roof a softer red with green copper trim, the stone trim light buff.
While the interior of the building differs little from the traditional planning

202

of big urban schools, the exterior is a brilliant exhibition of virtuosity that marks the high point of non-commercial architecture in the Chicago tradition.

Dwight Perkins left the Board of Education in 1910 and established the partnership of Perkins, Fellows and Hamilton in the following year. The firm prospered up to its dissolution in 1927 by following the ruling architectural fashion of the 1920's and designing in derivative styles. Perkins was interested in civic improvement beyond his professional responsibilities and was one of the group—including Burnham and Jensen—who brought about the establishment of the Forest Preserve District of Chicago and Cook County. This belt of recreational meadow and woodland now embraces fifty thousand acres. The small isolated rectangle of Forest Preserve land in Evanston was named after the architect.

The tradition of scholastic design established in Chicago by Dwight Perkins was carried on by Barry Byrne, who has designed a large number of Roman Catholic schools and churches in Chicago and the smaller cities of the prairie West. Byrne was born in Chicago and received only an elementary-school education before beginning his architectural career in 1901 as an apprentice in the office of Frank Lloyd Wright. He remained as a draftsman and later a designer until 1907. Wright, who could afford to be generous in those prosperous days, took him on wholly because of his self-acquired draftsmanship, a skill which Byrne had taught himself as a boy of early high-school age. He was associated with Walter B. Griffin and Marian Mahony (later Mrs. Griffin) from 1907 to 1910, when he went to Seattle to begin what proved to be an unfruitful three-year association with a local architect. He returned to Chicago and rejoined the Griffins as a partner in 1914. He established an independent office in the city in 1917 and maintained it until 1930, when he again left to practice in New York. By 1945 he was back in Chicago and now maintains an office in Evanston under the name of Barry Byrne and Parks.

Byrne has never wavered in his devotion to the Sullivan-Wright philosophy of architecture; yet in spite of this uncompromising adherence to an increasingly unpopular doctrine, he enjoyed a prosperous business in the 1920's, contrary to the experience of the other architects who tried to maintain the Chicago spirit. As an independent architect, he began largely with residential work but quickly established himself as the most imaginative designer of ecclesiastical buildings. His career formed a happier parallel to that of the older members of the Prairie school: the midwestern enthusiasm for a new American style flourished in the Archdiocese of Chicago until about 1923, after which date it survived only in the smaller communities of Wisconsin, Iowa, Minnesota, and the Dakotas. In these small towns, however, Byrne found kindred spirits among his ecclesiastical patrons and hence many opportunities to exploit his vigorous imagination. This is all the more remarkable when we recall two major characteristics of sacred architecture at the time: first, its unshakable adherence to Gothic and Romanesque forms of church design, and second, the enormous authority of the architect Ralph Adams Cram, an unreconstructed medievalist who was hostile to everything that had been done since the fourteenth century. Byrne's importance in the field, however, eventually received national attention: he became a director of the Liturgical Arts Society, an editor of *Liturgical Arts*, and a contributing editor of *Commonweal*.[39]

He enjoyed three large commissions in Chicago within a few years after establishing his own office. The first and largest was for Immaculata High School, built between 1921 and 1922 at 640 West Irving Park Road. This was shortly followed by two others: the Church of St. Thomas the Apostle, at 5472 South Kimbark Avenue, and St. Mary's High School, at 2044 West Grenshaw Avenue. Both were designed during the construction of the earlier school and were built between 1923 and 1924. They were his last commissions in Chicago until the west addition to Immaculata High School, which was opened in 1957.

This school best represents Byrne's highly specialized talent and most fully reflects his basic concept of design (Figs. 167, 168). Conspicuously situated along open land in the north half of Lincoln Park, the building is a framed structure L-shaped in plan, with one wing extending along Marine Drive and the open area between the wings facing Irving Park Road. The over-all form of the school constitutes another example of the organic-plastic approach in which the architect adapted to school design Wright's method of analyzing the house into its constituent functional elements and recombining these around a central formal motive. In the case of the Immaculata school, however, Byrne was specifically influenced in his visual treatment by one of the German pioneers of the modern movement, Hans Poelzig, whose earlier work reveals the principle of "total envelopment" provided through solid planes of brickwork, sloping roofs, and discrete window voids.[40] The extensive areas of tawny brick are the chief visual element in Byrne's school, and these are enhanced by the dense vertical patterns of the window groups, which are drawn into themselves, so to speak, and set off

[39] In fact, Byrne's reputation reached international proportions in the mid-twenties. He received a commission to design a church in Cork, Ireland (*ca.* 1926), after the Archbishop of Cork read Lewis Mumford's *Commonweal* article praising his work ("Architecture and Catholicism," *Commonweal*, I [April 25, 1925], 623–25).

[40] If there was a particular building of Poelzig's that influenced Byrne, it might have been the brick-walled chemical works at Luban, Poland (1912). For a brief discussion of Poelzig's work and his place in the modern movement, see Walter C. Behrendt, *Modern Building* (New York: Harcourt, Brace & Co., 1937), pp. 98–99.

from the solid areas by the Gothic arches at the tops of the vertical banks. Unlike the other works of the Chicago school, in which the roof either hides behind a parapet or sweeps out over the wall in broadly overhanging eaves, the Immaculata High School is capped by a prominent mansard roof that slopes up sharply from the wall planes but is strongly united with them. As in other commissions of Byrne's, the architect was associated with the sculptor Alfonso Iannelli, who molded the statuary and ornamental borders over the main entrance directly in the soft terra cotta (Fig. 168). Iannelli's earlier reputation in Chicago rested chiefly on the sculptural details that he executed for Frank Lloyd Wright's Midway Gardens (1913–14).

Of all the architects who belong to the Chicago school by virtue of their independence from traditional building forms, Irving K. Pond (1857–1939) and his brother Allen (1858–1929) are most difficult to place in any of the various streams of the movement. Born in Ann Arbor, Michigan, and educated at the University of Michigan, they established a partnership in Chicago in 1886.[41] They were soon drawn into the Chicago movement and in a few years were producing original work marked by their own unique stamp. One of the early designs was the Omaha Apartments, which we have already discussed.[42] Among their commercial structures in the central business area were the Kent Building, erected between 1902 and 1903 at 415 South Franklin Street, and the Illinois Bell Telephone Company's former Toll Building, completed in 1908 at 111 North Franklin. The first was a ten-story steel-framed block in the wholesale clothing district, owned for a number of years by B. Kuppenheimer and Company and known for a time by that name. It was demolished during the clearing operation for the Congress (now Eisenhower) Expressway–Wacker Drive interchange. The eight-story Toll Building, which now houses various service facilities of the telephone company, is typical of the Ponds' work (Fig. 169). The three narrow bays of the street elevation are bounded by broad, shallow, continuous piers joined at the top by a flattened arcade. The windows are grouped in pairs in two of the three bays, but in the third (south) bay the two windows are not uniform and are staggered because of the presence of the stairwell adjacent to the party wall. Two decorative features were to be repeated in the architects' later designs: one is a flat arch with the curve reversed at the ends, which is used as part of the tracery in the ground-floor windows, and the other is a row of pendants composed of little rectangular blocks set under the sill

[41] The Ponds' firm became Pond, Pond, Martin and Lloyd in 1925 and Pond and Pond and Edgar Martin in 1931. Irving Pond was active as an architect and an amateur acrobat until his death at the age of eighty-one. He was a passionate enthusiast of the circus all his life and wrote two books to record his love.

[42] For the Omaha, see p. 157.

of each of the large windows. The whole elevation is typical of the cellular wall treated as a shallow curtain, and the rather arbitrary ornament suggests that the Ponds were more determined to find an unusual way of treating the façade than to create a forceful expression of the commercial block.

But the Ponds' most valuable work in Chicago was concerned with social rather than architectural improvements. It grew out of their eighteen-year association with Hull House, which was founded by Jane Addams in 1861 and was for nearly thirty years housed entirely in the mansion of the Charles Hull family, built in 1856 at what is now 800 South Halsted Street. In 1890 Hull House began a major expansion of its facilities, which included the addition of ten buildings to the original quarters. All were designed by the Pond brothers and constructed at intervals up to 1908 in the form of a hollow square on the block bounded by Halsted, Polk, and Cabrini streets (Fig. 170).[43] The architectural character of these buildings was derived from that of the Hull mansion and was designed to harmonize with it. As a consequence, the Ponds had little opportunity to create original works and were forced to adapt the elevations of the various buildings to the traditional features of the 1856 house. The row of steep gables along Halsted Street and the disposition and outlines of the windows reveal the exigencies within which the architects worked. On the other hand, the grouping of windows, the smooth planes of brick, the diamond pattern in the brickwork, the odd shapes of gables and quoins, and the subdued horizontality of the projecting courses suggest the new ornamental interests of the time.

On February 15, 1961, the trustees of the University of Illinois decided to build their long-planned Chicago campus on an area extending west from Halsted on either side of Polk. The entire Hull House group was marked for demolition under the terms of this plan. The decision produced a bitter controversy that began when the citizens of the neighborhood protested the action at hearings before the City Council during the spring of 1961. The Historic American Building Survey made a complete graphic record of the entire Hull House group, and the Preservation Committee of the American Institute of Architects urged the university to incorporate the complex in its new campus. These activities bore sour fruit: on June 8, 1961, President David D. Henry of the University of Illinois recommended that the trustees retain the Hull mansion in the campus plan while sacrificing the other ten

---

[43] The successive Hull House buildings and their dates are as follows: Butler Building, 1890; Smith Building, 1895; Theater and Coffee Shop, 1897; Jane Club, 1898; Gymnasium, 1899; Apartments, 1901; Bowen Hall, 1904; Music School and Dining Hall, 1905; Boys' Club, 1906; Mary Crane Nursery, 1908. The Butler and Smith buildings, the Theater and Music School, and the Apartments were built as additions to the Hull mansion on Halsted between Polk and Cabrini streets and extend back to the alley west of and parallel to Halsted. The Jane Club and the Mary Crane Nursery faced Cabrini Street, and the Gymnasium, Bowen Hall, and the Boys' Club faced Polk Street.

buildings. In 1963 the trustees revised their decision and voted to include the refectory in the preservation plan, a consequence of the protests of the local residents and the Chicago Heritage Committee. The money to implement this act of generosity was to be raised by public contributions.

The value of Hull House rests only to a small degree on its architecture, which is of indifferent quality in the face of the main Chicago achievement. The destruction of the buildings means the loss of a valuable civic institution and a potent symbol. The present demoralization of the American city makes it obvious that the spirit and the accomplishments of Hull House need to be multiplied a thousand-fold. It was perfectly appropriate that Frank Lloyd Wright should have delivered his celebrated address of 1901 at the settlement house: here he described the degradation and the ugliness of the American city and called for an architecture that would use the machine in the service of beauty and dignity. The full measure of the disaster was most eloquently presented by Jessie F. Binford.

Dr. Henry's offer to preserve not Hull-House but just the old house of Charles Hull . . . does not solve the real issue of the location of the Chicago branch of the U. of I.; neither will it satisfy the people not only of Chicago but throughout the United States and foreign countries who cherish, as evidenced by their letters of appeal, protest and demand, the great heritage which Chicago and the world has in "Jane Addams and Hull-House." . . . As Archibald MacLeish said, "Hull-House was not a house it was an action. Jane Addams was not a reformer; she established a place in and around which a fuller life might grow for others and herself. Hull-House changed this city and this republic, not because it was a successful institution but because it was an eloquent action." . . . Jane Addams's old neighbors, their children, grandchildren and the later residents of the West Side, did not honor her merely in words but with eloquent, courageous action when political power and dogmatic undemocratic processes in city planning threatened their future and Hull-House. They understood why thousands of people visit Hull-House and always will, how there they feel the spirit of Jane Addams, her search for the enduring in human affairs, her responsibility for "the common life." Can Chicago and our state university afford to squander such a heritage?[44]

The fate of Hull House is doubly ironic in view of the subsequent careers of Irving and Allen Pond. They retained a steady devotion to civic amelioration throughout their lives, and their largest, best-executed commissions are university buildings, notably the student union buildings at the University of Michigan (1917) and Purdue University (1929). They continued to do commercial work in Chicago, but an increasing number of their commissions came from other cities of the Midwest.

[44] Letter from Jessie F. Binford, printed in "Opinion of the People," *Chicago Sun-Times*, June 20, 1961, p. 25.

Among the architects strongly influenced by the Arts and Crafts movement was Thomas E. Tallmadge, who designed a few commercial buildings among his predominantly residential commissions. He was born in Washington, D.C., in 1876, graduated from the Massachusetts Institute of Technology in 1898, and entered the office of D. H. Burnham and Company in the same year. He founded an independent practice with Vernon S. Watson in 1905. Tallmadge, however, was primarily interested in architectural history and devoted an increasing amount of time to the careers of author and teacher until his death in 1940. He was a professor of architectural history at the Armour Institute of Technology and the author of *Architecture in Old Chicago*, published posthumously in 1941.[45] An almost monumental example of the residential work of Tallmadge and Watson is the house originally built for John C. Linthicum between 1907 and 1908 at 1315 Forest Avenue in Evanston (Fig. 171). A representative of the few commercial designs of the architects is the little two-story shop and office building erected in 1910 at 608 Davis Street in Evanston (Fig. 172). The outrageous sign that now disfigures it almost eclipses the pleasing qualities of this unpretentious structure. It is marked by the extreme simplicity of surface characteristic of Tallmadge's houses: the flat, narrow bands of the brick spandrels alternate with wall-to-wall areas of glass set in such shallow reveals that the wall is transformed into a neutral curtain of the kind one can see less well done in many of the recent Chicago apartment buildings. The only ornament in the Davis Street building is the soldier course of brick in the top spandrel and the copper cornice above it.

The one area that resisted the architectural revolution of the Chicago school until well into the twentieth century was ecclesiastical building. Adler and Sullivan had broken the ground with the Anshe Ma'ariv Synagogue building (1890–91). This congregation is the Kehilath Anshe Ma'ariv (KAM) of which Adler's father, Liebman, was the first rabbi. Frank Lloyd Wright was the first to break the barrier and establish something of a movement when he designed the Unity Church in Oak Park (1905–6). He was soon followed by a latecomer to the Chicago ranks who had not even begun his independent career when Wright received the Oak Park commission. William E. Drummond was born in Newark, New Jersey, in 1876 and studied architecture for about a year (1897–98) at the University of Illinois. From the end of the century until 1908, he worked for varying periods in the offices of Schmidt, Garden and Martin, D. H. Burnham and Company, and Frank Lloyd Wright.

[45] Armour Institute of Technology and Lewis Institute were merged in 1940 to form the present Illinois Institute of Technology. Tallmadge's book covers the architecture of Chicago up to the Columbian Exposition of 1893.

He founded his own practice in 1908 and shortly thereafter established the partnership of Guenzel and Drummond.

Drummond's first major commission represents a radical break with the traditional design of churches and suggests that he was consciously following in Wright's footsteps. The First Congregational Church of Austin, built in 1908 on Waller Avenue at Midway Park, is a daring conception for an area that until recent years was a stronghold of architectural reaction (Fig. 173). The immediate ancestry of the forms appears to have been not only Wright's Unity Church but also his Larkin Building in Buffalo. The Austin church is reduced to three major elements: the high central block of closely ranked, narrow piers surmounted by a solid brick prism, and two identical wings that repeat the upper part of the central form. The nave is covered with a flat skylight carried in a single span across the enclosure by the side walls and a pair of brick piers at each end. Although a simple composition of rectangular planes, the open sweep of interior space and the direct statement of bearing wall and pier give the church a surprising power for its small scale.

There was little like the Austin church in ecclesiastical architecture for many years. Drummond's next commission in the field, the Methodist Episcopal Church of Maywood (1912), is more orthodox than the earlier design in its gabled end walls and traditional roof framing. The interior of the nave has some structural vigor in the exposed roof rafters, but the wall planes are excessively broken up by windows and decorative panels. Guenzel and Drummond recovered something of the earlier vitality in their design of the Lorimer Baptist Church, built in 1914 at St. Lawrence Avenue and Seventy-third Street (Fig. 174). The pitched roof ends in the familiar gables, but the grouped windows and the strong horizontal motive place it closer to the central tradition of the Chicago work.[46]

A small church close to the traditional meetinghouse form was Marian

[46] William Drummond submitted a project for the Tribune Building Competition (1922) that defies the descriptive powers of the historian. There is no question about the originality of the design or about the source of those parts that are recognizable as architecture. The main shaft of the skyscraper up to the sixteenth floor lies in the Chicago tradition: continuous piers alternating with narrow continuous mullions, generous openings in the three prominent elevations, the glass-filled bays of the three-story base, are all reminiscent of the Sullivanesque skyscraper of the nineties. The main shaft continues for several stories above the sixteenth, where it is increasingly loaded with ornament vaguely in the character of the Prairie school but extremely redundant, badly scaled, heavy and thick, and absurdly non-architectural. The whole thing culminates in an orgiastic tower that is simply fantastic. It does not appear to have been intended for functional purposes; it is given over entirely to immense ornamental panels either scooped out of surfacs or springing wildly from them. The general impression is of architectural caricature, possibly an expression of contempt for the competition in question. (There can be little doubt that some of the entries were motivated by this feeling.)

Mahony's Unitarian Church of Evanston, built on Chicago Avenue near Dempster Street between 1903 and 1904 (Fig. 175). The architect was one of Wright's draftsmen for eleven years and the wife and architectural collaborator of Walter B. Griffin. Her original design for the Unitarian Church was apparently more radical than the constructed building, more in the spirit of Drummond's Austin church, but was toned down to its relative orthodoxy by its unorthodox congregation. The pleasing little church, the only one of honesty and dignity in a city dominated by overblown ecclesiastical monuments, was demolished in 1960 to make way for a supermarket parking lot. Church building, as we have seen, proved to be one part of the architectural continuity uniting the late Chicago work with our own day through the many midwestern churches of Barry Byrne (see pages 203–5).

Among the little publicized architects of the late Chicago school who distinguished themselves locally by residential rather than commercial work were Walter Burley Griffin and John S. Van Bergen. Griffin was born in Chicago in 1876 and graduated from the architectural school of the University of Illinois in 1899. A great admirer of Sullivan and Wright, he began his professional career in the latter's office in 1900. In the few years of his independent practice as one of the Prairie group, he enjoyed a large number of commissions for suburban houses, of which at least seven survive in Evanston alone. Three of these bear the clear stamp of Wright's influence but at the same time are original works of high quality: the Carter House, 1024 Judson Street, 1910, and two houses completed for Hurd Comstock in 1912 on Ashland Avenue immediately below Church Street (Figs. 176, 177, 178). The characteristic features of the late Chicago work are the grouped windows, the vertical pattern of narrow openings, mullions, and wall panels, the widely overhanging eaves that seem to embrace the gabled end walls, and the low-pitched roofs. The heavy corner piers that tightly inclose the light and open wall areas are peculiar to Griffin's designs, although we have noticed a similar element in Elmslie's International Leather Company factory.

Griffin was the first Chicago architect to be awarded a commission from a foreign country when he won an international competition in 1911 for the plan of Canberra, Australia. He traveled to Melbourne in 1913 to supervise the construction of the new capital and a few years later decided to locate his office there. He did all of his subsequent work in Australia and India until his death in 1937. Wright followed Griffin to the Orient in 1916, when he began the design of the Imperial Hotel in Tokyo. Wright's last house in Chicago, still standing in excellent condition at 7415 North Sheridan Road, was completed in 1915. The departure of the two men was a prevision of the end for the Chicago school.

During his long stay in the Orient, Griffin's only contribution to American architecture was the project he submitted for the Tribune Building Competition in 1922 (Fig. 179). It was the only one in the spirit of Sullivan, Wright, and the late phase of the Chicago movement, but it was unfortunately well below the standard that Griffin himself maintained in his residential designs. The general verticalism and some of the decorative elements seem to have been composed out of the Chicago vocabulary, but the ornamental details are overscaled and not properly subordinated to the piers and window bands. The main emphasis is on the association of geometric masses in the form of attenuated rectangular prisms. The whole design suggests that Griffin was not at home with the high building: it is a confused reflection of odds and ends of the Chicago and the new European idioms and reminds us more than anything else of the avant-garde New York skyscraper in the days of Hugh Ferriss' fantasies and the black-and-gold fashion.

John Van Bergen almost came too late to enjoy a career as an original architect in the Chicago area. He was born in Oak Park, Illinois, in 1885, studied at the Chicago Technical College, and worked successively in the offices of Griffin, Wright, and Drummond before founding an independent practice in 1911. About 1921 he moved his office to Santa Barbara, California, where the climate was shortly to be a little more congenial to new architectural ideas. The intricate rectangular patterns that one finds in Sullivan, Wright, and Drummond distinguish Van Bergen's work. The best of his designs is a classic in the Wrightian idiom—the house built for Alfred Bersbach in 1914 on Michigan Avenue in Wilmette (Fig. 180). The dense vertical pattern of narrow grouped windows and mullions, disposed generally over the two main wings, is dominated by the widely overhanging horizontal roof planes. A later work, the house at 5730 Sheridan Road (1914–15), was a simplified version in stucco planes (Fig. 181). This house was demolished in 1960 for another of the many apartment buildings that are rapidly filling the remaining lake-side stretch of Sheridan Road. In 1920 Van Bergen prepared a design for the pavilion and boathouse in Jensen's Columbus Park, but a shortage of funds prevented the execution of what would have been his final work in Chicago (Fig. 182). The one surviving drawing is a bird's-eye perspective and is difficult to read in detail, but the basic formal element of the buildings appears to be a rustic variation on a row of piers dominated by the sweeping horizontal planes of the roof.

The Chicago school and its Prairie offspring died as active, unified movements about the time of the First World War. Wright's departure for Japan in 1916 marked the beginning of the end. Sullivan barely survived, unwanted in the city that once asked for the best that he had. In the city itself, the other leading figures produced their last original designs around the time of the Tribune competition of 1922. The rest either depended on commissions from the smaller midwestern towns, departed from the region to distant places, or surrendered to the new fashions of the twenties. A few isolated works of the decade following 1925 show that the old spirit lingered here and there. Among these, one clearly belongs to the central tradition of the Chicago school, but the others are difficult to place even in the heterogeneous work of the Prairie group.

Between 1924 and 1926 the Chicago, North Shore and Milwaukee Railway built an alternate high-speed line for its Milwaukee trains in the low-lying and then largely open land between the Skokie and the upper Des Plaines rivers. Backed in part by the Samuel Insull capital and still enjoying the heavy passenger traffic that the automobile was just beginning to take away, the company lavished money on roadbed, electrical equipment, and stations. The chief architect of the North Shore, A. U. Gerber, was given a free hand to design station buildings and waiting shelters in keeping with this generous spirit. Of these the Dempster Street Station in Skokie is the largest and best (Fig. 183). Built between 1924 and 1925, it served for a year exclusively as the terminal of the former Skokie branch of the Chicago Rapid Transit Company, then as a joint terminal and way station for both companies until the Skokie elevated line was replaced by a bus route shortly after the Second World War. The station building is 100 feet long and is solidly constructed of expensive and durable materials. The 12-inch brick walls rest on reinforced concrete footings. The hipped roof, covered with green tile, is extended north and south on cast-stone columns to provide deep sheltered areas at the ends of the station. For the rapid-transit trains on the south end, there was a reinforced-concrete island platform under a canopy also supported by cast-stone columns (this whole structure was demolished when rapid-transit service was abandoned). The terrazzo floor of the building rests on a 4-inch concrete slab continuous under the station and shelter areas. The formal character of the building in some ways belongs to the late Chicago movement—the close vertical pattern formed by the narrow windows, and the long horizontal lines of the roof and the sill at the base of the building are familiar elements. On the other hand, the exposure of the canopy beams and the roof rafters for decorative purposes and the brackets under the soffits are not common features of the Chicago work, although somewhat similar details appear in a few of the houses. The lively articulated pattern of the roof framing suggests the work of Maybeck and the Greene brothers in California around 1910. The North Shore company abandoned operations in January, 1963, but the station building has been leased to a local business establishment.

At the time the North Shore station was completed, shortly before both

European and American architecture became related parts of a new movement, a final work in the tradition of the eighties and nineties appeared in the
Loop. It is the largest building of the group comprising the Carson Pirie Scott
Annex, or Men's Store, located at the northwest corner of Wabash Avenue
and Monroe Street (Fig. 184). The store was constructed between 1926 and
1927 after the plans of Hubert Burnham and his brother Daniel, Jr.[47] The
annex has now expanded into two other buildings flanking it. On the north,
along Wabash, is the old Thomas Church Building, designed by Hill and
Woltersdorf and constructed in 1903 (four more stories were added between
1949 and 1950). On the west, along Monroe, is a former garage erected in
1940 after the plans of Louis Kroman. The façade of this structure is a glass
and limestone curtain in the cellular form of bay-wide windows and narrow
piers and spandrels. The remodeling of the garage, the strengthening of the
foundations, and the addition of a single bay to merge it with the store building were completed in 1950. The merging of the separate structures now
presents a continuous and nearly uniform elevation along the north side of
Monroe Street (Fig. 185). Thus two-thirds of the block from Wabash to State
Street provides us with an impressive and very late example of the great
Chicago tradition.

The construction and essential form of the Carson Pirie Scott Annex are
no different from those of many other buildings we have described. The
precedent was plainly the main store designed by Louis Sullivan at State and
Madison. Except for narrow bands of ornamental terra cotta at the sill and
lintel lines of each story and the scarcely noticeable classical garland at the
parapet, the architects of the annex depended upon the exact articulation of
the cellular wall for their architectonic effect. Although the proportions and
the whole system of dimensions are different from those of the main store, the
later building impresses us with something of the same clarity and grace. It
is lighter and more open but less powerful and far less rich in its detail. The
architects differentiated the first two stories from those above them only by
setting the windows flush with the outer faces of the piers and spandrels instead of placing them in deep reveals. The store is much superior to the non-
derivative commercial work of its time because of a simple characteristic:
the carefully handled articulated wall gives a sense of strength and provides
a lively play of light and shadow that are missing in the flat curtain walls and
vertical bands of the 1927 skyscraper.

The Carson Pirie Scott Annex is an isolated fragment in the tradition of
the Chicago school. By the time we reach the late twenties we can no longer
speak of an indigenous Chicago movement. The modern or non-traditional

[47] Burnham's sons had left Ernest Graham in 1917, when the latter founded Graham,
Anderson, Probst and White.

work of the time belongs to a national architectural development that had no regional roots. The most conspicuous examples are the stripped-down vertical skyscrapers—the Board of Trade, Daily News, Palmolive, Field, and others, their seemingly old-fashioned form still surviving in the huge Prudential Building of the mid-fifties. Anything else ought perhaps to be classified as unrelated parts of the precarious continuity maintained by Wright, Barry Byrne, and a few Californians between the original Chicago achievement and the new architecture largely derived from European forms. Such would be the case with the two delightful little pavilions that decorate the Rookery of the Lincoln Park Zoo (Figs. 186, 187). Designed by the landscape architect's staff of the Chicago Park District, the two structures were built in 1936 by the Works Progress Administration of the federal government. The Rookery formed part of a general improvement and extension of the Zoo property made possible by the public works program of the first New Deal administration. The pavilions are clearly in the spirit of Wright and the Prairie architects, although it would be difficult to find a specific parallel in their work. The ornamental frames and wings that spread upward and outward from the brick pylons of Wright's Midway Gardens (1913–14) lie closest to the pergola-like framework of the Rookery pavilions.

There is something ironic in the fact that Frank Lloyd Wright should have been the bridge to unite the Chicago group to the architecture of our own day. America is a commercial nation, and one would have supposed that the impersonal and public forms of our one native commercial style would have left the deepest impression on the building arts. The debt of Wright and his fellow spirits to the Chicago movement was essentially an aesthetic one translated into unique and personal and sometimes capricious terms. The great question, still largely unanswered by the historians, is why this brilliant and vigorous development should have contracted very nearly to the unpredictable talents of a single man. As we have noted, the creative drive of the Chicago movement spent itself by 1920, so that we may regard the time of the First World War as the turning point. The view that the virus of the Columbian Exposition sapped the strength and spirit of the Chicago architects is wholly unsupported by the facts. One must look to later and more profound causes.

The continued expansion of wealth and the parallel increase in the number of people who enjoyed a full academic education were important if ironic factors. The centers of population and industry might shift steadily westward, but the center of taste was steadily concentrated in New York. The major educational institutions of the Middle West were growing rapidly, and their graduate schools more rapidly still. They were determined to emulate the best of the East and to staff their faculties with the holders of doctorates from eastern universities. The result of this new eastward orientation was a great strengthening of the already powerful New York–Ivy League axis in all the arts, most particularly in the remunerative and laggard art of architecture. Thus New York came to be the cynosure of all hopeful young architects, not because of the plaster ephemeralities of the World's Fair but because New York and the Ivy League, for good reasons and bad, proved by the time of the First World War to be more irresistible magnets than they had ever been before.

Behind this latter-day attraction, from which the Chicago movement had emancipated itself earlier, were other social and cultural determinants. Growing wealth and its attendant conspicuous extravagance continued to be potent factors, but there were others that had to do with the emotional and intellectual life. The dichotomy between technology and art that had plagued the nineteenth century had not been resolved in the twentieth. Art was what one was taught in the best universities, or experienced in the museums and theaters of the East, or read in the avant-garde circles that had discovered Joyce and Eliot. As far as the graphic, literary, and dramatic arts were concerned, the new taste was right, and it is understandable that what seemed to be the same view came to prevail in architecture. Wealth and refinement turned to architects like Charles Follen McKim, educated, literate, at home in the salons of Europe; they certainly did not look to Sullivan, who drank whiskey straight, worried about democracy, and sounded like a radical. And after all, it was not easy to judge. McKim and his architectural and engineering associates had created a triumph in Pennsylvania Station: here were brilliant and daring feats of construction, sound planning, honorable historical precedents, the power of familiar monumental forms. The Bayard Building was scarcely noticeable by comparison. And who would expect an aesthetic experience on Bleecker Street?

By 1920 architecture as a symbolic as well as a technical and formal art came to be radically out of step with the new movements in literature, drama, and painting, although exactly the opposite seemed to be the case to the architects and their clients. The works of Sullivan and the late Chicago school, or of Behrens in Europe, simply did not look like art and did not play the role that educated people associated with aesthetic objects. Such architecture had to do with commerce and industry or with the odd tastes of prairie culture; it did not appear in galleries, concert halls, or schools. As for Wright, a twenty-year exile in Japan and the Far West erased the memory of him among midwesterners, and he was unknown in the East. Moreever, his art had no European counterpart, and Europe, after all, was the source of the exciting new ideas. The very taste that welcomed novelty and experiment in the literary and graphic arts remained blind to comparable

215

work in architecture. When it finally came to accept the new architectural forms, it did so chiefly because they were European importations.

Social changes tended to reinforce changes in taste and education. The explosive rise of the automobile after 1920 enormously increased the mobility of the urban population. The physical and cultural diversity of America could now be discovered at first hand. But instead of an enthusiasm for regional differences and an interest in perpetuating them, the opposite reaction occurred. Mobility led to the obliteration of regional distinctions and to a nation-wide standardization of dress, manners, and taste. The radio and mass journalism provided the subject matter for behavior and interest; the mass-production industries provided the physical material. The American passion for conspicuous emulation, now the basis for the myth of status, provided the inner motive. Since architecture is the most public of the arts, it was bound to be most immediately affected by the broad social and cultural changes. The best people and the wealthiest corporations wanted classical banks and Gothic skyscrapers, or both styles for collegiate building. And so, as a consequence, did everyone else. The architectural accomplishments of the most talented men were often impressive works of building art, and in some cases they were triumphs of structural technique and sensuous form. The unique building group along the Chicago River at the Michigan Avenue–Wacker Drive intersection furnishes the most conspicuous examples. But the architects were working the last vein of a mine that was nearly exhausted.

Changes in the intellectual and political climate of Chicago itself reinforced the effect of the national tendencies. The whole quality of civic life deteriorated in the decade of the twenties. The political corruption that came with the sudden expansion of wealth and with Prohibition and organized crime led to a radical decline in civic idealism and the growth of indifference and cynicism among the potential leaders of community life. The result was an atmosphere that gradually stifled creative work in the highly public arts of architecture, landscape design, and civic planning. The reaction that followed the international complexities and moralistic idealism of the First World War produced a hostility to the new and the alien that descended to the level of clownish burlesque in the idiocies of Mayor William Hale Thompson. In other areas, however, the city continued the long record of great achievements that began in the last decade of the previous century. The lake-front development was largely accomplished in the fifteen years following the war. The musical life of the community flourished as it never had before under the brilliant performances of the Chicago Opera Company and Chicago Symphony Orchestra. The universities and the great civic institutions rapidly expanded while steadily improving their scholarly and educational standards. The result was a perfect paradox, like American civilization itself, confused and anarchic, caught in a web of contradictory ambitions and ideals. The full meaning of this baffling pattern has not yet been elucidated. Out of it all, certain areas of culture in Chicago advanced to ever higher levels, while others—notably literature and architecture—declined to the point where genuinely creative work simply ceased to exist.

The Chicago school first achieved its greatness in the impersonal terms of commercial architecture, later in the more personal idiom of residential work. It was widely known for its offices and hotels, and its functional solutions were adopted everywhere. But the formal principles, if they were remembered at all, were denied by the leading architects of the 1920's. Thus the school had no direct influence on the development of architecture after the First World War. That development passed through two successive phases, one arising from native eastern precedents, the other from European influences. The first was the traditional phase, dominated by McKim, Mead and White, Cass Gilbert, and Raymond Hood in the East, and by Graham, Anderson, Probst and White in Chicago. The most powerful influence was undoubtedly exercised by Gilbert's Woolworth Building in New York (1911–13). The successive purifications of the Gothic skyscraper reached their culmination in the smooth verticalism of Hood's Daily News Building in New York and Graham's Field Building in Chicago. They made it seem that an American style for the high building had been achieved by 1930. But this short-lived form was denied further realization by depression and war. The rich and powerful expressions of it developed by Sullivan and refined by Wright were never further explored. When large-scale commercial building was resumed around 1950, the new European architecture provided very nearly the total vocabulary of forms.

In Europe around 1910 a modern structural art began to emerge chiefly in the work of Peter Behrens and Auguste Perret. The methods of construction and formal expression that they developed were essentially like those of the Chicago school. But there was no direct connection between the two groups, as there was between Wright and the Dutch architects after 1910. The new work in Europe and its older counterpart in Chicago converged at one point in the next decade. Walter Gropius, who had studied under Behrens, and his associate Adolph Meyer submitted a project for the Tribune Building Competition in 1922 (Fig. 188). Their entry was one of the few non-derivative designs to be offered. The starting point appears to have been the newsprint warehouse on the north side of the river behind the present Tribune Tower. The warehouse is a heavy-handed and strictly utilitarian example of the commercial architecture of the Chicago school. Gropius and Meyer narrowed the piers and spandrels, employed the Chicago window, refined away the minor details, added some pointless horizontal projections, and produced a coldly mechanistic skyscraper in the manner that Holabird and Roche had long before raised to higher levels. How many would have been happier if Gropius and Meyer rather than Hood and Howells had won this prize?

The brief contact that grew out of the Tribune competition proved to be abortive at the time, but twenty-five years later the principles of the Chicago school were unconsciously revived on such a scale as to constitute the essential character of most of the commercial and public building of our time. These principles were given their ultimate refinement in Chicago itself by one of the leading European pioneers of the new movement, Ludwig Mies van der Rohe. His many buildings on the campus of the Illinois Institute of Technology form the contemporary statement of ideas formulated in Chicago as early as 1879. The cellular curtain wall and the geometry of the steel frame emerge with almost relentless clarity in the two best buildings of the new campus, Alumni Memorial Hall (1945–46) and Crown Hall (1955–56) (Figs. 189, 190). Promontory Apartments, built between 1948 and 1949 on South Lake Shore Drive near Fifty-sixth Street, is a similar though inferior work of direct structural expression in concrete (Fig. 191). An unbroken if irregular line extends from the mature buildings of Holabird and Roche through the concrete structures of Richard Schmidt and the Tribune project of Gropius and Meyer to this apartment tower. The apartment buildings at 860–80 North Lake Shore Drive (1949–52) are the most celebrated examples of the glass curtain combined with a delicate but potent expression of the steel frame.

Derived from the Lake Shore apartments to a certain extent is the Inland Steel Building of Skidmore, Owings and Merrill, erected between 1955 and 1957 at the northeast corner of Monroe and Dearborn streets (Fig. 192). This remarkable exhibition of welded steel framing is wholly dedicated to the visual celebration of technique. On the other hand, the same architects' Hartford Fire Insurance Building, erected between 1960 and 1961 at the southwest corner of Wacker Drive and Monroe Street, is simply technique uncelebrated (Fig. 193). The column and slab frame of concrete clothed in polished gray granite represents the entire architectonic expression. One block north of the Hartford office is the Liberty Mutual Building of C. A. Eckstrom, a pleasing if undistinguished example of the cellular curtain of the Chicago school. A comparison of the two is instructive: the new building is a work of highly skilled engineering, but in its general visual quality it appears as an abstract and mechanized restatement of the older. The Hartford building, however, proved to be the first in a series of powerfully articulated designs distinguished by extremely wide bays. These buildings belong so clearly in the style of the Chicago work at the turn of the century that they soon came to be known collectively as the New Chicago school. The first of the buildings with wide-bayed cellular elevations of steel and glass is the Continental Center, designed by C. F. Murphy Associates and erected between 1961 and 1962 at the southeast corner of Wabash Avenue and Jackson Boulevard (Fig. 194). The Murphy organization, in collaboration with Skidmore, Owings and Merrill, carried the new principle to a climax in their staggering design for the Chicago Civic Center, placed under construction in 1963, a 648-foot tower with 87-foot bays covering the north half of the block bounded by Clark, Randolph, Dearborn, and Washington streets (Fig. 195).

A conspicuous feature of the hotels and apartments of the Chicago school is the oriel or projecting bay, which imparted a lively play of light-reflecting surfaces to otherwise sober elevations. It disappeared around 1915 because of improvements in electric lighting and was thought to be gone for good. Yet it was effectively revived in Chicago by Harry Weese in his designs for several buildings, most notably Stanley R. Pierce Hall, a dormitory built between 1959 and 1960 for the University of Chicago (Fig. 196). The same feature appears on a much larger scale in the Michigan Terrace Apartments, constructed between 1961 and 1963 at Michigan and Grand avenues from the design of William Schmidt and Associates. A variation on the projecting bay that suggests the triangular forms of the Manhattan Building appears in the twin apartment towers designed by Louis Solomon and John Cordwell for the northeast corner of the Sheridan–Hollywood–Lake Shore Drive intersection (1961–62).

The immense volume of postwar construction in Chicago includes impressive examples of all the forms and techniques of contemporary building. Except for structural innovations that came after the First World War, most of the fundamental elements were anticipated by Chicago architects and engineers in the marvelously productive years from 1880 to 1900. Thin shells and prestressed forms, load-bearing screen walls, and core-and-cantilever and suspended construction are developments in the technology of steel and reinforced concrete that followed the earlier stages of column-and-beam and flat-slab framing known to the Chicago builders at the turn of the century. Core construction, however, was first used by Frank Lloyd Wright for the S. C. Johnson Company's research tower at Racine, Wisconsin (1947–50), and its astonishing possibilities have so far been most thoroughly exploited in Bertrand Goldberg's Marina City project in Chicago (1960–63). This work alone is a stunning exhibition of the unparalleled and inexhaustible power in the city's great building tradition.

The new inventions in concrete have given the contemporary builder great advantages over his predecessors and have led to an architecture superior to the early Chicago work in a number of fundamental respects: elegance and purity of structural members and functional details; unprecedented lightness, buoyancy, and grace; diversity of internal arrangements and external forms; extremely wide spans with minimal supports. On the other hand, the curtain-wall architecture growing out of the older framing techniques seems increasingly poverty-stricken and is frequently inferior to that of the Chicago school. The monotony of the smooth curtain has led, as we have seen, to a strong revival in contemporary Chicago building of the cellular wall most prominent in the work of Holabird and Roche. The screens, trellises, angles, and serrations of the New Formalism lack the truly architectural richness of the Prairie school. Sullivan was in a class by himself, and it could not be expected that the building arts would produce another like him in a half-century. The vigorous structural emphasis in the work of Holabird and Roche— the continuous piers and deep reveals, the vivid play of light and shadow, the strong and steady rhythm commensurate with the scale of the big office block, and the power that unambiguously asserts the strength of the steel or concrete frame—these elements are fitting to a technological age, and we welcome their return in the new technical refinements of skeletal construction.

BIBLIOGRAPHY

ADLER, DANKMAR. "The Chicago Auditorium," *Architectural Record*, I (April–June, 1892), 415.

———. "Foundations," *Industrial Chicago*, I, 473–78.

———. "Foundations of the Auditorium Building, Chicago," *Inland Architect and News Record*, XI (March, 1888), 31–32.

ANDREAS, ALFRED T. *History of Chicago*. 2 vols. Chicago: A. T. Andreas, 1884–86.

BANNISTER, TURPIN C. "Bogardus Revisited," *Journal of the Society of Architectural Historians*, XV (December, 1956), 12–22; XVI (March, 1957), 11–19.

BAUMANN, FREDERICK. *Improvements in the Construction of Tall Buildings*. Chicago: Privately printed, 1884.

BEHRENDT, WALTER C. *Modern Building*. New York: Harcourt, Brace & Co., 1937.

BIRKMIRE, WILLIAM H. *Architectural Iron and Steel and Its Application in the Construction of Buildings*. New York: John Wiley & Sons, 1892.

———. *Skeleton Construction in Buildings*. New York: John Wiley & Sons, 1894.

BROOKS, H. ALLEN. "The Early Work of the Prairie Architects," *Journal of the Society of Architectural Historians*, XIX (March, 1960), 2–10.

———. "The Prairie School: The American Spirit in Midwest Residential Architecture." Unpublished doctoral dissertation, Art Department, Northwestern University, 1957.

BURCHARD, JOHN, and BUSH-BROWN, ALBERT. *The Architecture of America: A Social and Cultural History*. Boston: Little, Brown & Co., 1961.

BUSH-BROWN, ALBERT. *Louis Sullivan*. New York: George Braziller, Inc., 1960.

BYRNE, ARCHIBALD. "Walter L. Newberry's Chicago," *Newberry Library Bulletin*, III (August, 1955), 261–73.

Chicago and Its Resources Twenty Years After. Chicago: Chicago Times Co., 1892.

CHICAGO TRIBUNE. *The International Competition for a New Administration Building for the Chicago Tribune, MCMXXII*. Chicago: Chicago Tribune Co., 1923.

CHRISTISON, MURIEL B. "How Buffington Staked His Claim," *Art Bulletin*, XXVI (March, 1944), 13–24.

CONDIT, CARL W. *American Building Art: The Nineteenth Century*. New York: Oxford University Press, 1960.

———. "The Chicago School and the Modern Movement in Architecture," *Art in America*, XXXVI (January, 1948), 19–37.

CONDIT, CARL W. "Sullivan's Skyscrapers as the Expression of Nineteenth Century Technology," *Technology and Culture*, I (Winter, 1959), 78–93.

CONNELY, WILLARD. *Louis Sullivan as He Lived*. New York: Horizon Press, 1960. (Includes an extensive bibliography of critical and interpretive articles on Sullivan and a brief listing of manuscript collections of Sullivan's letters.)

DAVID, ARTHUR C. "The Architecture of Ideas," *Architectural Record*, XV (April, 1904), 361–84.

D[ESMOND], H. W. "Rationalizing the Skyscraper," *Architectural Record*, XVII (May, 1905), 422–25.

Dictionary of American Biography (articles on William Le Baron Jenney and William Holabird). New York: Charles Scribner's Sons, 1936.

EATON, LEONARD K. "Jens Jensen," *Progressive Architecture*, XLI (December, 1960), 145–50.

ERICSSON, HENRY, and MYERS, LEWIS E. *Sixty Years a Builder*. Chicago: A. Kroch & Son, 1942.

FERREE, BARR. "The Modern Office Building," *Inland Architect and News Record*, XXVII (February, 1896), 4–5; XXVII (March, 1896), 12–14; XXVII (April, 1896), 23–25; XXVII (June, 1896), 45–47.

FIELD, WALKER. "A Re-examination into the Invention of the Balloon Frame," *Journal of the Society of Architectural Historians*, II (October, 1942), 3–29.

Fireproof Building Construction: Prominent Buildings Erected by the George A. Fuller Company. New York and Chicago: George A. Fuller Co., 1904.

FLINN, JOHN J. *The Standard Guide to Chicago*. Chicago: Standard Guide Co., 1892.

FREITAG, JOSEPH K. *Architectural Engineering, with Special Reference to High Building Construction*. 2d ed. New York: John Wiley & Sons, 1901.

GEBHARD, DAVID S. "Louis Sullivan and George Grant Elmslie," *Journal of the Society of Architectural Historians*, XIX (May, 1960), 62–68.

———. "William Gray Purcell and George Grant Elmslie and the Early Progressive Movement in American Architecture from 1900 to 1920." Unpublished doctoral dissertation, Art Department, University of Minnesota, 1959.

GIEDION, SIGFRIED. *Space, Time and Architecture*. 3d ed. Cambridge, Mass.: Harvard University Press, 1954.

GILBERT, PAUL, and BRYSON, CHARLES LEE. *Chicago and Its Makers*. Chicago: Felix Mendelsohn, 1929.

HITCHCOCK, HENRY-RUSSELL. *Architecture: Nineteenth and Twentieth Centuries*. Baltimore: Penguin Books, 1958.

———. *The Architecture of H. H. Richardson and His Times*. Hamden, Conn.: Archon Books, 1961.

———. *In the Nature of Materials: The Buildings of Frank Lloyd Wright, 1887–1941*. New York: Duell, Sloan & Pearce, 1942.

HOLCOMBE, PAUL. *Depreciation and Obsolescence in the Tacoma Building*. Chicago: National Association of Building Owners and Managers, 1929.

Industrial Chicago. 4 vols. Chicago: Goodspeed Publishing Co., 1891.

JENNEY, WILLIAM LE BARON. "The Chicago Construction, or Tall Buildings on a Compressible Soil," *Inland Architect and News Record,* XVIII (November, 1891), 41.

―――. "Construction of a Heavy Fireproof Building on Compressible Soil," *Sanitary Engineer,* XIII (December 10, 1885), 32–33.

―――. "A Few Practical Hints," *Inland Architect and News Record,* XIII (February, 1889), 7–9.

JONES, JOHN H., and BRITTEN, FRED A. (eds.). *A Half Century of Chicago's Building.* Chicago: Privately printed, 1910.

KIMBALL, FISKE. "Louis Sullivan, an Old Master," *Architectural Record,* LVII (April, 1925), 289–304.

MANSON, GRANT C. *Frank Lloyd Wright to 1910.* New York: Reinhold Publishing Corp., 1958.

MENDELSOHN, FELIX. *Chicago—Yesterday and Today.* Chicago: Felix Mendelsohn, 1932.

MONROE, HARRIET. *John Wellborn Root.* Boston: Houghton Mifflin Co., 1896.

MOORE, CHARLES H. *Daniel Hudson Burnham, Architect, Planner of Cities.* 2 vols. Boston: Houghton Mifflin Co., 1921.

MORRISON, HUGH. "Buffington and the Skyscraper," *Art Bulletin,* XXVI (March, 1944), 1–2.

―――. *Louis Sullivan, Prophet of Modern Architecture.* New York: W. W. Norton & Co., 1935. (Includes a bibliography of the writings of Dankmar Adler and Louis Sullivan.)

MUJICA, FRANCISCO. *History of the Skyscraper.* New York: Archaeology and Architecture Press, 1930.

MUMFORD, LEWIS. *The Brown Decades.* New York: Harcourt, Brace & Co., 1931.

――― (ed.). *The Roots of Contemporary American Architecture.* New York: Reinhold Publishing Corp., 1952.

MUSEUM OF MODERN ART. *Early Modern Architecture in Chicago, 1870–1910.* New York: Museum of Modern Art, 1940.

NEWTON, ROGER HALE. "New Evidence on the Evolution of the Skyscraper," *Art Quarterly,* IV (Spring, 1941), 56–70.

OREAR, GEORGE W. *Commercial and Architectural Chicago.* Chicago: G. W. Orear, 1887.

PECK, RALPH B. "History of Building Foundations in Chicago," *University of Illinois Bulletin,* XLV (1948), 29.

PEISCH, MARK L. "The Chicago School and Walter Burley Griffin, 1893–1914." Unpublished doctoral dissertation, Art Department, Columbia University, 1959.

Pictorial Chicago. Chicago: Rand McNally Co., 1893.

Prominent Buildings Erected by the George A. Fuller Company. Chicago: George A. Fuller Co., 1893.

RANDALL, FRANK A. *History of the Development of Building Construction in Chicago.* Urbana: University of Illinois Press, 1949. (Includes an exhaustive bibliography of periodical literature on Chicago building within the area bounded by Lake Michigan, Roosevelt Road, Canal Street, and North Avenue, and a reprint of the Rand McNally Company's *Bird's-Eye Views of Chicago* [1898].)

REBORI, A. N. "The Work of Burnham and Root," *Architectural Record,* XXXVIII (July, 1915), 33–168.

ROOT, JOHN WELLBORN. "Architects of Chicago," *Inland Architect and News Record,* XVI (January, 1891), 91.

SCHUYLER, MONTGOMERY. "Architecture in Chicago: Adler and Sullivan" ("Great American Architects Series," No. 2, Part I), *Architectural Record,* V (December, 1895), 3–48.

———. "Architecture in Chicago: D. H. Burnham and Company" ("Great American Architects Series," No. 2, Part II), *Architectural Record,* V (December, 1895), 49–71.

SHULTZ, EARLE, and SIMMONS, WALTER. *Offices in the Sky.* Indianapolis: Bobbs-Merrill Co., 1959.

SKEMPTON, A. W. "The Boat Store, Sheerness (1858–60), and Its Place in Structural History," *Transactions of the Newcomen Society,* XXXII (1959–60), 57–78.

———. "Evolution of the Steel Frame Building," *The Guilds Engineer,* X (1959), 37–51.

STARRETT, THEODORE. "The Building of a Great Mercantile Plant," *Architectural Record,* XIX (April, 1906), 265–74.

STURGIS, RUSSELL. "The Schoenhofen Brewery," *Architectural Record,* XVII (March, 1905), 201–7.

———. "The Warehouse and Factory in Architecture," *Architectural Record,* XV (January, 1904), 1–17; XV (February, 1904), 123–33.

SULLIVAN, LOUIS H. *The Autobiography of an Idea.* New York: Press of the American Institute of Architects, 1922.

———. *Democracy: A Man Search.* Detroit: Wayne State University Press, 1961.

———. *Kindergarten Chats and Other Writings.* New York: Wittenborn, Schultz, Inc., 1947. (This edition includes six letters of Sullivan's.)

TALLMADGE, THOMAS E. *Architecture in Old Chicago.* Chicago: University of Chicago Press, 1941.

———. "The Chicago School," *Architectural Record,* XXIII (April, 1908), 69–74.

TSELOS, DIMITRIS. "The Enigma of Buffington's Skyscraper," *Art Bulletin,* XXVI (March, 1944), 3–12.

UPJOHN, E. M. "Buffington and the Skyscraper," *Art Bulletin,* XVII (March, 1935), 48–70.

WALKER ART CENTER. *Purcell and Elmslie, Architects*. Minneapolis: Walker Art Center, 1953.

WEBSTER, J. CARSON. "The Skyscraper: Logical and Historical Considerations," *Journal of the Society of Architectural Historians*, XVIII (December, 1959), 126–39.

WEISMAN, WINSTON. "New York and the Problem of the First Skyscraper," *Journal of the Society of Architectural Historians*, XII (March, 1953), 13–21.

———. "Philadelphia Functionalism and Sullivan," *Journal of the Society of Architectural Historians*, XX (March, 1961), 3–19.

WIGHT, PETER B. "Public School Architecture at Chicago: The Work of Dwight H. Perkins," *Architectural Record*, XXVII (June, 1910), 494–512.

WOLTERSDORF, ARTHUR. "Dankmar Adler," *Western Architect*, XXXIII (July, 1924), 75.

———. "The Father of the Skeleton Frame Building," *Western Architect*, XXXIII (February, 1924), 21–23.

Work of Purcell and Elmslie, Architects, Chicago, Illinois, Minneapolis, Minnesota, The. Chicago, 1915. (Reprinted from *Western Architect*, XXI [January, 1915], and XXII [July, 1915].)

Descriptions, illustrations, and technical details of individual buildings appear in the following periodicals: *American Architecture, Architectural Record, Architectural Review, Architecture, Brickbuilder, Engineering News, Engineering Record, Inland Architect, Inland Architect and News Record, Land Owner*, and *Western Architect*.

Architects' drawings of many individual buildings are preserved on microfilm in the Microfilm Project, Burnham Library, Art Institute of Chicago.

INDEX

[All bridges, buildings, railroad stations, and railroads are indexed by name under those general entries.]